6/8/12

MY MEDICINE

To Buzz,
   To a fellow patient, I hope
you enjoy my book. Keep up
All the good work.

Take care,

Rosenfeld

IRVIN ROSENFELD
MY MEDICINE

How I Convinced the U.S. Government To Provide My
Marijuana and Helped Launch a National Movement

Forewords by
MITCH EARLEYWINE, PhD *and* JUAN SANCHEZ-RAMOS, MD, PhD

OPEN ARCHIVE PRESS
SANTA BARBARA

Special limited edition first printing April 2010

OPEN ARCHIVE PRESS
2062 Alameda Padre Serra
Santa Barbara, CA 93103
(805) 963-3592

Founded in 1997, Open Archive Press endeavors to publish works that
enlighten the mind, nourish the spirit, and the challenge the conscience.

Frontispiece: Thelma Rosenfeld

Designed by George Delmerico

Printed in the United States of America
Cataloging-in Publication Data available from the Library of Congress
ISBN 978-0-9636380-9-0

FOREWARDS

No one has ever written a book like this, because no one else could. Even the most moving stories about a child's battles growing up with serious illness will only make modest suggestions about medicine while informing readers about a disorder. It's rare to get the details of the human side—the impact on family and friends, the confusion and frustration associated with the hunt for a diagnosis, and the struggles with painful symptoms and difficult treatments. Any family struggling with a sick child will find this book a superb guide for developing the persistence, patience, and optimism necessary to travel through the difficult labyrinth to appropriate medical care. Irvin Rosenfeld's tale of his family's hard work will inspire anyone.

But there's more to it all. Few others have required changing federal law in an effort to triumph over illness. For many reasons, this topic has not received the attention it deserves until now. Book-length works on battling this kind of byzantine bureaucracy are rare, which is what makes this work so distinctive. On its surface, the story is about medical cannabis, but it's more about standing up for individual rights. Lesser men would have deflated easily in the face of all of these obstacles. The fact that one person can persevere while keeping a great attitude is a great lesson for us all. Anyone who enjoys stories of the common man's successes over impossible odds is in for a genuine treat. I hope that Irv's bravery will be a guide for others to speak out for what they need. It's hard to imagine a better model.

It just so happens that Irv's illness, Multiple Congenital Cartilaginous Exostosis, the rare bone disorder that created tumors and complications galore, made his life unbearable without a plant that had been used medicinally for almost 5,000 years. Medical uses for cannabis date back to 2737 B.C., when the Chinese Emperor and pharmacologist Shen Neng prescribed the plant for gout, malaria, beriberi, rheumatism, and pain. News of the medication spread throughout the world. Legendary physicians from ancient Africa, Greece and Rome had prescribed this wondrous little gift of nature when medicine was in its infancy. Our founding fathers listed it as a treatment for symptoms just like Irv's back in the New England Dispensatory of 1764. Many authors assert that medical cannabis treatments would not have reached other countries unless they had meaningful efficacy. Dr. William O'Shaughnessy introduced the medication to Europe in the 1830s. By the early 1900s, some of the most prominent drug companies in Europe and America marketed cannabis extracts as cures for a variety of symptoms, including headache, nausea, cramps, and muscle spasms.

As new drugs developed left and right through history, a few standbys remained the best of their kind. But confusion, misinformation, economic hardship, and racist and classist attitudes derailed the progress of medical cannabis in the United States. The Marijuana Tax Act of 1937 put a damper on improving our understanding of the human body and its interaction with this plant. Fortunately, a few brave souls have kept important data rolling in. Many scientists, me included, have reviewed the extensive, modern research literature only to find that the plant is safe and effective medicine—far safer and more effective than popular pharmaceuticals that are ten times as expensive. The plant's impact on pain, nausea, vomiting, weight loss, muscle spasms, seizure, anxiety, and insomnia are undeniable. In our age of expensive health care, it's good to know that the plant is far cheaper than many alternative treatments, too. But there's scientific review and then there's real life; Irv's story is more persuasive than all the graphs and statistics in the world. There are times when the story seems unbelievable. How could our government keep people from maintaining their own health? How could people say the cruel things they've said, snub a medical patient so, or accuse honest health professionals of deceit? Truth is stranger than fiction, and Irv reveals it with wit and enthusiasm that is incredibly admirable.

—*Mitch Earleywine, PhD*
Professor, Department of Psychology
State University of New York, Albany

Irv Rosenfeld has charted his personal journey through the labyrinthine channels of governmental agencies that regulate and control drug use. His well documented account illuminates and reveals in harsh detail the absurd contradictions, paradoxes (and hypocrisy) of our drug laws. His odyssey begins with the revelation of a severe congenital medical problem that began in childhood and has plagued him to the present time. As a child, he bravely underwent numerous painful surgeries to remove bony tumors from his legs and arms and as a consequence was treated with a broad spectrum of analgesic medications. Irv was and continues to be an excellent patient who works closely with his carefully chosen physicians to overcome the limitations imposed by his condition. The chronic use of pain medications was frustrating to him for several reasons. He was often over-sedated but more importantly, he didn't receive adequate relief from muscle spasms and pain.

While in college he was exposed to recreational cannabis ("marijuana"), and to his amazement, he found smoking the weed provided relief from the painful muscle spasms. In fact, he was able to reduce the total amount of prescribed opiate drugs and eventually to completely stop their use when he smoked marijuana. He came to see this naturally-occurring plant substance as a medication, personally confirming what others have known for millennia across many cultures, including our own. Yet, medical use of this remarkable phytomedication is prohibited by the United States Federal Government because of a combination of social, political and economic factors.

The interaction of all the factors that led to marijuana prohibition in the US is not the focus of the book. The irony around which this book grew is the fact that a few individual patients were allowed to use medical marijuana provided by the National Institutes of Drug Abuse under a Compassionate Use Protocol. But Schedule 1 drugs, where marijuana is legally pegged, are stated not to have any medical value or have excessive abuse liability. Another irony is that scientists from NIH have been awarded a patent to use marijuana products as neuroprotective agents while at the same time another branch of government states that marijuana has no medicinal value! Even worse, the Federal government does not recognize the right of individual States (14 so far, with NY set to be the 15th) to permit the use of medical marijuana.

Although Irv's story doesn't blame physicians for marijuana prohibition, there is no doubt that American physicians as a whole are not very knowledgeable about herbal medications, and have not played a significant role in development of a rational policy on phytomedicines. This abdication of responsibility by the medical profession has contributed in part to the present state of affairs in which marijuana is legally misclassified and misunderstood by the professionals who should be prescribing it. Part of the problem is the medical education system which ignores an important part of pharmacotherapy. The scientific study of medicinal uses of plants, known as Pharmacognosy, has not been part of the American medical curriculum for at least three-quarters of a century. By contrast, the prescription of herbal medications by physicians in Europe and Asia is very common. The therapeutic use of herbs and phytomedicines has always been very popular in Germany.

About 600–700 different plant drugs are currently sold there, singly and in combination, in Apotheken (pharmacies), Drogerien (drugstores), Reform-hauser (health food stores), and Markte (markets). In addition to the self-selection of herbal products by consumers, about 70% of the physicians in general practice prescribe the thousands of registered herbal remedies, and a significant portion of the annual sales (about US$1.7 billion, a conservative estimate) is paid for by government health insurance. In 1998, 5.4 million prescriptions were written for a single phytomedicine, ginkgo biloba extract, a figure that does not include the substantial over-the-counter sales of the product.

Marijuana and its various formulations, when allowed to join the list of other legal phytomedications, has the potential to be a blockbuster both medically and economically. Already, the medical use of cannabis in several states has yielded interesting new ways to administer the plant product that obviate the need to smoke the burning weed. New generations of vaporizers and lipid-soluble extracts (that can be readily absorbed through mucous membranes) obviate the need for smoking and provide rapidly acting, titrable relief of symptoms. Beyond the medical benefits of marijuana, a legal medical marijuana industry would clearly provide an economic stimulus in the form of new jobs and new sources of lucrative tax revenue.

Irv's book should open the eyes of American readers to the inconsistencies and misguided US policy regarding medical marijuana. Hopefully all Americans who require medical marijuana will not have to follow the tortuous course forged by Irv and his pioneering legal marijuana users.

—*Juan Sanchez-Ramos, PhD, MD*
Professor of Neurology
University of South Florida, College of Medicine

PART ONE

ILLNESS AND ILLEGALITY

X-Rays Don't Hurt

I have told my medical history so many times in so many settings, but the most important time—the time my life depended on it—was early October 1982, in an office of the U.S. Food and Drug Administration in Rockville, Maryland. I had been given fifteen minutes to convince twenty medical experts assembled by the FDA that I needed Cannabis to treat my severe bone disorder.

On the drive to Rockville from my home in Portsmouth, Virginia, I thought about what to emphasize. Since 1971, when I was a college freshman, I had known that the street substance called "marijuana" worked better for me than all the drugs I had been prescribed by various doctors to relax my muscles, reduce inflammation and pain, and to help me sleep: Percocet, Darvon, Dilaudid (synthetic morphine), Methaqualone, Valium, Butazalitan Alka, and on and on and on...

None of the doctors who prescribed these drugs could prescribe the one that worked best for me—Cannabis—because the Federal Government deems it to have no medical use. But the FDA committee could, thanks to a little-known "Investigational New Drug Program" created in 1978. This would be my one chance before the committee. Dear GOD, be with me.

A 250-mile drive gives one a lot of time to think. I wondered how many thousands of hours I had worked to get this opportunity? How many times was I told that Cannabis wasn't a medicine and I was just wasting my time? All the setbacks and disappointments, yet I was about to get a chance, slim at best, to convince a panel of my medical need. I thought about all the people who had come into my life—both good and bad—because of my fight for medical Cannabis. I thought about how it came to pass that I was now taking on the U.S. Government. And I realized that I'd had no choice.

Upon arriving at the FDA Headquarters, I parked and found my way to the hearing room. Little by little, the hearing room filled to capacity. All these people had come to witness my hearing, to see for themselves how the FDA would respond to my plea.

It was now only minutes before I was to start. I blocked out everyone except for the most important twenty people, those that made up the committee. People say that when you are about to die, your entire life flashes before you. I wasn't about to die, but all of a sudden I relived my entire life and I almost burst into tears, but then I thought, how did all this happen to me just as the Chairman hit his gavel and said, "You may begin."

•

I was born February 26, 1953, to a middle-class Jewish family that already had two daughters, ages ten and six. My childhood was great. I got to do all the things boys get to do. I had all the normal childhood maladies, including the mumps, chicken pox, and the measles. I enjoyed playing all sports and excelled in baseball. I started playing Little League at age eight.

My hitting and fielding improved steadily. By age ten I was the starting shortstop on my team, "Crim Floor Covering," and batting leadoff. Life could not have been better. I went to school every morning and played baseball every afternoon. On Saturdays I would leave the house around 8:00 am. on my red 24-inch bike and not return until it got dark. The sport would change with the season—from baseball to football to basketball to dodge ball, and then, with the return of warm weather, baseball again. Life was simple in the sleepy little city of Portsmouth, Virginia.

In the Spring of 1963 I was in fourth grade and had not a care in the world. Trees and flowers were in bloom and our team, Crim Floor Covering was finally winning. Our next-to-last game was against the team we were battling for second place. I was ready for the challenge. Going into our final at bat, we were behind by one run. The first two batters were retired. The next got a base hit and the next got a double, putting the tying run on third and the go-ahead run on second with two outs. Up I stepped to bat. I hit the first pitch to right field for a single, scoring both runs to give us a one-run lead. All we had to do was hold them.

Their first two batters struck out. Their next batter hit a shot to deep right center for a triple. The tension was mounting. Their next batter hit a ground ball to me at shortstop, which I fielded and threw to first for the last out of the game. WE WON!!!! As I went to throw my glove into the air out of joy, my right arm was totally paralyzed. I could not lift or move the same arm I had just used to throw the ball to first.

I looked at my arm and everything looked normal. Then why couldn't I move it? I felt as if I was in a bad dream, only this was real. Time seemed to stop. My eyes locked in on my parents and then my coach. I guess they could see the fright, for they came running to me yelling "What's wrong?" I told them I couldn't move my right arm. It was totally paralyzed but there was no pain.

Maryview Hospital was across the street. We ran to the car and drove to the Emergency Room. This took all of about three minutes. By the time I got out of the car my arm was miraculously fine. We went in and explained to the doctor what had happened. He decided to take x-rays to see if anything looked abnormal.

So, there I was in a hospital for only the third time in my life. (The other time was when I had my tonsils out at age six.) I was taken to an x-ray room, told to lie down and relax. I was too naïve to be very scared. The technician placed a flat, black square under my right shoulder. She then went behind a screen and told me to hold my breath. Three seconds later it was over. That sure didn't hurt. She repeated this under my arm and wrist. Wow, that was easy! I was then taken back to my parents and we waited for the results.

A few minutes later, the doctor came out and said it looked as if I had broken my wrist when I was younger and it had healed wrong. He said there was a small, jagged bone on my wrist. The nerve had caught on it, causing the temporary paralysis but it had worked its way free and I was fine. Told not to worry, my parents and I got into our car and made the five-minute drive home. That was that or so we thought.

Over dinner my mother, who had worked many summers as a teenager assisting in her uncle Shipley's pediatric office, told my father that what the doctor said didn't make sense. She believed that if I had broken my wrist, even as a baby, I would have shown stress and pain. She looked at me and said, "I'm calling the orthopedic surgeon tomorrow and getting you in to see him." I had never been to this type of doctor but, being only 10, I thought it was no big deal.

The next afternoon I went with my mother to see the bone specialist. In the waiting room were kids my age immobilized by casts on their legs, or arms or other parts of the body. There were adults who could barely move. I wanted to leave. My mother went to the front counter and got forms to fill out. I sat there looking around, curious about what the other people were thinking. Here I was feeling healthy and fit, while others had pain all over their faces.

Every few minutes a nurse would call someone's name and they would make it towards the inner office as best they could. Wow, not to be able to walk! I'm glad I'm not like them. After about twenty-five minutes it was my turn. My mother and I walked to the examination room and sat down. A few minutes later a doctor walked in and identified himself as Dr. Kirk. He said hello to my mother, whom he knew, and asked what had happened. She told him the story and he agreed that it was unlikely I had broken my wrist and not shown any signs of it at the time. He turned and said "Son, let's take a look."

Dr. Kirk started feeling my wrists and arms. He said he felt a bump on my right wrist and then said he felt one on my left wrist. He manipulated my arms and shoulders and said he could feel bumps there, too. I was told to take off my pants. Now I was getting worried. He started feeling my legs and again said he felt bumps. The expression on his face became very serious as he said I had these bumps all over my body. He said we needed to have x-rays taken and to wait for the technician.

X-rays don't hurt, so no big deal. A few minutes later I was led to another room and had x-rays taken of every limb and body part. Then I waited with my mother for the results. After a while the doctor returned and started showing us the films. Neat—I had never seen pictures of bones. We viewed film after film and on each Dr. Kirk would point out these small bumps or growths that shouldn't be there.

After viewing the x-rays he took us to his private office. I still had no clue what was happening, nor what was about to happen. We sat down and Dr. Kirk, looking very stern, said "I know what is wrong with you." What did he mean? I'm fine! He said that I had a rare disease called "Multiple Congenital Cartilaginous Exostosis," which means that I had tumors growing on most of the long bones of the body. He said this condition was very serious and we needed to contact a research center, as he was not knowledgeable enough to recommend a course of treatment.

My mother reminded him that my great-uncle had been head of pediatrics at Johns Hopkins and that my uncle taught pediatrics at the Yale School of Medicine. We would contact them and see what they suggested. Dr. Kirk wrote down the name of the disorder and said we should call him back when we knew where I would be going for treatment. As we were walking out, I again looked at the other patients, not knowing that I would soon be just like them. I still was not that worried. After all, I was a healthy, normal, athletic ten-year-old.

"You Can Do This"

My mother started making phone calls the minute we got home. The first call was probably the hardest—to my father. She told him I had some sort of bone disorder and I needed to get to a research center as soon as possible. She was going to call her uncle, Dr. Shipley Glick, in Baltimore Maryland., and her brother, Dr. Sigmund Stein, in New London Connecticut.

She got in touch with both and relayed to them Dr. Kirk's diagnosis. Both said it was a rare disorder and that they would ask around to determine which medical center I should go to for treatment. Now I started to realize that there was something wrong with me and I had to accept the fact. I would have to play the hand I was dealt. (I had been playing poker since I was four.)

My father got home for dinner and not much was said. It wasn't that they were ignoring the situation; it was just that we didn't know what was going to happen. Then the phone rang and it was my Uncle Siggy. My mother repeated what he was telling her: the major center for this disorder was Boston Children's Hospital... He had already made the appointment... We had to be there in two days and I was going to be seen by the country's top specialist, Dr. William Green.

That night as I lay in bed, I thought about what was about to happen. My bedroom was completely dark. Not being able to see what's ahead was exactly how I felt about my life. The unknown was scary, but I realized I had no choice. Whatever was going to happen, I would be brave and make the best of it.

•

My family and I packed as if we were going on a vacation. Nothing was said about what lay ahead. This was just a drive to Connecticut with my parents to see my uncle and aunt, and, by the way, go to Boston to see what this disorder was all about. We were all scared but didn't want to show it.

I had never traveled this far before, so everything that happened was new to me. I remember going by ferry over Chesapeake Bay and playing pinball on board. That was fun and the time went by quickly. A ten-year-old has simple joys. The rest of the drive was uneventful except for what I was thinking. We got to Boston in the late afternoon and spent the night at a hotel.

Our appointment at the hospital was for 8:00 am. The sight of Boston Children's Hospital gave me confidence. I thought it quite special that there was a huge hospital just for kids. My father found a parking spot and we entered. At the admissions desk my mother filled out form after form after form. Dad and I were glad we didn't have to do them!

We sat down to wait our turn. I was starting to get used to medical offices. No matter what was to happen, I felt, this was the best possible place for me to be.

A nurse came out and said "Mr. Rosenfeld can come back now." I looked at dad and said, I guess you should go back. He laughed and said "She means you." So we all went back. I was taken to an examination room and we waited.

Soon the door opened and a team of doctors entered. They welcomed us and introduced themselves. I was asked to take off all my clothes except for my underwear. This was the start of learning not to be modest. They then began examining me all over. The doctors discussed all the "bumps" they felt and their approximate sizes. They ordered additional x-rays, and off I went with the technicians. I was now an old pro at this. They took film after film until they took the granddaddy of all films, one that was as long and wide as I was. That impressed me. It was an hour and a half before I was brought back to the examination room.

All the doctors returned, followed by a tall gray-haired man who introduced himself as Dr. William Green, head of Orthopedics. The other doctors seemed to look at him as if he were on a pedestal—as if he were more than their leader, almost as if he were a god. In time I would come to regard him that way as well.

Dr. Green confirmed that my disorder was called Multiple Congenital Cartilaginous Exostosis. He said I had bone tumors all throughout my body that would grow as I did. He looked directly at my parents and said that this was one of the worse cases he had seen. He proceeded to talk to them as if I wasn't there. He said I had more than two-hundred tumors, any one of which could become problematic, and that I would have to be the one to decide which tumors required surgery. Although what he was saying was shocking, there was something reassuring about his complete honesty and the tone of his voice.

"We will teach him everything he needs to know about this disease and, hopefully, how to survive. He needs to know as much as any doctor knows." Dr. Green then said something I will never forget: "He may not outlive his teenage years. With our help, he will have the best shot."

He looked straight at me and said, "You will have to battle this disease for the rest of your life, which I hope is a long time." My response was: "What do I need to know"?

Dr. Green talked to me as a doctor and as someone who wanted to be my friend. He repeated that the bone tumors would grow as I grew. I had more than two—hundred of these tumors and I would be the one to decide when to have surgeries.... I thought, "Surgeries, oh my god, what is going to happen to me?" Three things could necessitate surgery, he said. One: If a tumor starts growing very quickly, it can become malignant. Two: If a tumor starts growing toward an area where it would affect your normal pattern of development, it has to come out. Three: if the pain is too great, an operation will be necessary.

"You will have to learn these things," he said matter-of-factly. He opened up a medical text and handed it to me. "This is what a doctor learns about your disorder. But we don't know how you feel, nor what it's like to have it. Only you will know. So, we can teach you what's in the book, but that's only part of what you will need to learn to survive. Living with Multiple Congenital Cartilaginous Exostosis will change how you live your life. You have to learn to be more careful about things you do." He added something else I'll never forget: "Not only do you have to overcome this physically, but also mentally."

Everyone in the room was looking at me, wondering how I was going to react. I looked at Dr. Green and asked what he meant by overcoming it mentally. He said, "Don't let it win. When things get bad, always remember, you cannot give up or give in."

At that point I wanted to burst out in tears. Why me? Dr. Green must have realized how I was feeling because he put his arm around me and said, "You can do this... You have no choice." There was the doctor and the friend.

"Now the good news," he said. "God works in mysterious ways. I had a student named Henry Waive who had a fascination with your disorder. I would say that next to me, Henry has the best understanding and knowledge. He just got out of the Navy and is getting ready to go into private practice in, of all places, your home town! He'd been stationed at the Portsmouth Naval Hospital and fell in love with the area. For a kid as bad off as you are, you couldn't be in better hands. Henry Waive will consult with me every step of the way. I demand one-hundred and ten percent from all my students, and as of now, that includes you."

I knew at that moment that my life would never be the same. No longer was I the boy who only wanted to play ball all day, but the boy who had to learn how to play ball when I was healthy enough. I wasn't going to give in. Now the battle begins... Everyone in the room was looking at me and they must have picked up on my attitude because they were managing to smile.

We broke for lunch and didn't have to be back for two hours. The staff told us about a great deli just down the block, so off we went. Growing up in Portsmouth, I had never been to a world-class Jewish deli. As we walked in, a flood of delightful smells from all the different foods overcame all negative thoughts. I was going to order a hot corned beef sandwich from a real Jewish deli! The waitress brought out this huge sandwich and I ate every bite of it. I'm healthy now, I remember thinking. Whatever happens in the future will happen. Learn to enjoy the good times. Boy, that corned beef sandwich was great!

Back at the hospital that afternoon, interns and residents on Dr. Green's staff gave me a crash course on how to read x-rays and pointed out which tumors were most likely to cause problems as I grew. Medical books were put in front of me with fascinating graphics. There were pictures of cut-open bodies showing bone tumors before surgery and after. This is what is going to happen to me. Not a good thought for a ten-year-old kid.

Trying to read the books was difficult as I didn't understand half the words. The young doctors took their time and explained as much as they could. They treated me as if they were advising their little brother on what life was going to be like. We discussed what sports I could take part in. They approved of baseball, non-contact football, some basketball, golf—but no tennis, soccer, or track. I was warned never to ride a motorcycle. Don't drive a stick shift, don't roller-skate, don't ski...don't, don't etc. Information was coming at me from all directions. I had to grow up by years in only a few hours.

Dr. Green looked in and wanted to know how his new student was doing. The head resident said I wasn't ready to enter medical school just yet, but that I was a quick learner. I said I was scared about my future, but I truly believed that I was in the best hands possible. He put his arm around me and smiled. All this time my parents stayed in the background, but I knew they were there with me. They would always be there with me, but in the background. They also understood that I had to make all the final decisions.

When it was time to leave, I said goodbye to everyone and thanked Dr. Green. He said he hadn't pulled any punches and that I had handled everything well, considering what had been thrown at me. He then said "Irvin, you are going to do great." I never saw or talked to him again, but from that day on, his understanding and encouragement would always be with me.

Our drive back to Virginia was very quiet, almost as if nothing of great significance had happened. The fact that I was still healthy helped keep our spirits up. In fact, I felt like any other 10-year-old... almost. I kept telling myself that things were fine now and not to worry about the future.

"You Will Not Amputate..."

Because Dr. Henry Waive had not yet opened an office, our first visit was to his house, a 15-minute drive from ours. The door was opened by a man who seemed to me a giant. I was about four feet, eight inches tall and weighed about 80 pounds. Dr. Waive was about six feet, six inches and weighed about 270 pounds.

The examination took place in a bedroom. Dr. Waive told me to take off my clothes down to my underwear and to sit on the bed. After looking at the x-rays that we had brought back from Boston, he felt my bones from head to toe. For such a large man, his touch was surprisingly gentle. From the start he explained what he was doing and what he was looking for.

As he examined me, Dr. Waive asked about my family, what I enjoyed doing, and so forth. He also told us about himself. When he described studying under Dr. Green at Boston Children's Hospital, it was with respect and affection. I was feeling the same way—as if I, too, had become one of his students.

Dr. Waive spelled out what lay ahead. He made me feel special about being the first patient he'd seen since going into private practice. My mother and I left knowing that I had a very caring doctor and a new friend. From that moment on, I could call Henry Waive any time and for any reason.

Once a month, through the fall and winter of 1963-64, I went to Dr. Waive's office to be monitored. The tumors were growing slowly, as expected at that age. By March, as the baseball season approached, I still felt fine. But as I started practicing, I noticed that throwing a ball was bothering me. The tumor on my right wrist had not grown much, but it was in an area that affected my throwing. One of the reasons to have surgery was if a tumor bothered me a lot. The one on my wrist not only bothered me when I threw, it was starting to interfere with my writing.

The next time I went to Dr. Waive's, we discussed the situation. He agreed that surgery was appropriate and scheduled it for two weeks hence. My parents supported my decision. It was scary but I knew it was only going to get worse, and having the operation soon would give me two months to heal before our first game. Dr. Waive said I would be as good as new and could lead the league in hitting!

The surgery went well, the discomfort wasn't as bad as I'd expected. I recovered in time to play on opening day and that season I would come in fourth in the league in hitting. I kept going to Dr. Waive's office every month, with x-rays being taken every third visit. The tumors were growing, but at an unexceptional rate. I was in the fifth grade and was doing what other fifth graders did. I got up and went to John Tyler Elementary School. Three afternoons a week I'd go to Hebrew school at our synagogue,

Gomely Chesed. My spare time was spent on the ball fields of Portsmouth. And so my eleventh year went by.

I started sixth grade and that year, too, went by with no problems. I kept going to the doctor's office for checkups and x-rays. The tumors were still growing, but not causing any concerns. I was beginning to wonder if things were going to be as bad as I had been warned. Spring was about to start and you know what that meant… Little League! I was twelve-years-old and this was my last season. Most of the players on my team had been together since we were eight, and we were favored to win it all. I was the leadoff hitter and played mostly shortstop. I am proud to say that I did lead the league in hitting, but more important, Crim Floor Covering won the John Tyler-Port Norfolk Little League championship. My wrist was fine and I could run and play with minimal limitations.

After the season ended, I went on a camping trip through the Norfolk Jewish Community Center with twenty-nine other kids. We traveled by bus through Virginia and all the way up to Canada, camping out at a different place every night. We had three counselors for the fifteen boys and fifteen girls. Everyone had different duties each day. You either had to cook, clean up, or load the bus. My bone disorder kept me from loading the bus, so I cooked or cleaned. Every day I would feel each tumor to make sure all was well. The trip lasted one month. It was wonderful making new friends and seeing new places. And I had discovered girls, which made life even more interesting.

•

In September, 1965, I started Harry Hunt Junior High. It was in a three-story building, so changing classes meant climbing lots of stairs, which was hard on my legs. I started having a little trouble sitting for an extended time. Dr. Waive sent letters to the school and to my gym teacher telling them of my disorder and that I would have to limit what I could do. My friends knew I had a medical problem, but this was the first time they got an inkling of how serious it was. They would joke with me when I didn't do the exercises or strenuous activities. Years before, as a little kid in elementary school, I had been unable to get into the "lotus" position required by bomb drills. Now I knew why. My arms and legs were different, my body had limited flexibility.

Over the winter I started having minor problems with a tumor here or there—slight discomfort from certain movements that had not bothered me before——but the x-rays showed no inordinate growth and I was still able to do whatever I wanted. I was focused on preparations for my Bar Mitzvah, which was coming up in March. For five years I had been studying for this momentous occasion. In the Jewish religion, when a child reaches the age of thirteen, he or she becomes an adult. At that time you lead the entire congregation in services. Having been president of the Junior Congregation, I was very familiar with all the prayers and reciting them in public. Getting on a stage would be easy. The whole thing about becoming an adult seemed funny. Due to my medical problems, I already had!

My Bar Mitzvah was fantastic. Family from all over the United States arrived and we had a party that lasted all weekend. I remember looking at the more than five-hundred people and seeing Dr. Henry Waive, who seemed as proud of me as my father did. Both my great-uncle, Dr. Shipley Glick and my uncle, Dr. Sigmund Stein were there of course, and each took me aside for an informal examination in my bedroom during the course of that wonderful weekend. They didn't say much except that the tumors were getting bigger.

That summer I attended travel camp again. As one of the returning kids, I got to pick my duties. Just call me Chef Irvin... Every day was a new experience. We traveled from Virginia across the mountains of North Carolina, across the open plains of Texas, to our ultimate destination, the Grand Canyons of Arizona. I'll never forget the morning we started at 7:00 am. and hiked down to the basin of the canyon and then back up. We returned twelve hours later, tired and hungry. Cooking that night was quite a chore. When I went to bed, I was completely exhausted. I looked up at the sky and saw more stars than I had ever seen. I felt lucky.

We got back home as summer was drawing to a close. All that was left was a couple of weeks of relaxation, my regular visit to the doctor, and then the eighth grade. Did I mention that I had discovered girls? Baseball was no longer my sole interest.

My mother and I arrived at Dr. Waive's office on a Friday in late August and I went back to have the scheduled set of body films taken. I was anxious to tell the doctor about my summer travels. We were making small talk as he viewed the films. All of a sudden he stopped talking. He put the film of my left leg on an illuminated view box. Then I saw what he had seen. Oh my GOD! Here was a large mass in my upper calf where before had been a small tumor. It appeared that the large tumor was growing inward towards a major growth center. The look on Dr. Waive's face was one I had never seen. He looked at me and I knew what that x-ray was saying: SURGERY!

Dr. Waive said I would need to check into the hospital on Sunday and surgery would be as early as he could get an operating room. He said this tumor had grown way too quickly in a very bad area and that there was a danger of malignancy. He said I could lose my leg.

Now I realized what Dr. Green and all the other doctors were worried about. I had done everything right and still look what happened! A tumor had grown inwardly—which I couldn't detect. Since I had these tumors all over, I reasoned, if one went malignant, others could too. I refused to be chopped up; I would rather die. This was something I had thought about since my first session with Dr. Green in Boston. When you are thirteen, the thought of losing one leg, then another, than one arm, than another,... It just can't happen. I looked at my mother, then at Dr. Waive, and said "If it is malignant, you will not amputate my leg."

Dr. Waive knew I was serious. He promised he would not amputate my leg without my permission. He would wake me up and go over all my options. He said he owed me that. From the beginning, doctors wanted me to make all the decisions and that's the way it would be. I felt better. Dr. Waive warned that even if the tumor was benign, the operation was not going to be easy and recovery would be long and painful. He said "Irvin, I'm being completely honest with you, I'm worried. You will have to learn to walk again and you may never be as well as before."

I could tell my mother was trying hard not to cry. So was I. There was nothing else to be done but leave his office and drive over to Maryview Hospital and pre-register. As I was walking to our car, I was very aware of each step. How we all take walking for granted. My whole life was going to change... if I was to have a life.

That night the rest of my family was informed of the situation. I tried to be as grown-up as possible, but tears were shed. Sunday came, and I packed a bag and went to the hospital. I was worried and scared. If I didn't wake up, so be it. Life had been great and that's all there is.

On Monday, the day of the surgery, I said goodbye to my parents and thanked them for all they had done. I was wheeled to the operating room where I saw Dr. Waive. I wished him good luck and he wished me the same. I was then put under.

When I woke up, there was Dr. Waive looking over me with a big smile. At least I knew I wasn't dead. And I still had both my legs! He proceeded to say that he was ninety-five percent sure that the tumor was benign. It was so large that to get it all he had to stretch the main nerve in my leg. This would result in nerve damage but I should be able to learn to walk again. I didn't know what he meant. Learn to walk again?

I didn't realize at the time, but this was the start of a new phase of my life, one in which I would have to find ways to reduce pain, loosen muscles, and be able to sleep. In other words, from now on I would have to rely on medicines—a term I prefer to "drugs." To me, taking "drugs" has always had a bad connotation, but when you are sick, you take medicines. After all, I never asked for this to happen. It was not my fault.

Once I got out of the hospital, my thoughts were focused on returning to school. I tried, but I could not do it. Besides the overwhelming pain, I couldn't get around on crutches because of the tumors in my arms. I was as- signed to Homebound Teaching, a program run by the Portsmouth School Board and paid for by the State of Virginia. Teachers would come to my house in the afternoon, after they taught their regular classes. I would be schooled like this for the eighth, ninth, tenth, eleventh, and twelfth grades.

My social life may have suffered, but my education didn't. When you are the only student, you go through the material as fast as you learn it. I could have done the whole school year in three months, but my teachers would come up with strategies to stretch out the material. In between operations, when I could walk, they would take me to Old Dominion University in Norfolk where I learned to help them do research for their masters theses. Little did I know how helpful that would be in the years ahead.

So, on the eve of eighth grade, at age thirteen and a half, I had to learn to live with the inability to walk on my own, severe pain, and pain-related insomnia. I was prescribed Demerol for pain, Parafin Forte for muscle relaxation, and something else for sleeping. I didn't like how I felt on them, but I was a lot worse without them.

On one visit Dr. Waive asked my mother if I had ever had any alcohol. She said that our family got together every Sunday night and by tradition the men and my mother had a shot of bourbon. I had been doing this with the men since I was about six or seven. Dr. Waive brightened up and said that he would prefer me taking small drinks of bourbon at night to all the other medicines. He was hesitant to prescribe the dosages of narcotics that adults are routinely given for severe pain and insomnia. He knew how much I would need in the future and was concerned about tolerance building up. So, a little bourbon became another medicine for me.

How I Invented the DARE Program

When the cast came off my leg in late October, my mother became my physical therapist. Every day she would put me through a regimen of exercises designed by Dr. Waive, and little by little, I made progress. I went from being unable to bend my knee to—by early December—taking small steps without any help. Meanwhile, other tumors were growing in the same leg. I didn't want to think about them. It was taking all my energy to try to heal from the operation and regain my mobility. Every day was a struggle… but by spring, I was able to walk around without assistance.

Homebound teaching had kept me up to date with my fellow students. I knew I would not be able to return to school that year, but I was looking forward to the ninth grade—the start of high school- and the presence of girls. Being the only student in your class does have its drawbacks. In late August, I joined a youth organization under B'nai Brith called Aleph-Zad-ic-Aleph, or AZA for short. There was a sister group called B'nai B'rith Girls or BBG. There were chapters all over the world. It seemed like a good way to meet girls—and indeed, I did meet a special one. More about her later.

I started ninth grade at Woodrow Wilson High School but soon was missing days because of my condition. I now had another large tumor above my left knee. It got worse and surgery was performed in November. After the operation Dr. Waive said he'd removed all the tumors in the area, large and small. Recovery was not as bad as it had been the last time, but it was no walk in the park. My mother again served as my therapist and my friend. She had spent her summers as a teenager in Baltimore working with Uncle Shipley and acquired some nursing skills. Sometimes she was a tough as a Marine Corps drill sergeant, other times she was as gentle as… my mother.

I was again put on homebound teaching and assigned some of the same excellent teachers. Paul Butler, who was a History teacher at Woodrow Wilson, taught me many subjects, including Latin, English, and History. I told people I attended "Rosenfeld's Academy."

AZA became my outlet for making new friends. When I could get around, I would go to events put on by the different groups. The kids understood what I was going through and were very sympathetic. I ended up becoming president of my local AZA chapter, and later on, state president. Since I was never able to attend public school on a regular basis again, I made the most of being able to travel around the country visiting different chapters. When I was away and got hurt, I would have to explain to doctors what I had and what I needed done for treatment. I educated quite a few doctors. I was not going to let my bone disorder control me. I would be the one in control.

One of the best parts of AZA and BBG were the conventions at hotels around the country. It was nice having 150-200 girls in the same place. The only chaperones were advisors to the chapters, some paid staff, and the officers. We all followed most of the rules. One rule was "no alcohol," but mine was known as "Irvin's cough medicine," and my use of it was tolerated.

My attempts to minimize the pains and be able to sleep involved taking pills during the day and drinking "cough medicine" most nights. Many times I would think how bad this bone disorder was and I found it difficult to remember what life was like before my leg operations. At times I would feel sorry for myself, which was only natural. I could no longer do things that I used to take for granted. It was hard putting up with all the problems... But I would also realize how lucky I was to still be alive to fight the battle. And I always had my family to lean on.

I ended up having three operations on my left leg during my five years of homebound teaching. During early fall and spring, I would attempt to attend a class or two in regular school so I could see my friends. I could only do this on days I could walk. It was nice to be in a classroom environment, even if only for a few hours. The principal, teachers, and guidance counselors were all understanding and helpful.

It was during these years, 1967-1971, that marijuana and other illicit drugs started turning up in schools. The teachers would comment on the contrast of my use of legal drugs—out of medical necessity—while healthy kids took illegal drugs by their own choosing. I found it strange that these kids didn't appreciate their good health. I envied them having a choice. I approached the school administration about giving a talk making the point that healthy kids should be thankful and not take a risk with illegal drugs. (The DARE program didn't exist, yet. I "invented" it.)

The school thought it was a great idea. I soon found myself in front of classes holding up a baggy full of prescription bottles saying "Look at me and see all the legal drugs I have to take. Be thankful you are healthy and don't do illegal drugs." Marijuana was the illegal drug used by most. I had never tried it. It was illegal, therefore I would not use it. No illegal drug could possibly be beneficial. ,

I also started talking to the kids in AZA and BBG about not using illegal drugs. I was a walking billboard for the anti-drug movement and proud of it. At least my bone disorder has enabled me to carry this important warning.... It's always good to feel useful, especially when you think you've turned a negative into a positive.

•

I made the Honor Society when I was in the eleventh grade and went to the induction ceremony at school. (I graduated 5th. out of 465 seniors at Woodrow Wilson High School, where my records were kept.) My parents were very proud. I still wasn't sure if I was going to outlive my teenage years, but day-by-day, life was good.

Nights were often painful. There was something about the dampness that made it hurt too much to sleep. On many a warm night I would get out of bed, walk across the silent street and down a small embankment to a bed of pine needles I had made alongside a creek that ran along the border of our property. The sound of the moving water was peaceful and very calming. Cars almost never came by and the suburban neighborhood was completely safe. I would look up through the pines at the star-filled sky and wonder what the future held in store for me. On these nights, I usually would fall asleep as the sun was coming up.

•

It was during my senior year that I started entertaining the idea of going to college. The fact that I was going on eighteen meant that I had almost reached my full height. I was all of five foot four and weighed about one-hundred-ten pounds. At my February appointment, Dr Waive and I discussed my college prospects. He advised that a warm climate might be best, given my condition. He suggested South Florida, perhaps Miami. I thought that was a wonderful idea, especially since I had a girlfriend there from my Jewish Youth program. Thanks to AZA and BBG, I had girlfriends in several different cities.

During spring break, I flew down to Miami to check out colleges and my girlfriend, Cathy. The trip was a complete success. I had a great time with Cathy and I decided to go to Miami-Dade Community College, south campus. I flew back to Virginia and anxiously waited for graduation. I was excited about living in a new city and being back in a regular classroom setting. My plan was to spend two years at Dade and then, if my health allowed, transfer to the University of Virginia. Beyond that, I thought about studying and practicing law.

In the back of my mind were some major doubts. Could I physically handle the demands of living on my own in an apartment and attending classes at the college? My family thought I should try. Dr. Waive pointed out that I had made it this far and the worst was now behind me. No matter what happened next, I had beaten the odds.

An Interesting Game of Chess

I loaded up my brand new, blue 1971 Plymouth Duster, which my father had bought me, and headed south on the one-thousand mile drive. I had all my possessions that would fit in the car, including a TV and a stereo—everything an eighteen-year-old freshman needed. The drive was difficult. I would stop every half hour to stretch my legs.

Reaching the Florida state line was very exciting—I made it! But then I saw a sign that said, "Miami 325 miles." Oh well, at least I was in Florida.

I stayed with some friends of the family for a couple days until I moved into my own one-room efficiency apartment near the campus in South Miami. "Dade," as it's called, was then rated the top junior college in the country. The student body of more than five-thousand was diverse, with large Jewish and Hispanic contingents.

The residents of my apartment complex were mostly college students. I had gotten in touch with Cathy and she moved in with me for what was to be three weeks until she went off to college.

Things were going well between us when "it happened". She pulled out some joints and lit one up. I went ballistic. How could she use an illegal drug when I had to take all these narcotics? I told her to throw it away—I was not going to break a law! She had no intention of complying with my order. I gave her an ultimatum: either she threw out her marijuana or I wanted her out of the apartment. If only I knew then what the future would hold for me! Anyway, she moved out and we would never be lovers or friends again. I have always wished it had ended differently.

So, there I was, a thousand miles away from home, in a strange city, getting ready to attend regular classes for the first time in six years. I've always made friends easily, so I wasn't worried on that account. There were about 60 apartments, two-thirds of them occupied by students.

The day after Cathy left, I went out to the pool to swim and socialize. The students were very nice and seemed just like me. I was invited back to one of their apartments to drink some wine and smoke some pot. I politely said no and off they went. Almost all the students in the complex, I would soon find out, drank wine and smoked marijuana. I had no problem with the wine but I could envision being arrested because of the pot.

School started and I felt almost normal for the first time in six years. I was going to classes just like everyone else. Only one thing was exceptional: I had been given a special pass for the teachers' parking lot, which was closest to my classes. (It was the era before handicapped parking.)

I quickly started making friends, but it seemed as if in every crowd, socializing involved drinking and smoking marijuana. It was the norm, not the exception. I was on a regimen of seven very strong and potentially lethal prescription drugs but refused to be around marijuana. I wasn't going to break the law.

The first three weeks of school went by rather fast. I was taking the normal freshman classes: World History, Humanities, English, Math, World Art, and Golf. I was doing well in all of them, but I was starting to have physical problems. Even though I had Demerol for pain, Sopor 300 mgs (Quaaludes) for sleep, Valium and several other medicines for muscle relaxation, I was scared of tearing muscles as I walked and I was kept awake by pain night after night.

I had many acquaintances but no new friends. One night as I lay in bed, I reflected that marijuana was the stumbling block. So I made up my mind that the next time I was offered some, I would join in. This was the first time in my life that I ever gave in to peer pressure. I didn't feel good about it, but I had been alone all those years on homebound teaching and I wanted to make friends. If I had to smoke marijuana to be accepted, so be it. The marijuana didn't seem to be harming anyone around me. The kids who smoked it conversed intelligently, and weren't transformed into weirdos or zombies. They were as serious about their schoolwork as I was and studied as hard as I did.

The day after making my decision, I went swimming at the pool. As usual, there were other students enjoying the beautiful, warm weather of South Florida. It started getting dark and one of the girls invited us to join her and her roommate for a bite to eat and drink. When I accepted, she mentioned that people would be smoking pot. I told her I had decided I wanted to try it. About six of us headed for her apartment. Within minutes, someone produced a joint. I was instructed to inhale and hold the smoke in my lungs for as long as possible. I took a rather large puff and promptly started coughing. Everyone laughed and said that was normal. "Next time take a smaller puff..."

I did as told and this time I was able to hold the smoke in my lungs. We all took turns taking puffs. My new friends seemed to be enjoying themselves immensely. I wasn't. That's when they explained to me that you may not get "high" the first few times you smoke.

The rest of the evening went as if marijuana had not been present. We ate, drank, and talked. "Marijuana is no big deal," I thought, as I walked back to my apartment. I thought about Cathy—how ridiculous my bossiness must have seemed to her.

Over the next several weeks I would join my friends for our evening swimming and get-togethers. There would be a little grass, which we all passed around. I still was not getting "high." I suspected that my friends were somehow self-inducing this mysterious state. To me, not getting high was unimportant. I was now making friends, which was the reason I started smoking grass in the first place. Besides, I could always have a little bourbon to get a buzz.

One afternoon at someone's apartment, I got into a chess game with my friend Steve. I preferred backgammon, but Steve loved chess, so chess it was. We were all talking about classes, sports, politics, music, and gossip—the things that college kids talk about. Of course we were smoking. The game went on for about half an hour. I had lost again, but then I realized something astonishing: I had been sitting down for thirty minutes! This was the first time in five years that I had sat still for longer than ten minutes. My normal routine was to sit for ten minutes, then stand for ten minutes to relieve the tension in my legs, then sit, then stand.... How could I have sat still for thirty minutes? In what combination had I taken my prescribed drugs to allow this? But wait, I hadn't taken any pills for the last six hours. I had no idea why I had been able to sit.

Just then, the joint was passed to me. I looked at it and a light bulb went off: I wonder if marijuana relaxed my legs? Even though I was not getting high, maybe marijuana had other advantages. But how could an illegal drug possibly be better than my arsenal of prescription drugs? The reality was that I had sat for a long period of time and I hadn't taken any drugs, just smoked marijuana.

•

The next morning I called Dr. Waive to let him know my hypothesis. He laughed at first. Like most doctors of his generation, he had been taught absolutely nothing about marijuana in medical school. I told him about sitting through a half-hour chess game and my logical conclusion: marijuana had somehow worked as a muscle relaxant. I told him I intended to do research on the subject.

He realized I was serious. He knew that I had been a vocal opponent of marijuana, and if I now thought it might have some benefits, it was not because I was looking for an excuse to indulge. My parents, too, were surprised by my news, but understanding and supportive as they'd always been. I also called Uncle Shipley and Uncle Siggy—neither of whom knew that marijuana had medical use, both of whom said they would look into it.

I couldn't wait to get to the school library myself. I was grateful that several of my high school teachers had taken me to the Old Dominion library to help them do research for their masters theses.

I spent four hours that afternoon looking through material related to marijuana and its use as medicine. Even without the Internet, I struck gold. I learned that marijuana had indeed been known to the medical profession by its Latin name, Cannabis, and that it had been used in many cultures for medical purposes.

In fact, Cannabis was used in tincture form in the United States from 1860 through 1937 to treat a variety of disorders, including muscle tension, inflammation, and pain! It had been manufactured and distributed by Eli Lilly, Merck, Squibb, and other major pharmaceutical companies. I even discovered that there was a farm on the campus of the University of Mississippi where Cannabis was grown under U.S. government auspices for medical research. I still wasn't sure that it was Cannabis that had enabled me to sit for an extended period, but I knew that I had to do a lot more research—including smoking more.

I told my family what I had learned. Cannabis had been used to treat many disorders before it was banned by the Federal Government in 1937. The ban was not the result of any medical findings, but rather a political move. In the early decades of the 20th century, according to what I read, marijuana was used for recreation almost exclusively by Mexican immigrants and African Americans. By passing laws against its cultivation and possession, the white establishment in the Southwest could criminalize and control these segments of the population and undermine their potential power as citizens.

I learned that Cannabis was known as "hemp" when grown for fiber.

Even though hemp contained virtually no THC—the active ingredient that makes marijuana psychoactive— it was seen as a threat by many large corporations. Because hemp was a great fabric for clothing, it represented competition for the cotton industry and the petrochemical companies such as DuPont, which introduced nylon in the 1930s. Hemp could also be used to manufacture paper, which was a threat to the lumber industry. Cannabis had been banned for political and financial reasons, not to protect the health of the American people!

•

For the next three weeks, I used Cannabis almost every day and my health improved dramatically. I was able to sit and walk with less muscle tension and pain. I was able to cut back on the amount of prescription medication I was taking, and generally felt better. School was easier and I was making many new friends.

I maintained a cautious, scientific attitude, however. Perhaps the warm South Florida weather was responsible for my improved health, I told myself. To test this, I didn't smoke for a week—and started going downhill. The pain and muscle tension was worse and I found myself taking more of my prescription drugs without positive results. The weather had been warm and beautiful, but my condition worsened.

I went back to smoking and within several days my condition improved. Another three weeks passed and I felt like a new person. It amazed me how much better I felt. I could move around without the feeling that I was about to tear something. My sleep improved and I wasn't taking nearly as many pills. I conducted this experiment two more times with the same results. The week without Cannabis brought many more problems; the other three weeks I felt like a normal, healthy person. It was now very clear to me that Cannabis was a great medicine and that I had to have it.

•

During this time I had an experience that could have cost me my life. A couple of girls from school had heard about a man who sold marijuana in quantity at a good price—$100 for four ounces. (It was then $40 an ounce, when available around campus.) I wanted to save money and assure myself of a steady supply, so I ordered four ounces and offered to drive them to make the purchase.

We drove to a neighborhood I wasn't familiar with in North Miami and picked up the seller on a street corner by pre-arrangement. He said the marijuana was at his buddy's house. We drove a few blocks and the next thing I know he pulled a gun out and demanded my money, which I gave to him very quickly. He threatened to shoot us but didn't. I had never been that scared in my life. One of the girls peed on herself—this was definitely not a setup. An important lesson was learned: never try to buy marijuana from someone you don't know.

Despite this upsetting incident, I was really enjoying my college experience. It was great being back in a regular class environment. The work was tough, but I was doing well. My health was the best it had been since before my second operation. I started playing a little basketball and I even took bowling as a college class in the spring semester. My careful self-monitoring revealed no new tumors and my existing ones were no longer growing. I was cautiously optimistic that I was going to live. I still had to be somewhat careful how I moved because muscles and veins over my tumors could easily tear. When this did happen, however, the pain and inflammation was less severe—thanks to Cannabis, apparently.

As much as I was enjoying college, I knew what I had to do. My health came first. I had to pursue my right to medicate with Cannabis, and Virginia was the place from which to do it. Not only was Virginia close to the center of power, it has a historic tradition of honoring the rights of the individual. (Patrick Henry's famous line, "Give me liberty or give me death," was the state motto.) Moreover, it was my home base.

I talked to Dr. Waive about collaborating on a scientific study based on my case. We would study the effects of using Cannabis along with Dilaudid, the powerful morphine derivative which I took for pain. We would see if

Cannabis enhanced the effects of Dilaudid so that I could take less to control my pain.

Taking heavy narcotics disrupts your sleep, changes your appetite, can cloud your waking hours and make you lethargic. If we could document a safe, effective method of reducing the required dose of narcotics, countless patients might be helped.

Since my disease was so rare, and my disorder had been so well catalogued, I would make the perfect study patient. Dr. Waive said he would sign any forms or protocols put in front of him, but his responsibilities to other patients meant he would not have time to design the study or to fight my political and legal battle. I agreed to do all the work.

I talked to my family about leaving school, coming back to Virginia, and applying to the Federal Government for permission to use Cannabis. While they were not happy about me dropping out of college, they knew how much better I was doing physically because of Cannabis. They also knew I didn't like being labeled a criminal—I was not raised to break the law. My plan was to leave after the upcoming summer semester.

My social life, which had been non-existent when I arrived in Miami, had become lively and interesting. I was part of a group of about 30 people who gathered regularly at a friend's house in Coconut Grove. The group included people of various nationalities, backgrounds, and interests. Some were students, others had jobs. The main thing we had in common was Cannabis—which all the others called marijuana, of course. They smoked to get high and I smoked to get relief. We were all friends and would do whatever we could to help each other. It was really tough to say goodbye to them. My friend, Paul Herrera, gave me a going-away present: a plain, black plastic tray to roll joints on. I still use that tray to this day, thirty-six years later. I bet more Cannabis has been rolled on that tray then any other in the world! The sad part is I lost contact with all those people, including Paul. I wish I could tell them the rest of my story.

The Supply Problem

The drive North on I-95 seemed to take forever. I was feeling ambivalent. In my heart, I didn't want to leave beautiful, warm Miami and I told myself that one day I would move back. I'd spent a very productive year there. I had learned to live on my own, to take care of myself, to make new friends. I had made the Dean's list. Most important, I had been introduced to a drug that had changed my life. Cannabis was definitely helping me to feel and function better. I was taking fewer pills and suffering fewer adverse effects. If only it were legal, I could have stayed in college.

But Virginia—home—is where I belonged for the next part of my life. It was going to be nice to be with my family again, and to be closer to a girl who lived in Richmond named Debbie Glick. I planned to move back into my old bedroom, get a job, attend classes at Old Dominion University, get reacquainted with Debbie… and convince the Federal Government that I had a right to medicate with Cannabis.

I thought about how God had helped get me to this point. Even though I had this severe bone disorder, God made it that I got treated by the best doctors in the country. He made sure that I got a great education and he brought Cannabis into my life. Somehow, I knew one way or another, I would prove to the Government that Cannabis was the only medicine that really worked for me. God had kept me around for a reason. I hoped that was still his plan.

I pulled into my driveway and I was home. My family greeted me like I had just come back from the war as a hero. They'd had more doubts than they'd let on about whether I would physically survive college. I guess I'd had a few doubts myself.

It was funny smoking Cannabis in the house for the first time and having my parents wonder what that smell was. I told them and said "I think you better get used to it." They laughed and reiterated their support for me. They also reiterated their doubts about my getting cooperation from the Feds. I replied "God has kept me around for a reason and has opened my eyes to a wonderful medicine. One way or another, with God's help, I will win."

The next day I had an appointment with Dr. Waive. We were much more than patient and doctor, we were friends and genuinely glad to see each other. After a lot of small talk, he examined me from head to foot. No new tumors had developed and the existing ones had stopped growing! A full set of x-rays had confirmed what he thought. Dr Waive conveyed the news with a big smile: from now on the odds were going to be in my favor.

He too had begun doing some research and recognized that Cannabis indeed might be having a beneficial effect in my case. I described in detail the experiment I had conducted, using Cannabis for three weeks and then stopping for a week—at which point my condition would worsen. We discussed the possibility of getting the Federal Government to supply me with Cannabis from their farm in Mississippi. The study I had in mind would determine whether using Cannabis as an adjunct medicine would allow me to decrease my use of the drugs I had been prescribed. I would write the study protocol. All I needed Dr. Waive to do was sign it.

He said he would be glad to review, edit, and sign any study plan that I designed. He knew that the odds were against my gaining access to an illegal drug, but he wasn't afraid to help. He slapped me on the back and asked how I planned to get started. My next step, I told him, would be a request to Portsmouth Police Chief Ron Boone, that I be provided with confiscated Cannabis while I was applying to the Federal Government. I needed to obtain a steady, ample supply without breaking the law. (Although it wasn't my main goal, it would also save me a great deal of money not having to buy my medicine on the black market.)

Fortunately, Portsmouth was a small enough city so that through my school, my synagogue, Little League and other community institutions, many people knew about my situation. They knew I had a rare bone disorder and was lucky to be alive. They knew I came from an upstanding, law-abiding family. Many even knew that I had been an advocate against marijuana. The leaders of Portsmouth's medical community respected Dr. Waive and would be inclined to take seriously any project with which he was associated. If Chief Boone were to check out my reputation, I thought he would give my proposal his serious consideration.

Moreover, I had learned that our city incinerator was used to dispose of most of the marijuana confiscated on the East Coast. Because of this, there was always plenty available.

•

That night I told my parents that I intended to approach Chief Boone. They said I had chutzpah—the equivalent of "balls," in English.

My appointment was at 10:00 am. I was there by 9:45 am. I hate to be late. I had never been inside a police station. I wasn't nervous at all because I wasn't doing anything wrong. All Chief Boone knew about meeting with me was that Dr. Waive wanted him to. A few minutes after 10:00 am., he ushered me into his office and we talked briefly about Dr. Waive, who had also treated some of the chief's family members. I told him I had been Dr. Waive's first patient in Portsmouth and that I felt I owed my life to him. When the chief asked the reason for my visit, I asked him to let me fully explain my request before he responded. He agreed.

Here goes... "Chief Boone, I am here today to plead my case for you to turn over to me confiscated marijuana for medical use." I told him my whole story to date. I said that Dr. Waive had also researched the medical uses of Cannabis, and was willing to conduct a formal trial to determine whether Cannabis would enable me to cut back on my prescription drugs. I told him we would seek Federal support for such a trial, but until that came through, I needed a legal supply of Cannabis.

Chief Boone took me seriously. He said he would check with "the powers that be" and get back to me soon. I thanked him for his time and effort, gave him my phone number, and left.

A major concern was finding a source for getting Cannabis until Chief Boone came through—or in case he didn't. I had brought three ounces back with me from Florida, but that amount wouldn't last more than three weeks.

Fortunately, cousins of mine were able to locate a source and I arranged to buy some. Breaking the law made me very uncomfortable, but going without medical Cannabis jeopardized my health.

I started working for my father in his furniture business. My father and a partner owned four furniture stores and a warehouse in the Portsmouth area. They sold and leased moderately priced furniture and bedding. My first job was in the warehouse, helping out wherever needed. I then graduated to making sure that deliveries went out correctly and that new freight was checked for damage and properly stored. I enjoyed working with the other employees and was soon treated as one of the gang.

I would usually go to lunch with my father and Howard Caplan, his partner, then return to the warehouse, go up to the roof—it was a four-story building— and take my medicine. One day as I was smoking, lo and behold, there were two Norfolk, Va., police officers looking at me through binoculars from an eight-story apartment complex across the highway. Almost immediately I heard the thwack-thwack-thwack of a helicopter approaching—a police helicopter. I put out my medicine and went down to the third floor and got back to work. I expected the police to show up any minute, but for some reason they didn't. After that I made sure to smoke in an area not visible from the building across the way.

Each day I would get up, smoke my medicine and go to work. One day Chief Boone invited me back to his office. He had checked out my references and everyone vouched for me. He had heard comments such as, "If Irvin Rosenfeld said it worked as a medicine and if it helps him, then by all means give it to him... He's lucky to be alive and if marijuana helps, then help him." He was impressed by the unanimous response.

I then asked him the million-dollar question: "You are going to provide me with my medicine so I don't have to deal with the criminal element, aren't you?" I didn't like the look on his face. He said, "After talking to the city attorney, we are not going to be able to turn over confiscated marijuana to you. Not only would we be possibly breaking Federal law, but the main reason stated by the attorney was the possibility of catching some unknown disease from potentially tainted marijuana. He was afraid that if you got sick, that you could sue the city. I'm really sorry because I do believe what everyone said about you and that it must help."

I had prepared for a no answer, but not quite in that way. I offered to sign a release indemnifying the city: I would not sue over any sickness which might come from contaminated marijuana. I also said I thought I could tell if something was wrong with a batch of Cannabis. The chief said he already had asked the city attorney about getting a letter from me and the attorney said no, we could still be sued. He said how sorry he was that he couldn't supply my medicine, but the Chief added: "Promise me that you will never sell marijuana, and if you ever get bothered by any police, have them call me and I will explain your situation. You are not a criminal."

He seemed genuinely sorry but I understood that his hands were tied. I thanked him for all the time he put into checking me out and for being in my corner. I reminded him that until Dr. Waive and I could get our study written and approved, I was left with no choice but to deal with the criminal element to get the marijuana I need. He said, "I'll be pulling for you." I shook his hand and left.

Driving home I kept thinking, "Why does everything have to be so difficult?" Here I had survived a disorder that doctors said could kill me. I had discovered a substance that worked better than any other drug or combination of drugs... but I wasn't allowed to obtain it! After a moment of feeling sorry for myself, I began focusing on my research protocol.

That night I told my parents that Chief Boone would not be supplying me with confiscated Cannabis. We knew it had been a long shot, but I tried. Getting the Federal Government to approve my scientific protocol was also a long shot. But I had no choice. Dinner that night was not the celebration I had hoped for.

Civilian Life

The next several months found me working during the day learning all about the furniture business, and trying to research and write my protocol by night. I was trained in sales and worked at all of my father's retail outlets. I was also spending as much time as possible with beautiful Debbie Glick.

Debbie and I had known each other for more than four years. We had gone from being friends to being boyfriend and girlfriend, back to friends, and back again to lovers. When I was a senior in high school I used to go to Richmond almost every weekend and stay at Debbie's house. I became close to her mother, and there were days that I would drive to Richmond knowing Debbie was in school, just to visit with her mother.

During my year in Miami Debbie's mother, Beatrice, was diagnosed with liver cancer and I flew to Virginia several times to see her and to be there for Debbie. The very last time I saw Bea, she said she was sorry she wouldn't be around to see us get married. Since I had always been honest with her, I said I was not going to marry her daughter. She smiled and said, "Yes you will." When I moved back to Virginia, I realized that she had been right.

•

I briefly enrolled at Old Dominion University in Norfolk. Returning to the campus where I used to help my teachers do research, I thought about how much my situation had improved. Before, I had medical problems with no help in sight. Now my problems were fewer and less severe—and I hoped that medical Cannabis would help me get even better. Unfortunately, working and going to school was more than I could handle physically. With an eye towards getting married in June, I chose to keep working.

I had been able to secure a reliable source of quality Cannabis. It was expensive, but I had to have it. The tumors were no longer growing, nor were any new ones forming. Life wasn't bad. I was enjoying my job and was making new friends. I started playing some basketball at Old Dominion. I wasn't very good, but it was fun and it kept me active. I could only play half court because running was difficult. My doctors had told me I had to beat the disease mentally as well as physically. Not giving up on sports was one of my ways of doing both.

One day I received a notice from the draft board: my lottery number was two. (1972 was the next-to-last draft of the Vietnam War. An all-volunteer Army would soon be implemented—proof that our Government is capable of making major policy changes when old approaches aren't working.) I called Dr. Waive who said he would send my medical records to the board. He added, to my surprise, that he could not reassure me of a "4F" exemption because he had recently learned of a patient with a severe spinal disorder whom the Army had seen fit to accept.

Arrangements were made for me to be examined by an Army doctor in Richmond. I arrived at the armory at 7:00 am., was told to halt by a guard at the entrance, then directed to the doctor's office. My records were sitting on his desk. He gave me a grave, sad look, and said, as if he was telling me the worst news possible, "Son, we're not going to be able to take you. This bone problem is just too serious."

For his sake, I tried to sound disappointed: "Are you sure?"

He nodded.

I had to hang around the armory to take a written test given at 11:00 am. A bus from Portsmouth arrived with all the guys who were going to have their physicals. Many of them were friends of mine. "I'm already out," I said, sounding the opposite of disappointed.

That night Debbie and I decided to get engaged. "Make love, not war," was a popular slogan back then, and I lived up to it.

Marijuana had been categorized as a "Schedule 1" drug (potentially harmful and having no medical use) when Congress passed the Controlled Substances Act in 1970. A Presidential commission was expected to review marijuana's status as a drug without medical use, but did not. (The commission did, however, call for "decriminalizing" small-scale possession.)

Writing a protocol in the format required by FDA turned out to be quite difficult, although the study design was quite simple. Dr. Waive and I hoped to show how my intake of Diluadid and other drugs would be diminished with my use of Cannabis on a regular basis. The study would take two years and Dr. Waive would file reports every six months. If the findings were positive, then the study could be renewed.

In March, 1973, I gave my draft to Dr. Waive. He made a few changes and submitted it to the FDA. We did not want to be seen as challenging the marijuana prohibition; we were merely seeking an exemption—approval for a study of one patient and one patient only. We could substantiate the severity of my very rare disorder. The FDA would not have to worry about opening "Pandora's Box."

I was glad to see the trees turning green and everything coming back to life that spring. My year in Miami had spoiled me. It seemed as if every day there had been warm and sunny. My physical condition, while better than it had ever been in Virginia, was not as good as it had been in Miami, and this I attributed to the weather. When you wake up and your first feeling is one of pain, the cold seems to make it worse. You don't even want to get out of bed. I really missed living in Miami.

My weekdays were consumed by work and my weekends were spent with Debbie. We had decided to get married on June 24, 1973. Except for an occasional call to the U.S. Food and Drug Administration to check on the status of my research project, life felt orderly and normal.

What A Way To Start A Marriage

Our wedding in Richmond was a great occasion. All my family and friends were there to celebrate. The only person missing was Dr. Waive; one of his children was being confirmed that day. I had an appointment scheduled with him the following Friday, at which I planned to tell him all about the wedding.

Debbie and I went on a five-day honeymoon to Williamsburg and to my sister's house in Raleigh, North Carolina. Debbie was now around me all the time and subjected to my Cannabis use. While she realized how beneficial it was for me, she hated the second-hand smoke. I'm lucky it wasn't a deal-breaker! We made up ground rules. I would not smoke in our bedroom. If I smoked while driving with her, I would wait 30 minutes before smoking another.

We got back to Norfolk on the night before my appointment with Dr. Waive, and stayed together for the first time in our new apartment. My right ankle was bothering me, but I figured it was just a basketball injury. I slept really well that night.

I wasn't due back at work until Monday, so we had a leisurely morning. I smoked my medicine and was in a good mood. It was summertime and the weather was nice and hot, just the way I like it. My appointment was for 3:00 pm. I got there a little early to tell the staff about my wedding. I then went back toward the x-ray room. I saw Dr. Waive as he was going in a room to see another patient. I told him my right ankle was bothering me. He told me to tell the technician what x-rays to take and that he would see me in a few minutes.

I had the films taken and waited for the doctor. The technician brought the films out so the doctor could see them. Since he was still with other patients, I figured I might as well read them. I took the first film and popped it into the viewer. I looked at the x-ray and cringed. Oh my God... there was this huge tumor encasing my ankle that had never been there before. I knew right away what was about to happen.

Dr. Waive appeared, looked at me, and knew something was wrong. I couldn't speak. He looked at the film and his head dropped. He said, "I don't know where that tumor came from, but you know what this means."

I said, "I guess I need to check into the hospital Sunday."

He put his hand on my shoulder. "I thought we were finished with all this," he said. Me, too.

I got into my car, lit a joint and drove around for about an hour. All I could think about was I was no longer a kid. I'm married and working. What was I going to do? I did everything that I had been taught and yet here was a brand new tumor that three months ago was not even there. This should not have happened. I went to my parent's house which was where Debbie was and broke the news to them. We spent Friday and Saturday night at the apartment and Sunday afternoon I checked into Maryview Hospital.

Surgery was performed bright and early Monday morning. I woke up in the recovery room and saw Dr. Waive smiling. He said he had to break my tibia and fibula in two places to get the tumor out and the pain from this operation would be worse than I had experienced in the past. I was in the hospital until Wednesday, then went back to my parents' house to begin my recovery. What a way to start a marriage!

For several days after surgery I couldn't smoke because it hurt my fresh incision. It wasn't until Thursday that I could smoke again and by that time, my body really needed it. Strange how the same substance one day can hurt and another day provides such relief. I was learning more and more about the effects of Cannabis. I had to learn how to walk again and rehabilitate my ankle. It was a month before I could go back to work. It would be a year before my ankle felt right.

During recovery I had a lot of time to think about my scientific project and the obstinacy of the Government. I was being given synthetic morphine and any other potentially lethal pharmaceuticals that I wanted, but my doctor could not give me the medicine that I needed. It just didn't seem right.

The FDA continued to ignore my application and I didn't have the energy to do anything about it. Surgery takes a lot out of you. I was still able to find Cannabis, but I couldn't afford all that I needed, so my intake of pharmaceuticals increased.

Six months after my operation, Dr. Waive contracted Hepatitis from a "stick" from a needle in the course of performing an operation on a sick patient, a danger faced by all health care workers. He was told the damage to his liver had been nearly fatal, and to stay home for two months so he could fully recover. I told him to be a good patient and do as he was told. After one month, I got a call from his office saying that he had come back to work and would not listen to anyone about going home. The staff was hoping he would listen to me, since I was his first patient.

I got Dr. Waive on the phone and asked him who I should use as an orthopedic surgeon after he died. I told him he was being selfish. His family and all his patients counted on him—he had some nerve to put himself at risk. He said his patients needed him now. I had always told Dr. Waive that even with all my operations, one day he would be visiting my grave. I now told him, "I guess I was wrong. I'll be visiting yours."

Three months later, that's exactly what happened. Dr. Waive died. Not only had I lost one of my heroes, but I had lost a true friend. It was so sad seeing his wife and five children at the funeral. The entire community showed up to pay their last respects. Almost everyone in the area was touched by this great man. He died at age 47—much, much too soon.

Finding the Right Doctor

What was I going to do? I no longer had a doctor to conduct my study, even if the FDA approved it. I also had to find a new orthopedic surgeon. Dr. Waive had taught me enough so that, in his absence, I would be able to explain to other doctors what needed doing. I thought that maybe one day he or I would move away...

I was treated by Dr. Waive's partners, who continued to prescribe Dilaudid, Valium, etc., but declined to take on my study. Over the next year, I met with many doctors but none open-minded enough to agree to be the researcher.

In the summer of 1974 I noticed a brand new tumor starting to grow on my pubic bone, an area of the body that one knows intimately. Within a week the tumor was the size of a cherry and growing rapidly. Dr. Waive and Dr. Green had taught me that any tumor that grows that quickly needs to be taken out. I made an appointment and went to one of Dr. Waive's partners. He said the tumor couldn't be new, it had to have been there for some time. I explained that is one area of the body one notices all the time, and this was a new tumor. After we reviewed old x-rays, he agreed with me. This did not instill a great sense of security.

I called my Uncle Siggy, the pediatrician in Connecticut. He had graduated from medical school with a doctor who was now head of orthopedics at the University of Virginia, Frank McCue, MD. Uncle Siggy arranged for me to see Dr. McCue the next day.

Debbie and I got in the car and drove the five hours to Charlottesville. I was very quiet during the trip. I didn't want to talk about what was to happen. I kept thinking: why was I developing these new tumors when the authorities said the worst was over? I wondered how many other tumors might crop up. Here I had just been married a little over one year and I was about to go through my second operation. I thought I had beaten this disease... I was wrong.

I met with Dr. McCue and his staff. The tumor was now the size of a lemon and they agreed that surgery was needed and offered to perform it there. I was reluctant to get stuck in a hospital more than two hundred miles from home. I was given a referral to a surgeon in Norfolk, Dr. David Young, and we headed back. The drive home was just as long and just as quiet. I didn't want to talk about how I felt. The new tumor hadn't caused me any pain, but it was growing wildly. So I was going to have to have another operation and I couldn't do anything about it. That was a low, low point.

I called Dr. Young's office and was given an appointment the next day. I brought all the relevant information and x-rays with me. I met Dr. Young and brought him up to date. He proceeded to look at the films and examine me, all the time asking questions about the disorder. When he finished, he said he would be willing to operate on me, but he did not want me as an ongoing patient because the case was so complex. (I had told him about my marijuana use but he showed little interest.) He offered to perform additional surgeries, as needed, but he would not monitor my condition or treat me on a regular basis. He said this matter-of-factly, pulling no punches. Again, I had no choice. I would have to let a doctor I had only just met, and who would not take me on as a patient, operate on me. What a strange world.

I went into the hospital that Sunday and was operated on the next day. The tumor was now the size of my fist. The tumor had grown from nothing to the size of my fist in less than a month. I couldn't take the chance of malignancy. Right before he put me under, he informed me that I may wake up with a catheter and not be able to urinate. I looked at him and thought what a time to tell me this. I wished him good luck and out I went.

When I came to in the recovery room, the nurse said the procedure had gone very well—everything seemed to be working properly— and I should be fine. I breathed a sigh of relief. Dr. Young came in and told me the same thing. He had removed the entire tumor and it didn't appear to be cancerous. He also said I should have a complete recovery. I went back to him a week later to have the stitches removed and I never saw him again. Sure enough, he did a great job. I fully recovered.

After I got better, I still needed to find an orthopedic surgeon that I could talk to and rely on. A Dr. Joel Mason was recommended as a competent surgeon who also had a good bedside manner. I went to see him and he reviewed my file. I asked him if he knew any reason why those last two tumors had developed. He had no idea.

My right ankle was bothering me again, so I asked to have some x-rays taken. Sure enough, the tumor in my ankle had grown back, even worse than before Dr. Waive had operated on it. By this point I was not shocked; it was like I expected that to happen.

Dr. Waive was dead; I just had an operation on my pelvis, and now the tumor had reappeared in my ankle. It was like, I just could not win. Dr. Mason looked at the x-ray and advised that surgery might not be possible now that the tumor was encompassing my tibia and fibula three inches above my ankle and most of the ankle bone itself. I was not about to go through surgery again until I knew why these new tumors were forming when they shouldn't.

After examining me, Dr. Mason thought that what I really needed was a doctor who could be my everyday doctor. One who could take care of all my prescriptions and my general health. He said, "You know your condition better than any orthopedic surgeon and you know when something needs looking at." He recommended that I call an endocrinologist by the name of Charles Goldman.

It turned out Dr. Goldman's parents knew mine, and that he knew my older sister, Gayle, with whom he'd gone to high school. The family connection put both of us at ease.

I told him my medical history in detail. When I told him about the recent, unexpected tumors, he looked at me thoughtfully. He asked me to hold out the back of my hands. He looked at them and then pointed out how my little finger on my left hand was smaller than the one on my right, which was not normal. He asked me to hold out my arms. He pointed out a curvature that was not normal. He felt my neck and said it was shorter than normal. He looked at me and said, "I think I know what is wrong."

He went over to his bookshelf and pulled out one of his medical texts. He shuffled through, found the page he was looking for, and started reading out loud: "...a variant of the syndrome Pseudo Pseudo Hypoparathyroidism, prevalent in people who have Multiple Congenital Cartilaginous Exostosis. The patient can develop new tumors at any age and existing ones can grow at any time."

I felt like a great weight had just been removed. Dr. Goldman didn't understand why I was smiling when he had just read me a potential death sentence. I was relieved because at last I had an explanation of why tumors kept forming. I had been to major research centers and been examined by specialists, and here was a doctor who just looked at me and knew what I had!

I asked Dr. Goldman if he would take me on as a patient. He said, "Let's go over what you need me to do and I will decide." He proceeded to examine me from head to toe, noting where all my bad tumors were and how they affected me. We then discussed all the medicines I was on. He agreed that they were the best available and had been appropriately prescribed.

Dr. Goldman said he would take me on as a patient and that together we would do the best we could. Then I told him about my discovery of medical Cannabis. I told him what I had learned about the history of Cannabis in this country and about the scientific study I was planning to conduct with the help of Dr. Waive. (Dr. Goldman was another of Dr. Waive's admirers.)

He asked how the FDA had responded. I said they had basically ignored us, but that I'm not one to give up. I made sure he knew that I had done all the work myself and that Dr. Waive only had to make a few small revisions before signing his name. I knew I was taking a chance of scaring him off.

Dr. Goldman said that I should bring him what I had written up. He would do some research on medical marijuana and we would discuss the subject at our next appointment. Hearing him say "your next appointment" filled me with hope. I had a new doctor who cared about me and was willing to be open-minded about my treatment. The next day I brought all the paperwork so Dr. Goldman could review the study.

My next appointment was thirty days later and he was totally prepared. He had studied all my material and had read up on medical Cannabis. He said he believed me and thought we should try to get the study approved. That was music to my ears! I could now proceed with a doctor who understood what medical Cannabis was about and who was also going to be my treating physician.

Ever since Dr. Waive died, it had been very difficult to get doctors to write prescriptions for the powerful narcotics I used. Doctors are very reluctant to prescribe Dilaudid, etc., especially to patients they aren't seeing regularly. Dr. Goldman was willing to write the necessary prescriptions and he shared my hope that access to medical Cannabis would enable me to decrease my use of those dangerous pharmaceuticals.

For the next two years, Charles Goldman would examine me once a month. We monitored all my bone tumors, and thank God none were growing. We started keeping records of how much Dilaudid and other medicines I would take when I had very little Cannabis compared to when I was able to afford and could find enough for my medical needs. He quickly realized that I took a lot less when I had plenty of Cannabis. He also came to share the frustrations Dr. Waive and I had with FDA. Every six months or so, in response to my prodding, an official would send Dr. Goldman a letter saying that I hadn't been to a certain research center or hadn't tried a certain type of therapy. Their stalling seemed to have no end.

Caught Up in the "War on Drugs"

One morning in the Spring of 1976 I picked up the Virginian-Pilot and read a brief story about the start of a trial involving a man named Robert Randall who claimed to be using Cannabis as a treatment for glaucoma. He had been arrested for growing marijuana in his Washington, D.C. backyard and intended to cite "medical necessity" as his defense. I wasn't alone—there was someone else who recognized the medical value of Cannabis!

I hoped to meet Robert Randall someday, and two years later I did. He had started going around to college campuses under the auspices of NORML—the National Organization for the Reform of Marijuana Laws—telling his story and discussing the use of marijuana as a medicine. It was in April, 1978, that I first heard him speak at Old Dominion University. He was very articulate. He had a Master's in Rhetoric from the University of South Florida and knew the subject very well.

Bob, who was then twenty-nine, had been diagnosed with severe glaucoma at age twenty-four. At the time of his diagnosis he had recently arrived in Washington, D.C., with ambitions to be a political speechwriter but his "day job" was driving a cab. His ophthalmologist prescribed all the available drugs but his intraocular pressure kept rising. He was advised that he would be blind by age thirty. Then he discovered—just as I had, after smoking it in a recreational context—that marijuana eased his symptoms. In Bob's case, it eliminated the visual "haloes" caused by glaucoma.

That discovery made it crucial that he have a regular supply, but black market sources would come and go. In 1975 a marijuana seed sprouted in a flowerpot on his deck and, as Bob put it, "this 'volunteer' was the obvious solution to my problem—grow enough marijuana to cover the dry spells.'" He was growing four plants on the deck when D.C. police raided the apartment and arrested Bob and his wife to be, Alice O'Leary.

Bob then paid a visit to the Washington headquarters of NORML, which had been founded in 1970 by a young lawyer named Keith Stroup, with a $5,000 grant from Hugh Hefner of Playboy Magazine. NORML had filed suit in 1972 challenging the Controlled Substances Act classification of marijuana as a "Schedule 1" drug—meaning dangerous and of no medical use. But the Feds had ignored the suit, and NORML had shifted its emphasis to pushing "decriminalization" bills in state legislatures.

Stroup gave Bob some government contacts, and one of them forwarded a report from the National Institute on Drug Abuse (NIDA) that made reference to a 1971 study by UCLA opthalmologist Robert Hepler, MD, who had successfully treated glaucoma patients with marijuana. Bob went to Los Angeles and spent ten days being tested by Dr. Hepler, who confirmed that only inhaled marijuana reduced his intraocular pressure. He came back to Washington with a letter from Dr. Hepler documenting his desperate situation.

Instead of accepting a plea bargain and paying a fine for misdemeanor possession of marijuana, Bob decided to fight the criminal charges, citing "medical necessity"—a legal principle that justifies breaking the law when obeying it would result in a greater harm.

But even acquittal wouldn't solve Bob's problem of obtaining a legal supply. Alice O'Leary suggested that he ask the Federal Government to provide him with some of the marijuana being grown for NIDA's research purposes. In May, 1976 he petitioned the Drug Enforcement Administration (DEA) and the Department of Health, Education and Welfare (now Health & Human Services) to provide him marijuana.

In July '76 Bob made his medical-necessity argument in D.C. Superior Court. Judge James Washington, former dean of Howard University Law

School, ruled in his favor four months later.

In August Bob learned that a physician affiliated with Howard, John Merritt, MD, was interested in studying marijuana as a treatment for glaucoma. Bob became his patient, and NIDA agreed to deliver to Dr. Merritt, c/o the U.S. Public Health Service pharmacy, a tin of 300 pre-rolled marijuana cigarettes for use by his patient.

Although the Government pressured Bob to show his gratitude by not publicizing the fact that he was using marijuana legally, he decided to carry the message as far and wide as he could. This is how he summed up his attitude: "Having won, why go mum? There were sick people to save. Better to trust my fellow citizens and shout into the darkness than rely on a devious Government dedicated to a fraudulent prohibition."

•

I first met Bob at a speaking engagement at Old Dominion University. He talked for about an hour and a half to an audience of almost three hundred people, then answered questions for another half hour. When he had finished, some twenty people surrounded him to ask more questions. I was one of them. I waited until I was the only one left. I introduced myself and started to tell him my story.

At first, I could see him thinking, "Here's another person who wants marijuana." But when he heard that I had submitted a scientific project to the FDA, his whole attitude changed. He was now listening intently. I told him how I had applied to the FDA in 1973 and been stonewalled. This did not surprise him. I told him about my bone disorders and how I discovered that Cannabis worked for me. I basically told him my whole life story. After I finished, he said, "You've been working on your study for five years. How would you like to work another five years?" My answer was, "Whatever it takes."

Bob and I continued talking in the hallway outside the auditorium. He told me more details of his life, his criminal case, his fight to get legal marijuana through NIDA. He said the Government had no intention of ever giving marijuana to anyone else, but if anyone had a chance, it was me.

Bob suggested that we turn my study into what he called a "Compassionate Care Protocol." Instead of trying to prove that Cannabis works as a medicine, my doctor would state that none of the conventional medicines work and that he believes Cannabis could. "This way the Government doesn't have to agree that Cannabis is a medicine," Bob explained. "They are just having compassion for you. All a qualified physician has to do is believe that a Schedule 1 drug could be beneficial, and the Government could allow a doctor to try this for a patient to see if it works."

Bob offered to help me construct a Compassionate Care Protocol based on my medical records. He repeated that the Government did not intend to issue medical Cannabis to anyone else. I reminded him that the Government never intended to give medical Cannabis to anyone at all, but he had proved them wrong. "The fact that you are willing to help me says that I have a chance."

That night I shared my excitement with my family. I was no longer alone. The only person in the United States to receive medical Cannabis from the Federal Government was going to try and help me! They were glad that I was upbeat but I could see in their faces that they thought I was in for more disappointment.

I called Dr. Goldman the next day and told him all about Robert Randall and his suggestion that we turn our study into a Compassionate Care Protocol. Dr. Goldman acknowledged that all the drugs he was prescribing had marginal effects and that Cannabis enabled me to decrease my use of them and achieve better effects. He said he would sign off on the protocol if Bob and I did all the work. I told him not to worry, we would handle it. I was putting a lot of faith in Bob although I hardly knew him.

Dr. Goldman and I got all my medical records together and sent them off to Bob. He and Alice O'Leary were now working for NORML, handling inquiries concerning the medical use of marijuana. For the next several weeks, I would talk to Bob or Alice on a daily basis. They would have questions or would need more medical records. I was very impressed with the seriousness of their approach.

It took them about two months of steady work before we had a protocol that we thought was ready to present to Dr. Goldman. He said he couldn't believe how well it read and how convincing it was. He readily signed it, along with a mountain of forms to be sent to the FDA, the DEA, and the NIDA.

In order for me to get Government-issued Cannabis, first the FDA had to approve the protocol. Then the DEA had to approve of my doctor and myself. The DEA also had to approve the pharmacy or office to which the Cannabis would be shipped and held. Only after these approvals had been granted would the NIDA ship the medicine. Simple... Right!!!

We mailed everything off (there was no Fed Ex back then) and started the wait. I contacted the FDA 10 days later to confirm that they had received my paperwork and was told they had not. So we re-sent it by registered mail.

That package they got.

•

Weeks and months went by without any word. Every time we contacted them, we got the proverbial answer, "We are still investigating your condition." Bob had warned us about the stall tactics the FDA would employ and I reminded him that I was all too familiar with their ways.

My health was holding steady. I was relying on Cannabis supplied by Bill C., whom I had met through a cousin. Bill sold marijuana to supplement his income and to pay for what he smoked. He understood that my use was medical and he didn't try to take advantage of my situation. In fact, it made him feel good to be helping me out. He would typically sell me a quarter pound of high-quality Cannabis from Colombia, Jamaica, or Mexico for $80. I was using about five ounces a month and could have used twice that if I could have afforded it.

After six months went by I contacted the FDA and was told they had not come to any conclusions. I knew I had to come up with another battle plan because, regardless of my medical needs, I had been caught up in the "War on Drugs."

A Small Victory

By early 1979, thanks to Bob and Alice's efforts, several states had passed laws to allow doctors to prescribe Cannabis for pain caused by cancer or glaucoma. Bob thought there was a chance of Virginia passing such a law.

With the help of the state chapter of NORML, public hearings were organized around the state. Bob asked me to testify at the hearing in Norfolk. I had never gone public with my use of medical Cannabis and now Bob wanted me to say that I used it daily in defiance of State and Federal law. This truly scared the shit out of me. I owned my own furniture store with my father, so I didn't have to be worried about losing my job. I could still be arrested for possession however, and my arrangement with Chief Boone might not keep me from being prosecuted. I was just too scared. I told Bob I would come to the hearings and listen.

Debbie and my parents agreed that testifying would be too risky. I really felt very bad about letting Bob and Alice down after all they had done for me, but they understood. Bob was a legal Federal patient and I wasn't. I was also disappointing two local attorneys, Michael Goode and Claude Scialdone, who had helped me in putting together my protocol and to arrange the public hearing in Norfolk.

The day of the hearing was beautiful, weather-wise. It was early spring and flowers were starting to bloom. I walked into the hearing room and saw Bob, the two attorneys, and many other people, including local and state police. The state representatives came in and the hearing was called to order. They started off with some opponents of the proposed statute, then Bob and the attorneys spoke in favor of it. Bob explained how Cannabis worked and that other states had passed laws identical to the one Virginia was considering.

The law had two main purposes, he said. It was a way of telling the Federal Government that Virginia supported access to medical Cannabis—which the Federal Government controlled— and it would shield a small group of patients from arrest under state law. The representatives asked him many questions and Bob answered them all in a very convincing way.

The last speaker before lunch got ready to talk. Before he did, the chairman said that anyone else who wanted to speak should sign up during the lunch break if they hadn't already. My friends looked at me hoping I had changed my mind, but I was not about to speak publicly.

The last speaker identified himself as the head of narcotics for the Virginia Beach Police Department. He stated that if the law got passed, he would have many more illegal prescriptions to track down. The chairman asked how the officer would go about solving the existing problem of illegal prescriptions. "If we could close all the pharmacies," came the reply, "there would be no more illegal prescriptions."

When the chairman asked how sick people would get their medicine, the officer responded that it wasn't his problem. I couldn't believe what I had just heard and I wasn't alone. What would I or any sick person do if there were no pharmacies? How would we get the medicines we needed? That was the last straw. I went to the clerk and signed up to speak after lunch. I was scared, but at least there were friendly attorneys there to help me if I got arrested. I looked at Bob and he had a big smile on his face.

We all went to lunch and my allies tried to assure me that with Chief Boone on my side, I probably would not be arrested; and if I was, he most likely could get the charges dropped. I noticed they said "probably" and "most likely." I didn't enjoy my lunch. I trusted Bob and he assured me it was the right thing to do. He explained that sometimes you just have to do what's right even if the consequences aren't good. He said, "Irvin, you are fighting for a medicine you need. You've come so far, but you and I know there is still a long way to go and you may never win. So you need to fight for yourself and most important, you can do this." I thanked him for his pep talk and asked if he would visit me in jail.

We went back to the hearing room and sat down. I waited for my turn.

The committee had several more opposition speakers, including the head of the State Police and the head of the Virginia Crime Commission, Lew Hurst. I listened to what they said and kept thinking about what I would say. After they finished, the chairman said the next speaker is Irvin Rosenfeld, from Portsmouth.

This was my first time speaking in public. Little did I know that it would be the first of hundreds of talks I would give on the subject of medical Cannabis. I walked up to the front table, sat down, looked at the committee and identified myself. I started telling them about my bone disorders and how I was lucky to still be alive. I told about my homebound education, provided free of charge by the state. I also told about all the legal prescriptions I had been taking since age thirteen, and that closing pharmacies would most likely kill me. "Just because there is a problem with illegal prescriptions doesn't mean you should penalize sick people." I pointed out that we have a problem with obesity, and if we closed all the supermarkets and restaurants, the problem would be solved.

I told the committee that even with my severe bone disorder I co-owned a furniture store with my father. I told them I had been married for almost six years. I told them about my major surgeries. What it felt like to go under, not knowing if you were going to wake up with both legs. I described being an advocate against marijuana during high school and how I talked to fellow students about staying away from illegal drugs. I told about going to college and how quite by accident I discovered the medical aspect of Cannabis. I told about the doctors in my family and how they and I had researched Cannabis and found that it was prescribed in tincture form in this country from 1860 through 1937. It was manufactured by leading drug companies, such as Eli Lilly and Merck. It was used for treatment for many medical problems, such as pain and inflammation, and to help provide muscle relaxation.

Those were the effects that Cannabis had on me—without any negative side effects. I was not getting "high" or euphoric. I had finally found a medicine that worked without giving me that drugged feeling. I kept wondering how far I should go. I knew that what I said could change everything...

I proceeded to tell the committee about my daily use of Cannabis and how my intake of more harmful, potentially lethal drugs had diminished. I told them about the prohibitive cost and how I could not afford to buy all I needed on the black market. I also told them how I didn't like dealing with the criminal element to get the medicine I needed. I told them of my years of efforts to get the Federal Government to supply my medicine, first by planning a scientific study and then recasting it as a "Compassionate Care Protocol." One does not ask for a devastating disease, I said, but one has to learn to cope the best way one can. "This medicine has changed my life and I had to tell you the truth, no matter what the ramifications are."

I thanked the committee for their time and hoped they would have a positive recommendation. As I turned to walk back to my seat, the local and state police officers followed me with their eyes. My heart sank. I sat down and the next thing I saw was the head of the State Police and the head of the Crime Commission walking over to me. I thought, "I've done it now, I'm about to be arrested."

They sat down and the head of the Commission asked, "Do you realize what you have just done?" I told him, "I did what I had to do." He again asked, "You have no idea what you just did, do you?" I said, "Look you can arrest me, but I had to tell the truth." They both kind of snickered and the chief said, "You really don't know what you have done. By testifying before this committee, you are afforded immunity from prosecution. We are NOT here to arrest you, but to ask you how we can help."

To say I was in shock was an understatement. I was not being arrested and two of the highest-ranking police officers in the state were asking me how they could help. God had done it again. Miracles do happen. Bob and my other two friends could not hear what was happening and you could see on their faces expressions of "What did we get him into?" Then they saw me smile and—noting that no handcuffs had been employed – figured things couldn't be all that bad.

I thanked the state officials for wanting to help and told them the best thing they could do was to get behind the bill and see that it passed. I then asked them why they wanted to help me. Their reply was very simple, "We want to stop crime, not to harm patients. We believe your story and you've gone about this the right way. How could we not help?" I almost started crying. I thanked them again and shook their hands. They got up and went back to their seats.

I later learned why the head of the Crime Commission was so sympathetic. His name was Lew Hurst and his son had been a Norfolk police officer. One night Lew Hurst, Jr.'s unit conducted a drug raid at a house that had been incorrectly targeted. The officers entered with a warrant and were going up the stairs when the resident, who kept a gun in his bedroom, fired a shot through the bottom of his door, trying to scare them off. It hit Officer Hurst in the head, killing him. As a result of this tragic, botched raid, his father, the commissioner, had become skeptical about the "War on Drugs." I was an indirect beneficiary.

After another hour of pro and con speakers, the hearing ended. I got up and went to each committee member and shook their hands and thanked them for their interest. I got a lot of positive feedback from the members. I said goodbye to my two new friends, who I hoped to see again in Richmond when the bill was voted on in committee. They reiterated their support.

I walked over to Bob, Claude, and Michael and acted like nothing much had happened. They asked, "What happened over there when the head of the Crime Commission and State Police came over to you?" I said, "You're not going to believe this, but they said I had immunity and wanted to know what they could do to help." They were also in shock after hearing this. Bob said, "Strange how some things happen."

I went home and told my family what took place. They, too, were quite surprised by the outcome. They couldn't believe I wasn't in jail. Neither could I. For the first time, I could see in their faces a belief that maybe I was moving forward and just maybe society was changing its attitude. Here I had two of the highest- ranking state officials wanting to help me. I now had three government officials on my side. Granted they were state and local, not Federal, but it was a start.

That night I went to bed feeling good about having won for a change, even if it was just a small victory.

Education of an Activist

Over the next several months, hearings were held around the state and widespread support for medical Cannabis was expressed. In response, our opponents started a campaign of their own to maintain complete Prohibition.

The climactic hearing was held in Richmond, where a Senate committee would decide whether to send the bill to the full Senate, or kill it. The last time I had been at the statehouse was on a visit with my fourth grade class. Now I was walking in as participant. I felt very important, I could make a difference.

The bill that had been agreed upon by the joint (no pun intended) committees protected only cancer and glaucoma patients. It was expected that the patient would go to a pharmacy, present the prescription, and be told that it could not be filled because the Federal Government controls the production and distribution of marijuana for medical purposes. The patient's attempt to comply with Virginia law would shield him or her from arrest if he or she then tried to fill the prescription from a street dealer. I had complained to the committees that, never having had cancer, I would not be protected by such a law. I was reminded that benign tumors could become cancerous at any point, therefore I was protected. It was a gray area, but I supported the final wording.

The Senate hearings were scheduled to run from 1:00 pm. to 5:00 pm. Both sides were well represented. The head of the State Police and Lew Hurst, the head of the Crime Commission, were there and had drummed up support, as promised. I was very moved by these law enforcement officials who understood that marijuana had bona fide medical uses. It was good to have them on my side!

I would have two opportunities to speak, once along with other speakers in support of the bill, and then again giving the final "pro" argument before the vote. I was playing an important role in what could be historic legislation. I was no longer scared to speak my mind. I was becoming a force in the state for the passage of this bill. During the next four hours, not only did I testify publicly, but I also lobbied the Senators privately in the hall. My opponents were also hard at work. This being the first time I had ever lobbied, I watched other people to learn the correct protocols. I had quite an education that day. I met State Senators and their staff, did interviews with the media, and talked with my opponents.

The hearing ran late. Five o'clock came and we still did not know if we had enough votes to get the bill out of committee. A lot was on my shoulders, but I felt up to the task. Around 5:40 pm., Senator Peter Babalas asked to speak. He was one of the oldest and most respected Senators in Virginia. He had not asked any questions or spoken at all during the hearing. He and his staff had purposely not spoken to anyone, for or against the bill. We didn't know why until he turned on his mike and said, "Gentleman, I have cancer and I am being treated at Sloan Kettering Cancer Center in New York. If it wasn't for the marijuana they give me to take away my nausea, I would quit my treatment. Nothing else worked."

There was dead silence. No one had any idea that he had cancer. Here was one of the most senior Senators in our state saying that he was using medical marijuana. God had to be around again. I felt that I had been vindicated and validated—yes, marijuana is a medicine. I still wasn't sure of the vote, but I was a lot more confident.

There were a few more questions, and then I was called as the last pro speaker. I walked to the podium, looked into each Senator's eyes and then started. I told them how today had been a learning experience for everyone involved, both pro and con. I told them this was a medical issue, one that should be resolved by patients and their doctors. I said, "You've heard from the patients, the ones using medical marijuana. We are not criminals. Please enact this law so we won't be labeled that way." I again looked into the eyes of each Senator and thanked them for their understanding and compassion. Senator Babalas had a smile on his face. I knew then that I had done well.

The last speaker in opposition got up to the podium and started berating Senator Babalas for using marijuana. He said that medical marijuana was "a hoax" and "evil." Whatever support the opposition may have had evaporated when Senator Babalas was addressed so disrespectfully. The Chairman called for the vote and there was not one vote against! We had won the first battle. I thanked everyone for their support, especially my friends in law enforcement. It didn't really hit me what had been accomplished until the drive home. We had discussed medical marijuana in the State capitol and had won. The bill then passed the full Senate and House and Governor John Dalton duly signed it into law.

I had become a part-time political activist. I ran my furniture store with my father, tried being a good husband to my wife, and smoked the marijuana I bought from Bill. I hadn't had a new tumor develop or an existing one grow for more than five years. I still had to take numerous prescription drugs, still could not afford to buy all the marijuana I needed. Worse yet, there were times that I couldn't find any marijuana to buy and had to rely on my prescribed drugs.

·

On July 1, 1979, the day the new state law went into effect, I went to Dr. Goldman, got a prescription for marijuana, and then went to my pharmacist, who said he could not fill it. I had complied with Virginia law. Now I had to get my prescription filled wherever I could—in other words, "the street." I was no longer a criminal under state law, which felt pretty good, but I was still breaking Federal law, however, and to change that I needed the FDA to stop stonewalling us. We had done everything we could to meet their various demands, but the stall continued. Then another idea came to mind.

Legal Support

I had the state of Virginia behind me, why not the law school at the University of Virginia? Bob Randall had been able to convince Steptoe and Johnson, a top-flight Washington law firm, to sue the Federal Government on his behalf; maybe I should try the same route. My cousin Donald Hornstein was a student at UVA Law School. We were close, having grown up together in the same neighborhood and being only a year apart in age. Donald was intrigued by the idea and approached one of his law professors, Richard Bonnie, on my behalf. Professor Bonnie was co-author of a book, "The Marihuana Conviction: A History of Marijuana Prohibition in the United States." He definitely would understand my situation. He also knew of my family, as he was originally from Portsmouth.

When I talked with Richard Bonnie, he said that the involvement of the University of Virginia Law School might get the Federal Government to respond. I asked, "Does that mean you will take my case?" His reply: "We will be glad to help. I think it would be a good lesson for my students and I do believe you need this... Write your history up and anything else you feel is relevant and send it to me, along with all the names of people in the government you think we need to contact. We will make our own list of who to contact and go from there."

Since my father and I worked together in our furniture store, he over heard all my conversations. After I hung up with Professor Bonnie, he smiled and commented about my chutzpah, which he said I got from my mother. I said, "Pop, I think I got it from both you and her." I then called Debbie and told her the good news. While she was happy for me, she was still cautious because she knew how far we still had to go. That night we celebrated. Any step in the right direction was worth celebrating.

I wrote up what Professor Bonnie had requested and mailed it off. It was now the fall of 1979. More states were passing laws in favor of medical Cannabis, so it was in the news more than ever. The way things are going, I thought, maybe Cannabis would be legal for medical use within about five years. I truly believed that the FDA would eventually agree with my doctor and give me Cannabis.

Richard Bonnie drafted a letter in support of our protocol and submitted it to the FDA. The FDA acknowledged that the letter had been received and promised to respond at a later date. Gee, did that sound familiar! They were going to try to stonewall the University of Virginia Law School. I told Richard that, but he said we have to give them time.

The fall of 1979 turned into a cold, barren winter. Neither Dr. Goldman nor Professor Bonnie heard a word from the government. Every time I tried to contact the FDA I was told they were still investigating alternative medicines for my condition. I pointed out that to date they had not recommended anything new. Their standard answer was, "We are still researching..." I thought, Bullshit! Bob was right; they have no intentions of ever giving medical Cannabis to anyone else.

Once a month I went to see Dr. Goldman. None of my tumors had grown and I was in pretty good shape, for a person with a severe bone disorder who was taking all kinds of medicines including Diluadid 4mg. Dr. Goldman was amazed how much less of the prescribed medicines I took when I was able to secure enough Cannabis. We both hoped that, with UVA Law School on our side, 1980 would be our year.

•

In early January, I called my Congressman, William Whitehurst. He had been a history professor at Old Dominion who for years hosted a weekly show on PBS. When he decided to run in 1969, both parties wanted him. He ran as a Republican and was so popular that the Democrats didn't even run anyone against him. Rep. Whitehurst would serve nine terms.

My call was directed to a staff aide who handled medical affairs. I explained my goal of getting the Federal Government to provide me with

Cannabis. I told her that the precedent had already been set by Robert Randall. I said I had the support of my doctor, Charles Goldman, and the Law School at UVA, and that I had helped get the state law passed. She asked me several questions, but obviously didn't know much on the subject. She requested materials to get her up to speed and told me to contact her in a week. I thanked her for her time and said I would get her the material. I also said "I bet if you help me, that FDA will ignore you, too." Her response was, "We will see." I dropped off the information and waited.

The FDA seemed to be able to do whatever they wanted to do without worrying about the repercussions. Were they afraid that if my protocol was approved I would be encouraged to speak out about the benefits of Cannabis? I had always thought government agencies were there to help the people. How wrong I was. I was beginning to think I needed to expose them, to embarrass them into ending their unrighteous stalling tactics.

I waited the week and called back. "Congressman Whitehurst and our staff would be happy to help," I was told by his aide. "You and Dr. Goldman have done everything the right way and it's wrong of FDA not to respond. We are going to write a letter on your behalf and inquire as to the long delay." I thanked her and reminded her of my prediction that the FDA would stonewall the Congressman, too. "I hope I am wrong," I added.

That night, knowing I had a U.S. Congressman on my side, I wondered how long it would be before I became legal. Debbie cautioned me not to get my hopes up. She had a good point. The Federal decision makers did not care about my personal wellbeing, they cared about enforcing the prohibition.

Over the next six months, FDA gave Rep. Whitehurst's office vague reassurances that they were "working on the issue." To my dismay—but not to my surprise—the Congressman's staff showed no defiance. "We have to give them more time," I was told.

In May, I testified in Richmond before the State Crime Commission about street prices for marijuana and how hard it was to find. I felt quite strange talking openly about marijuana with all the state police and government officials present. However, my old friend, Commissioner Lew Hurst, chaired the meeting and treated me like a law-abiding citizen. He was not happy to hear how the FDA continued to ignore us.

That winter I experienced more physical problems and I had to cut back on making some deliveries—a critical part of the furniture business. I had to be more careful how I moved for fear of tearing a vein. Muscle tightness and pain were worse. I would take more of my prescribed medicine, which made me feel drugged at times. I needed to smoke more Cannabis, but either I couldn't find enough, or couldn't afford what I needed. The FDA's stall of my application seemed increasingly outrageous. My disorders are real, Cannabis works, end of story. Why did everything have to be so difficult?

By year's end we were still no further along than in the spring. Congressman Whitehurst's office still wanted to believe that the protocol was being worked on behind the scenes. UVA was not as naïve. Richard Bonnie knew that the FDA was just going through the motions. I suggested maybe it was time to sue the FDA the way Steptoe and Johnson sued on behalf of Robert Randall. That suit had been filed on a Thursday and the Feds gave in the next day. Why don't we do the same?

Professor Bonnie replied it was still too soon to go that route. "I know how long you've fought for medical Cannabis," he said, "but the FDA could still argue that they need more time. We have to play their game, for the time being." I didn't like his answer, but he was my attorney, so I listened to him.

Getting a Hearing

Another year went by. A deadly new disease was identified as Acquired Immune Deficiency Syndrome—AIDS. President Reagan and Pope John Paul had been shot and survived. The first woman was appointed to the Supreme Court—Sandra Day O'Connor. The world kept changing, but

Bob Randall still remained the only medical Cannabis user recognized by the Federal Government.

My condition, while not good, was not getting any worse. None of my tumors had grown in years. Dr. Goldman was treating me and we both knew that if I could get enough Cannabis, I would be relatively well off. I had no need to see an orthopedist.

1982 marked the tenth year of my efforts to get government-issued Cannabis and the fifth year since we had changed my scientific project to a Compassionate Care Protocol. I remembered how Bob had warned me in 1978 that it might take another five years, and there were no guarantees we would win.

Periodically I called Professor Bonnie to see if there were any steps we should be taking. One day, much to my happiness, he said, "We have given the FDA more than enough time to come to some decision. It's now time to let them know we want an answer or we will begin a lawsuit. I will co-ordinate this with Congressman Whitehurst's office so as to have a greater impact. We will let them know, 'Enough is enough. You have kept the patient in limbo long enough. It's time to let the courts decide.'" This was music to my ears.

Bob and Alice were glad to hear what was being planned, but they reminded me that the end of my struggle was not necessarily near at hand. (I can hear Bob now telling me how naïve I was.) The courts could still take forever. It seemed that for every step forward I would take, I would fall back three. Oh, well, at least I didn't fall back four!

Professor Bonnie and the Congressman's office decided to give the FDA until September before we filed suit. "Why give them that much time after all the time they've had?" I asked. He replied, "We still have to play the game the right way." "Why do we have to play the game right when they don't?" I wanted to know. "We need to look good for the courts," was the answer. After waiting this long, what's another eight months?

The next several months went by slowly with still no movement by the FDA. About once a month I would talk to the Congressman's office and would be told that negotiations were ongoing. I expected communications between them and Dr. Goldman to increase, but that wasn't the case. One day in June Professor Bonnie mentioned that his third-year law-students had been working on my prospective suit since January. "I didn't expect them to give in," he explained.

I asked him what he thought our chances would be in court. He said he didn't know. He also didn't know if he could get the documents filed by Steptoe and Johnson in connection with Bob Randall's suit. "Those records would make our job a lot easier," he said. "However, UVA Law School is no pushover. We don't like to lose and the FDA knows this." I thanked him and waited for the next shoe to fall.

At the start of August, Professor Bonnie wrote a letter to the FDA saying we were going to file suit. About two weeks later I got a call from him at the furniture store. I could hear a note of shock in his voice and got very worried. He said, "You're not going to believe this, but the FDA is going to hold a meeting for you before their entire committee that decides which protocols get approved."

He said I would have fifteen minutes to plead my case. The meeting was scheduled to take place in early October in Rockville, Maryland, at the FDA headquarters. He would tell me the exact date as soon as he found out. I didn't know if this was a positive development or a way for the FDA to turn me down. Professor Bonnie said he thought it was another stall tactic. "After they turn you down, we will proceed with the courts," he added.

I hung up the phone and told my father. He asked if I thought I could convince a group of doctors in fifteen minutes. I smiled and said, "I have no choice."

I called Bob and Alice to tell them the news. They predicted that the FDA committee would turn me down. They were glad UVA was preparing to proceed with the suit. Bob said, "The FDA is in a huge building and since these are public hearings, I am going to place posters all through the halls inviting people to attend. I'm also going to invite the media so we can have a public record which UVA will be able to use in court." Mainly because of Bob and Alice's organizing efforts, Thirty-four states had passed medical marijuana laws by the end of 1982, however no one was actually able to get medical Cannabis. But the Federal Government controlled Cannabis and was not about to allow its use.

I didn't sleep much that night. All I could think about was how best to use my fifteen minutes to convince a panel of doctors that Cannabis was the best medicine for me. I wasn't scared. I was wondering if maybe I had a chance to win.

The Doctors Decide

My hearing with the FDA committee was scheduled for the first Tuesday in October at 1:00 pm. Professor Bonnie said he was going ahead with plans for a suit on the assumption that I would be turned down. Bob and Alice also thought my chances of being approved were slim. I thanked them for their honesty and reminded them that stranger things had happened. Maybe God would lend a hand.

The weeks before my hearing went by slowly. Each day I would get up and go to the furniture store thinking about what I was going to say to the doctors in Rockville. I had learned early on that it is best not to read a speech because you lose eye contact with your audience. I wanted to look each committee member in the eye. It would be harder for them to say "no" if they recognized me as a legitimate patient who had tried all other medicines and found that Cannabis worked best.

When the big day arrived I kissed Debbie goodbye and was on the road at 6:00 am. Five hours later I arrived in Rockville and went directly to the FDA headquarters. (I always try to get to a meeting early so I can get the lay of the land.) I couldn't believe how big the building was, but I didn't feel intimidated. In the lobby was a bulletin board with an announcement giving the time and room number of my hearing.

I found my way to the hearing room, which was empty. The room had chairs for about 100 people and three long desks, side-by-side, facing the audience. This is where the committee members would sit, I assumed. About 10 feet away was a desk with a single chair and microphone. That undoubtedly was for the witness—me. I felt surprisingly at ease as I waited.

Bob and Alice arrived around 11:30 am. It was great seeing familiar faces. Bob said he had invited TV and print reporters along with "some other interested parties" whom he didn't identify. He told me what points to stress to the media after the committee turned me down.

People started trickling in and finding seats. As reporters arrived, Bob or Alice would introduce me to them and we would start answering questions. At one point I looked around and the room was almost full. There were people in hospital garb, in fancy suits, in workaday clothing. I found this interest in my case almost perplexing. If the Federal Government was so against medical Cannabis, why had so many of its employees showed up to hear it discussed?

At 12:55 pm., I took my seat and forgot about the audience. As far as I was concerned, I was alone in the room waiting for the committee to arrive. Right on schedule, in walked the twenty doctors. They were all in suits and looking very professional indeed. I tried immediately to start making eye contact with individuals on the panel.

They took their seats and the chairman started speaking. He thanked everyone for attending and explained what this hearing was about. He stated I would have fifteen minutes to testify. At that point committee members would be allowed to ask questions. He then lifted a gavel, slammed it down, and invited me to begin.

I said good afternoon, stated my name, and thanked the chairman and the committee for the opportunity to explain why I needed medical Cannabis. I told them, as succinctly as I could, the story you have been reading. How at an early age I had been diagnosed with a debilitating disorder. I had undergone terrible operations and been put on narcotics and relegated to homebound schooling for grades eighth through twelfth. I was an advocate against illegal drugs, especially marijuana.

My doctor suggested I might feel better in a warm climate so I went to school in Miami, where marijuana was readily available. I only tried it in response to peer pressure, and got no euphoric effect.

One day I found myself absorbed in a chess game and realized that I had been sitting for half an hour. It was the first time in five years that I had sat motionless for more than ten minutes. Since I hadn't taken any pills, I could only attribute it to that "garbage" I had smoked for social reasons. I soon learned that marijuana did indeed have recognized medical benefits. It was known to doctors by its Latin name, Cannabis. Cannabis-based tinctures and salves had been widely used in this country from 1860 through 1937, for muscle relaxation and to relieve inflammation and pain. Major companies such as Merck and Eli Lilly had marketed Cannabis prior to Prohibition.

I did not want to believe that an illegal substance was more effective than the drugs my doctor had prescribed. As a reality check, I would use Cannabis for three weeks and not use it for one week. I improved for three weeks, then relapsed. I did this experiment for four months with the same results and concluded that Cannabis worked much, much better than my prescription meds. But, I was raised a law-abiding citizen. I didn't like being labeled a criminal for using Cannabis as a medicine. So I left college after three semesters and went back to Virginia to try to convince the Federal Government to let me use the most effective medicine available for my conditions.

For five years I tried unsuccessfully to get the FDA to approve a study with me as the patient and my doctor as the researcher. Then I changed my study to a "Compassionate Care Protocol." Charles Goldman, MD, an endocrinologist, had been tracking my use of Cannabis and Dilaudid for ten years. He determined marijuana enhanced the effects of Dilaudid, enabling me to take much less of this debilitating narcotic. Cannabis also enabled me to reduce by about half my use of other muscle relaxants, anti-inflammatories, and sleeping pills. Whereas those pills made me feel drugged and sluggish, with Cannabis I felt coherent and sharp. I reiterated that I get no euphoric effect from Cannabis, just alleviation of my medical problems.

I concluded by saying, "Gentlemen, I have very rare disorders and I'm lucky to be alive. I learned to live with my diseases knowing that they could kill me. All I ever asked of any doctors were for them to be honest with me and do the best they could. After all, they are just MDs, not G,O,D's. I was lucky enough to discover a natural plant that works best for me—and that's Cannabis. I have used this medicine successfully for over eleven years. I have done everything possible to take the crime out of the picture, from getting a state law passed in Virginia allowing medical use of Cannabis (but with no provisions where to get it as the Federal Government controls all production and distribution) to my scientific study, and now my Compassionate Care Protocol. My doctor can give me all the Dilaudid and any other potentially lethal and addictive pills I want. If he can do this, then why can't he be allowed to give me Cannabis? Dr. Goldman wants what's best for me. Please allow him to help me."

I thanked the committee and said I would answer any questions. A gentleman in the audience wearing a white coat was recognized by the chairman and stood up to address me. "I really don't have a question, but a statement," he began. "I'm a visiting oncologist from Venezuela studying pain treatments and I have learned that the best pain treatment you have in this country is Dilaudid, just like in my country. The fact your doctor and you have studied the effects of Cannabis as an adjunct medicine with Dilaudid, and have found that Cannabis allows you to take less Dilaudid with better results, is amazing. This needs to be studied further with a steady supply of Cannabis."

As he sat down, the impact of his statement could be seen on the faces of the committee members. How could they go against such logic?

There were no more questions from the audience, no questions from the committee members. The chairman looked at the doctors seated to his left and they all seemed to avoid meeting his gaze. He turned to his right and his colleagues there did the same. He seemed somewhat lost as he thanked me for my presentation. I don't know how he knew a consensus had been reached, because none of his colleagues had even made eye contact with him, but he said he was speaking for the entire committee and that my protocol would be approved.

What!? Did I just hear right?

All of a sudden flashbulbs started going off and people were coming up to congratulate me. Bob and Alice were beaming as they came over to give me a big hug. We looked at each other, shook our heads, not believing what had taken place. The number of Federal patients had just doubled!

I did numerous interviews and had my picture taken over and over again. This being before the era of cell phones, I excused myself and found a pay phone from which to call Dr. Goldman and thank him for his indispensable help. At one point I looked for the visiting oncologist, but he had gone before I could thank him. Was it just luck he had been there and said what he did, or something more? He was there for a reason. God only knows.

We finished all the interviews and I called my wife to give her the good news. Then Bob, Alice, and I walked out to the parking lot and said our goodbyes. We wondered how long it would take to get my first shipment of medicine. We weren't sure that the FDA would actually comply with the committee's recommendation. I took a last look at the building, which didn't seem so intimidating now, got in my car and started the motor. Then I screamed at the top of my lungs, as I pounded on the steering wheel, "WE WON!"

PART TWO:

LEGITIMACY AND ACTIVISM

My First Shipment

The drive home was glorious. I was on I-95 but it felt like I was riding on Cloud 9. I lit up, realizing that from now on I would not have to worry about how to get my medicine, or the possibility of running out. No more having to find a dealer and pay Prohibition prices. The FDA had recognized in my case, as in Bob's, that marijuana is a "new drug" worthy of "investigation." (I wasn't upset by the reality that it was a plant that had been used medicinally for thousands of years.) From now on, the government was going to keep me supplied. What a country!

One thing that did upset me was that countless Americans were still prohibited from medicating with Cannabis, no matter how much they were suffering, no matter how much it might help them. Bob and Alice were working to help others gain access to Federal marijuana, and I offered to do whatever I could to help the cause.

Back in Portsmouth Debbie was waiting at my parents' house. As I told them what had happened, they had huge smiles on their faces. All those years, all the setbacks, money, aggravation, despair, all that effort spent on a battle no one thought I could win... and now I had! It was a dream comes true. Yeah, I cried. Everyone was in a wonderful mood at dinner. My father joked that with enough of the right medicine, maybe I would be able to put more effort into our furniture business. I said I expected to—and wasn't joking.

That night lying in bed, I thought how easy my life as a Federal patient would be. If only I knew. I had no idea what really was going to take place in my future. I never imagined all the trials and troubles that were going to occur to me because I was a Federal patient.

•

The next day I called Dr. Goldman to let him know what was to happen in the months ahead, as it had been explained to me by the FDA officials.

His application for a Schedule 1 license would be approved by the FDA immediately. The DEA would be notified and would inspect the area where my can of government-issued Cannabis would be stored. Our backgrounds would be checked for criminal activity. Once the FDA and the DEA had signed off on their requirements, then the NIDA would ship one can containing a 30-day supply to his office. I would come to his office weekly until he was assured that the government Cannabis was effective and exerting no negative side effects. At that point he could allow me to have the entire month's supply. Subsequently he could order three cans at a time, reducing the paperwork involved.

•

Next, I called Dr. Waive's widow. I had first gone to their house as a ten-year-old kid. I told her how important her husband had been in my life and how much I owed him. She said, "No, you don't owe him anything. He lived to help people. All you need is to continue to do what he lived for. Remember him and do what's right."

I also called to thank Congressman Whitehurst's staff. They said they intended to contact the FDA to make sure the shipments started in a timely manner—a stark reminder that my victory was conditional.

For the rest of the day, between customers, I was calling everyone with an interest in my case: Chief Boone, Paul Butler, the cantor and rabbi at Gomely Chesed, staffers at the Woodrow Wilson High School and the Virginia Crime Commission, and many friends.

When I got Richard Bonnie on the phone I tried to sound disappointed. He asked how the hearing went. I replied, "What do you think?" He started talking about our next step, which would be taking the FDA to court. I interrupted to say, "I don't think we need to do that.... because... WE WON."

He asked, "But do you trust them?"

I said, "I think we can."

Over the next several weeks, the DEA agents showed up at Dr. Goldman's office and approved his security arrangements. The FDA sent Dr. Goldman his Schedule 1 license along with order forms for Cannabis, which he filled out and mailed to NIDA. And on November 20, 1982, Dr. Goldman called to say the magic words: "Irvin, it's here. "The Can" has arrived. You need to come to the office." My God, after eleven years of effort, my legal medical Cannabis was here!

I drove over, walked in, and took a seat in the waiting room—just another patient. When it was my turn the nurse opened the door and said, "Dr. Goldman is ready for you." I walked back to his office where he was beaming triumphantly, holding up a tin can, about six inches in diameter and five inches high, as if it was a winning lottery ticket. Which, in a way for me it was.

It had been delivered by a new company called Federal Express. The label on the can identified it as "Marijuana Cigarettes." A package insert was included, just as one would expect with a conventional medication. One difference was that mine included instructions for returning the can itself to NIDA (a requirement that would be dropped after several years).

The can was sealed with wax around the top and Dr. Goldman had to use a screwdriver to remove the lid. He pulled out a thin piece of styrofoam, revealing approximately 300 perfectly rolled Cannabis cigarettes. He took out several and handed them to me with instructions: "Go outside and smoke two, then come right back."

I did as the doctor ordered. I went to my car, lit up, and took a puff of my first legal Cannabis cigarette. It was somewhat harsh but my feeling of success was undiminished. I smoked them both and reported to Dr. Goldman that I didn't feel any euphoria, but could feel my muscles relax.

He checked my vital signs, which were normal. We talked for a few minutes so he could say I was perfectly coherent and could operate dangerous machinery—in other words, drive my car. He then gave me 68 more joints and said to come back in a week.

I drove home feeling perfectly legitimate. I was a normal law-abiding citizen with a new drug that the government had an interest in investigating.

Debbie and I went out to dinner that night to celebrate. Later, as we lay in bed watching Johnny Carson, a commercial came on for Federal Express. "We will deliver anything from three ounces to 70 pounds," said the ad. We cracked up. I wondered if anyone at FedEx knew that the package they had delivered to Dr. Goldman in Norfolk, Va., contained legal marijuana.

•

The package-insert that came with my can of government-issued Cannabis described the contents in great detail. The average weight of each cigarette was given as 910 milligrams, which equates to about 20 cigarettes per ounce. (The amount per cigarette was reduced in 1991 to 734 mg.)

The plant strain was said to be "Mexican and Special Hybrid." Moisture content: 11.4%. Delta-9 THC content: 3.95%. Other cannabinoids listed were Cannabidiol, Cannabinol, Cannabichromene, Cannabicyclol, and variant forms of delta-9-THC. The rolling paper was from the Ecuster Paper Company, #12853. (I wondered what #12852 was like.)

An instruction stated, "Cigarettes should usually be treated to raise the moisture content prior to use. Please refer to the attached document, 'General Information on Marijuana Cigarettes from NIDA and their use in Therapeutic Programs.'"

The 'General Information' (a separate sheet) included the definition of marijuana in the Controlled Substance Act: "all parts of the plant Cannabis Sativa L., whether growing or not; the seeds thereof; the resin extracted from any part of such plant; and every compound, manufacture, salt, derivative, mixture or preparation of such plant, seeds or resin.

"The term 'marijuana' as applied to street material includes preparations of the whole plant as well as those, which include only the flowering tops of the plant. A popular and potent street preparation known as 'sinsemilla,' results from careful manicuring of the unfertilized flowering tops of the female plant."

"For the purposes of this information sheet, marijuana will refer to the preparation produced by the Research Institute of Pharmaceutical Sciences at the University of Mississippi under contract to NIDA. In this preparation, the entire male and female plants excepting stems are dried and passed through a coarse sieve to produce a mixture of large leaf particles, small leaves, bracts, and flowers."

In other words, NIDA marijuana would be less potent than the "street preparation" of manicured, unfertilized flowering female tops.

"Marijuana cigarettes supplied from NIDA are manufactured on a modified tobacco cigarette machine. They look like a standard tobacco cigarette and weigh about 0.9 grams. They are packaged in cylindrical cans, which contain approximately 300 cigarettes per can.

"Cigarettes are stored frozen at the Research Triangle Institute. Prior to placement in storage the moisture content of the cigarettes is reduced from the high level necessary for smoking to approximately 10%..."

I smoked my 10 cigarettes per day and was doing well. After a week I returned to Dr. Goldman's office and was examined again. He decided I was thriving, so he gave me the rest of the pre-rolled Cannabis cigarettes and said, "I'll see you in three weeks. Go help my secretary with the next order form. Only put in for one can. We'll request more later."

Busted!

In February, 1983, Debbie was asked to attend a business conference for her company in Orlando, Florida. I was invited along and readily agreed.

This would be my first time traveling as a Federal patient. I phoned the FDA official who oversaw my protocol, Dr. Ed Tocus, who confirmed that I was allowed to travel in any U.S. territory with my Cannabis. He advised me not to check it through but to keep it on me at all times.

Then I called Chief Boone to discuss what would happen if I were stopped by a police officer who didn't believe I was a Federal patient. The chief agreed to put together a "rap sheet" on me explaining that the Portsmouth Police Department had certified that I was a Federal patient not breaking any laws by possessing marijuana.

The flight from Norfolk to Orlando went smoothly but the weather was disappointing. Debbie and I soon realized we had not packed warm-enough clothes. We were in Florida, only it felt like winter-time in Virginia, cold and ugly. I ended up attending the conference instead of heading for the pool. I learned quite a bit about the self-storage business.

•

The last night was a banquet at a large restaurant/nightclub in downtown Orlando called Church Street Station. All 450 attendees, nicely dressed, were bussed from our hotels to the gala affair. We were directed to the second floor where Debbie and I sat down for dinner with some of her acquaintances.

As the meal ended, many people lit up cigarettes, pipes, and even cigars. (This was when you could still smoke in a building.) My legs were hurting and I dreaded going out into the cold night air in my lightweight suit with no overcoat. "Dr. Tocus said I could take my medicine wherever cigarettes are allowed," I told Debbie. "I think I'll take it right here." She urged me to go outside, but going out in the cold would have caused more pain than relief, so I compromised and went to the men's room instead.

No sooner had I gone into a stall and lit up than a bus boy walked in and recognized the smell.

"Hey, lemme have some of that!"

"I'm sorry, I can't do that," I told him, "this is medical use."

He walked out and notified a policeman who happened to be on the premises. The officer came into the bathroom and said, "Is that marijuana you're smoking?"

I said, "Yes sir," and came out of the stall. I explained that it was legal marijuana provided by the Federal Government. He got on his walkie-talkie and said, "Yes, sergeant, there is a person smoking marijuana, but he said that it's provided by the Federal Government."

I heard the response loud and clear: "WHAT THE FUCK? I'LL BE RIGHT THERE!" The first cop was a nice guy, but soon there arrived a sergeant acting like the meanest drill instructor from the Marine Corps. "What the fuck is this?" Every other word out of his mouth was "fuck"

I said, "Sir, there's a Federal program that I'm under. I'm from Virginia—"

He interrupted me. "Son, you're in Florida and Florida law supersedes Federal law."

"You can verify my story by calling the Portsmouth, Virginia Police Department to get my rap sheet. I'll pay for the call."

"Fuck that," the sergeant replied. "Son, you're in Florida and you're under arrest!"

"Look," I said to the sergeant, "I've got seven cigarettes in this bag. Back in my hotel room, I've got a tin can with about another two-hundred and fifty marijuana cigarettes rolled by a machine. There are Federal Government labels on the can, plus I have other government materials. If you're going to arrest me for seven joints, why not go back to my hotel and get it all?"

This offer didn't interest him. He pulled his handcuffs out and I kept trying to explain. "Sir, excuse me. If you want to arrest me, I will not resist. I'll follow you wherever you want me to go. But right now, there's a problem. I have bone tumors all through my body." I pointed to a large bump on my right wrist. "If you put those handcuffs on my wrist and I have a problem with these tumors, I'm going to sue you for assault and battery. Sir, I've not raised my voice, I haven't said a foul word, and I'll go where ever you want me to."

Meanwhile, of course, everybody at the conference had seen these policemen going into the men's room. Only my wife could figure out what was happening.

As the officers led me downstairs, I made eye contact with Debbie but didn't get to say a word. I had told her that if I ever got arrested, I would injure my ankle on purpose so I could be taken to a hospital. (Just twisting it is enough to cause a hemorrhage.) I would rather defend my rights from a hospital than a police station.

They put me into a police car with a bench instead of a back seat, and there I lay for fifteen minutes before the nice policeman drove me to the station. Thank goodness he had left the heat on.

As I got out and was stretching my legs (with the nice cop's permission), another police car pulled up and unloaded a man in handcuffs who was spitting at the cops. I watched them lead him into the building up a step and through a back door. That would be my place to twist my ankle.

And so, as I was led in, I intentionally tripped and fell.

"I've injured the tumor in my ankle and I can't move," I said.

A nurse was summoned from within the station. I lay there as cops came and went. Finally the nurse arrived and I told her about my bone disorder. She saw my ankle hemorrhaging. I asked her to get me to a hospital. She went off, saying, "I'll be back."

As I lay in the doorway, more police arrived with suspects under arrest. They just stepped over me.

An officer removed my tie and belt. I felt that was quite funny. What did they expect me to do? I told myself it was a unique experience and I should try to appreciate it.

I kept telling the police, "Call the Portsmouth Police Department. I'll pay for the phone call. They've got a rap sheet on me and you'll see that I'm not breaking any law." But nobody made the call.

The nurse finally came back and said, "I talked to the doctor by phone. He said it didn't sound that bad and that you could walk." I said, "Oh, you talked to a doctor by phone and he made a diagnosis by phone. Isn't that interesting? I'm sorry, I can't walk."

The policemen standing around me had no idea what to do. Just then, who drove up but Sergeant "WHAT THE FUCK?" The nice officer explained the situation: "Well, sergeant, he was stepping into the building and his ankle gave way and you can see how it's hemorrhaging and the nurse went off and the doctor said it didn't sound so bad, but how can a doctor make a diagnosis by phone?"

The sergeant said, "What the fuck, I'll get his ass up." He took out his nightstick and started smacking it against the palm of his hand. I said, "Sir, right now you think you have a legal arrest. You don't. I'm a Federal patient and whether you believe it or not, Federal law supersedes Florida law. Monday morning I'm going to contact the U.S. Attorney General's Office and tell them what happened. They're going to contact Tallahassee. Tallahassee's going to contact Orlando. Orlando is going to contact you and they're going to want to know why you arrested me. Right now it's a problem, but nobody's been hurt that bad—except that I can't walk. If you touch me with that nightstick, I will prosecute you for assault and battery and I mean it. And there are witnesses."

There were about ten cops watching. The sergeant reluctantly put his nightstick back in his belt. Someone remembered that they had a wheelchair available, and I was lifted into it, wheeled into the station and placed outside a cell.

I was seeing some bad things—prisoners being hit by the police, prisoners spitting at the police. Whenever anyone went by I would tell them, "Call the Portsmouth Police Department, I'm legal, I'm not breaking any law." But nobody would.

They wheeled me into a room where I was fingerprinted and photographed as I kept thinking, "This is a unique experience, try to appreciate it."

Debbie and some associates had arrived by cab. Unbeknownst to me, they were standing outside saying the same things that I'd been saying on the inside: "He's not breaking any law, he's legal."

After almost three hours there was a shift change. A woman with many stripes on her arm came over to me and said, "What's your story?" I repeated the story that I had told to twenty other cops. She said, "I believe you and I want you out of here."

I said, "I want to be taken to the hospital." She replied, "We can't get you to the hospital, but your wife's down there telling the same story...What if we post bail at $250?" They had taken my wallet, which had about $500 in it—maybe they thought I was dealing. She said, "If we get her your wallet, she can post bail. I want you out of here."

And that's how my first arrest ended. They gave Debbie the wallet, she posted bail and they let me out. They wheeled me to a cab, which we took to the hospital. I was examined in the emergency room and released.

•

On Monday morning I called the FDA and told Dr. Tocus what had happened. He put me in touch with an FDA attorney and I told him the story. Since Bob had never been arrested, my experience in Orlando was a first. The lawyer said, "I hope we can handle it."

Wednesday I got a call from a judge in Orlando who said that the circumstances of my arrest were "unusual." He wanted to know if I had told the sergeant about my status under Federal law. I said, "Yes sir, I explained I was part of a Federal program. He said Florida law superseded Federal law, and none of the other officers would go against him. He also refused to call the Portsmouth, Virginia Police Department to confirm my story."

The judge said, "We're really sorry about this. Your record is being expunged and your bail money is being sent back along with four marijuana cigarettes."

I said, "Excuse me? Four cigarettes? There were seven."

"Well there are only four now," said the judge.

I said, "I guess three were taken by someone."

"We're really sorry about this," the judge repeated, "and we hope you won't take this further."

I said, "Sir, I was wronged, very much so, and I want an apology from that sergeant."

"You'll get it," the judge promised.

And I did, in the form of a letter. I have no idea whether or not the profane sergeant wrote or signed it himself. I didn't pursue the case because I lived in Virginia and had been warned that every time I was scheduled to appear, the hearing could be postponed.

That was my first experience of being arrested. It happened just four months after I was admitted to the "Investigational New Drug Program" as it was called. I had remained calm and collected—I had no choice. I didn't get upset or raise my voice. My main frustration was that no one would call my hometown police department. I figured one cop would call another cop, but I figured wrong.

One good result was that the FDA sent a letter to the Florida's Orange County Court citing the Federal statute that protected me. To this day, I carry a copy of that letter with me at all times.

Does The FDA Care?

In June, Dr. Goldman had to send the FDA his first six-month report evaluating my response to government-issued Cannabis. He filled out in detail a five-page questionnaire that Bob and I had drafted as part of my protocol. Dr. Goldman was pleased with how I was doing and proud to be involved in cutting-edge clinical research. He assumed the FDA would be collecting data on a growing number of Cannabis users.

Three weeks later, during my regular monthly appointment, he asked if the FDA had commented on his report. I said the FDA might not want to publicize data contradicting marijuana's status as a Schedule-1 drug with no medical value. He asked for the name of our contact at the FDA.

Up to this point, I had done all the communicating with the FDA. I explained that Dr. Tocus was overseeing our protocol. Dr. Goldman asked me to get him on the line, which I did.

"It's nice to finally get to talk," said Dr. Goldman to his colleague. "I want to thank you for all your help. As you saw in my report, Irvin is doing much better now that he has an adequate and reliable supply of Cannabis... The main reason for my call is, somehow a copy of that report was misplaced. I was hoping you would send back a copy for my records."

Dr. Tocus was equally cordial, but said he would not be able to provide a copy of the report. He suggested that Dr. Goldman be more careful next time about keeping back-ups. This was our first indication that the FDA was not serious about coordinating a real investigation into the effectiveness of marijuana as medicine.

Dr. Goldman asked me to call our contact at Congressman's Whitehurst office. I got her on the line and he asked her to get him a copy of his report through the Freedom of Information Act. She said she would try, but it was hardly surprising when it turned out that she could not.

When it came time for Dr. Goldman to file his next six-month report on my condition, he wrote on each of the five pages, "IT'S WORKING," in big red print and signed it at the bottom. "If they're not going to use the information," he said, "why should I take my time to fill it out?"

Although his reasoning made sense, I was worried about what the FDA would do. Fortunately, they didn't do anything, and Dr. Goldman filled out future reports simply and quickly.

•

Life became relatively uneventful. I would go to my doctor's office every month to pick up my government-issued medicine. Every three months he would conduct a thorough examination. My health was good and my intake of other medicines decreased. Everything we had stated in my protocol was coming true. I worked at our furniture store and lived a normal life made possible by smoking ten Cannabis cigarettes per day.

In late October 1983, I got a strange phone call from a doctor at the Portsmouth Navel Hospital, Dr. Waive's alma-mater, saying that as a Federal marijuana patient, was there any person that was around me a lot who had ingested my second hand smoke but who had never smoked marijuana before and would be willing to take a urine test. I asked, "Why do you want to know?" He replied, "An Admiral tested positive for marijuana and said it must be from second-hand smoke from a party he recently attended. We want to back up his story, hence my question." Thinking of Dr. Waive, I told the doctor how my father and I worked together eight hours a day and he was subjected to my smoke daily.

I told Dad the story and asked if he would submit a sample. Pop said, "Sure, if they come here."

The next day two navy corpsmen showed up with a bottle which Pop filled and off they went. A week later the doctor called and asked again, "Are you sure your father has never smoked marijuana?" Yes, why? "Your father tested negative."

Years later I reiterated the story to Al Byrne, an ex-naval commander and he said, "There wasn't any Admiral that tested positive, just the Navy wanted to know if one could test positive from second-hand smoke and you were available." That's probably the first and only time the Federal Government has ever done any research at all into my use of Federal Cannabis.

•

In November 1984, Ronald Reagan was re-elected President of the United States much to my chagrin. A crack cocaine epidemic was escalating. Government policy was summed up in the phrase "Just Say No," which first lady Nancy Reagan used in response to a student's question about illicit drugs. The Administration made no distinction between marijuana and hard drugs with addictive potential. This bothered me since I knew from personal experiences how different medical marijuana was from cocaine or heroin. I wondered what personal experience on this subject President Reagan or his advisors had.

From Virginia I was doing what I could to educate people while Bob and Alice were doing their best trying to inform politicians that marijuana was a useful medicine, but hardly anyone seemed receptive to such a message.

Marijuana prohibition had been imposed by a legally awkward tax act in 1937, passed over the objections of the American Medical Association. (The history is recounted in a great book called "The Marihuana Conviction" by Professor Richard Bonnie, my friend and supporter, and Charles H. Whitebread, II, his colleague at the University of Virginia School of Law.)

The Controlled Substances Act of 1970 created "Schedules" to categorize drugs according to their safety and usefulness. You would think scheduling decisions would be up to doctors and scientists, but the Controlled Substance Act left them up to law enforcement—specifically, the Drug Enforcement Administration, which is under the Department of Justice. The DEA had placed marijuana on Schedule 1, a category for dangerous drugs with no medical value.

NORML had sued DEA Administrator Jack Ingersoll back in 1972 to get marijuana moved to Schedule 2 (potentially harmful drugs with recognized medical uses). The government had been stalling all these years. President Ford came and went, President Carter came and went, and now Ronald Reagan was in the White House. It was the "Just-Say-No" era.

Mattress Madness

Things had not been going smoothly on the business front. In late 1984 we lost the lease on the building in which we had our furniture store. We'd had a great location across the street from the only mall in Portsmouth. We tried another location, but it wasn't profitable. So my father and I closed the business we had been running for eleven years. The worst part was not working with my father anymore, as I really enjoyed working together with him.

I contacted a friend of my sister Susan who managed a store for the chain "Mattress Discounters." They required a drug test and I informed them about my situation. I tested positive for Cannabis and was hired. They had no problems with my walking outside to smoke.

That Christmas, my wife, her sister, her teenage niece, and I arranged to stay at a timeshare in Daytona, Florida. We expected warm weather and a spacious apartment. Instead, we found ourselves in a small apartment and the weather was freezing.

•

We as a group weren't getting along well, so one day I got in my car and drove almost 300 miles down to Miami to have lunch at my favorite restaurant, Shorty's Barbecue. I got there around 10:30 am. and they weren't open yet. I drove around and saw a mattress store called "Mattress Madness." I figured I would stop and kill some more time.

It had a layout similar to the store I was running in Virginia—a one-man operation. I started talking to the manager and he realized that I had experience in the business. He said the company had stores in Miami, Ft. Lauderdale, and Palm Beach, and was always looking for good employees. He suggested that I talk to one of the owners at the main warehouse in Ft. Lauderdale. I figured, why not? I had a great lunch, and then followed his directions to the warehouse.

The only employee there when I walked in was waiting on a customer. I looked around the store and felt at home. Just then, another husband and wife walked in. I went over and asked if I could help them. They said they were looking for a firm queen-size mattress for a good price. I took them over to a set priced at $599. They tried it out and loved it, but said the price was too high. I told them we had a sale going on and I could sell them that set today for half price and would also throw in the metal bed frame.

The owner was listening to me and was fine with what I was doing. They decided to take it. I turned the customers over to the owner and started helping the couple he had been with. As he was writing up the ticket, I sold his couple a set. He wrote up both tickets, handed me a set of keys and asked if I could go around to the other side of the warehouse and tie each set onto the top of their cars. "No problem," I replied. I opened the door, found the sets of bedding and some rope, and proceeded to tie each one down. When they drove off the owner asked, "When can you start?"

I explained my situation in Virginia. He offered me my own store to run and more money than I'd been making. Since I had always wanted to move back to South Florida, the offer was tempting. He told me the store was due to open January 21, 1986 and to just let him know. I told him about my use of legal Cannabis. He had no objections. I thanked him and said I would let him know in one week. I got back in my car and drove back to Daytona.

The offer was tempting because I tend to feel so much better, physically, in a warm climate. But moving would mean being 1,000 miles from family and friends, and Debbie would have to give up her great job at a real-estate company and managing thirteen self-storage facilities. One of my concerns was whether I could find a new doctor and a new pharmacist to maintain my supply of government-issued medical marijuana.

After much thought, I decided to try. Our plan was for Debbie to stay in Virginia while I started work in Florida and got a sense of whether it would be worth establishing ourselves there. Dr. Goldman agreed to remain my doctor until I found someone in Florida to take his place (assuming we decided to move permanently). I called the owner of Mattress Madness to make sure the job was still available. He was happy to hear from me and said the store was due to open in two and a half weeks. I drove south excited but scared.

•

I left the Friday before I was to start working and drove straight through. It had been fifteen years since I had driven to Florida, heading for college and unsure of how things would turn out. Would I be able to live on my own without hurting myself? Now I was older and again unsure of how things would turn out. The major difference was, this time I had effective medicine to help me. I had not had any surgeries for eleven years. My health was stable and I felt a lot stronger.

The store I had been assigned was in a strip shopping center on University Drive in Sunrise. There was a shoe store on one side and a small restaurant on the other. The first day at work I met the other owner and he, like most people, was amazed I could use Cannabis legally and that it didn't impair my ability to function. I smoked four Cannabis cigarettes during the eight hours we spent at the store that day. He observed I was no different after smoking. "I would have passed out," he said.

Upon arriving in Ft. Lauderdale I stayed with friends for a few days, then rented a room that soon turned out to be unsatisfactory. I went back to "Rentfinders" and looked through other offers of rooms to rent. I noticed one was near my store but the woman who had placed it, Fay, was looking for a female who didn't smoke. I gave Fay a call anyway. I explained how I was a married man recently arrived in Ft. Lauderdale by myself to see if Florida would work out. I needed to rent a room and her house was near the store I was running. She said I could come over and talk with her.

I knocked on the door and a woman in her early thirties answered. She said hello and seemed friendly. I thought to myself, "This is a nice house and plenty big."

She invited me in and we started talking. I told her all about myself except for the bone disorders and my medicines. She told me she was divorced with two sons who lived with their father close by. She said she had a boyfriend in Vancouver, Canada, whom she would visit for weeks at a time, and he would come down occasionally. She had not thought of a guy sharing her house because her parents would flip out if a man answered her phone. They were strict Muslims and didn't believe in a man and woman sharing a house without being married. I thought, "Great, now we have another major difference."

We continued to talk and got along well. If I were to rent the room, she said, I was not to answer her phone. I told her I was Jewish and asked if that would be a problem. "Only if my parents or my sister found out," said Fay. "She is a member of the PLO [Palestinian Liberation Organization]. My parents have been living in occupied lands under Israeli control... As long as they don't know, it should be okay." She told me how they had sold her into marriage at age fourteen. I looked at her in amazement, but to her it was just the way it was in her culture.

Then I told her about my bone disorders and the medicines I used, including Cannabis. I showed her my prescription and explained how I got the Cannabis from the Federal Government. She was intrigued and sympathetic. She asked, "Will you promise you will only smoke outside?" I asked, "Does that mean you'll let me move in?" She nodded and said, "You need to move in tonight. I'm leaving tomorrow for three weeks to go to Vancouver." I said, "You don't even know me and yet you're going to trust me with your home." She replied, "Can I trust you?" I answered, "Of course you can."

I moved in and stayed there for seven months. Six days a week, I would go to work. Running a store by myself, it was easy to stand out back and take my medicine. If a customer walked in I would just put out the joint and go wait on them. On my day off I would relax and go to the beach. It was good to be back in South Florida. While I missed my family and friends, I knew I was going to stay. In Virginia I would wake up in pain and the weather for the day would be "high of thirty degrees with a chance of sleet and snow" and I wouldn't want to get out of bed. In Florida I would wake up in pain but the weather would be beautiful with a high of eighty degrees. Life's not so bad.

Debbie flew down at the end of February and surprised me for my birthday. We had a great time. She saw how much I loved being in Florida.

I flew north once in this period to see Dr. Goldman and pick up my supply of Cannabis. He had explained to the government that I was living in Florida for health reasons and requested a shipment of six cans instead of three—which they provided.

Debbie gave notice that she was leaving in September. Tom Nicholson, her boss was disappointed but understanding. We put the house up for sale and started planning a new life in Florida.

One night in August, Fay and I were watching the evening news when a story came on about Israelis attacking the PLO. "Your people are killing my people," she commented. It was time to move out.

I enjoyed my time at Fay's house. She was only in town about half the time. We got along well and enjoyed each other's company. Her two boys, ages twelve and sixteen, were likeable, as were her friends—many of whom who were police officers. It was always fun educating them about Medical Cannabis. I never had any problems with them.

Career Moves

In late August I took a week off to fly home and help with the move. Debbie and my best friend, Marc Silverberg, did a wonderful job getting our house in Portsmouth ready to sell. Her company listed the house and in several weeks, it sold. We had a yard sale and disposed of the furniture we were not taking. I rented a twenty-four-foot truck and packed it full. It was Cannabis that enabled me to do all the strenuous work that needed doing.

Because of the stress on my legs, Debbie and I took turns driving the truck and our car with our two white German Shepherds, Lady and Tyoga, and our white Cockerpoo, Angel. The drive took two days and was hard on my condition. As bad as it was, I could only imagine how bad I would have been if I hadn't had the right medicine. We arrived, unpacked, and started our new life in a rented house in North Lauderdale.

Debbie settled in little by little. It took her some time to get used to being around the second-hand smoke again. She never liked being around it in Virginia but knew how well it worked, so she tolerated it. She landed a job with the computer company that had provided support for her thirteen self-storages. They had a software program to handle the bookkeeping and daily operations of each site. This job was perfect for her and allowed her to travel all over the country and even to Australia. She would eventually come to like living in South Florida as much as I did.

I was glad to get back to work. I worked six days a week and was feeling well. I started looking for a Florida doctor to take over my protocol by asking the people I knew if they had any suggestions. The few physicians that were mentioned all turned me down. After four months of looking, I contacted an old high school classmate who had become a respiratory specialist with a practice just south of Ft. Lauderdale. As a favor, he agreed to take me on as a patient.

Bob and Alice helped get the correct forms and mailed them to me. I took them to the doctor and we filled them out. We sent them along with a form signed by Dr. Goldman to the FDA, the DEA, and the NIDA, and waited.

1987 arrived and Dr. Goldman put in a re-order for my Cannabis. I flew back to Virginia, visited my family and friends for a weekend, and flew back uneventfully with A LOT of Cannabis in my carry-on bag.

Over the next several months, the FDA issued a Schedule 1 license to my new doctor, the DEA inspected and approved the storage facility in his office, and in April they signed off on the transfer and notified NIDA.

This was now the second time that the DEA had to inspect an office to start the ball rolling for me to get my medicine and both were done in a respectable timeframe.

While I was having success in transferring my protocol, business was not going well as my bosses had over-expanded. The handwriting was on the wall; Mattress Madness was not going to make it. As the highest-paid employee, I was the first laid off. The timing could not have been worse—we had just purchased a new house.

•

I now had to decide what to do for a living. I was sick of the retail business. Working the long hours and most holidays was getting old. But what other marketable skills did I have?

Since the age fourteen, I had traded stocks for my family and friends. I had been confined to the house after my first operation and was often bored. I decided to take the $3,000 I had received in Bar Mitzvah presents and invest in the market. My mother had driven me downtown to the only brokerage firm in Portsmouth, Mason and Company (today Legg Mason) to open an account. The manager was surprised—not many kids opened brokerage accounts back in 1967—and told me I could come to the office anytime.

I wound up hanging out there a lot throughout my teenage years. As an investor, I was generally successful and found the environment exciting. From 1967 to 1971, I turned my \$3,000 to \$12,000. Now, at thirty-three, I wondered if I could make a living doing what was once just an extra-curricular activity.

I responded to a "Help Wanted" ad from a firm called R.L.R. Securities. I was advised that to become a stockbroker I needed to pass a difficult six-hour test given by the National Association of Securities Dealers (NASD), which only about fifteen percent of applicants pass. R.L.R. would hire me provisionally. I would have a month to study before taking the test. I would mostly likely fail the first time and would have to pass the second time, or be fired.

Because my bone disorders prevented me from sitting for hours at a time, R.L.R. contacted the NASD to request that special arrangements be made for me to take the test, which was to be given in an auditorium at Miami Dade Community College. They put me on the phone to explain that I used medical Cannabis supplied by the Federal Government and needed to smoke ten times a day, and that I couldn't sit or stand for long periods. The NASD official was quite taken aback, but I gave him phone numbers for the DEA, the FDA, and NIDA and he was able to verify my status as a Federal patient. Arrangements were then made for me to take the test in a separate room so I could smoke Cannabis and stretch my legs as needed.

I went to a prep service, bought my books, and started studying. Since I had been around the market for over twenty years, I figured it shouldn't be difficult. How wrong I was. The book is one thing, reality is something else. For the next three weeks, I made phone calls for the firm during the day and went to class three nights a week. I read and studied every waking minute. The fourth week I was in class from 9:00 am. to 5:00 pm. and studied late into the night.

The morning of the test—Saturday, June 20, 1987—was sunny and warm. I smoked two Cannabis cigarettes on the forty-five minute drive to Miami. My legs felt pretty good as I pulled into the parking lot of my alma mater, and I parked in one of the same spots I had used as a student. Good memories came back to me. I walked to the auditorium and found the woman I had been told to contact. I told her I was feeling well and thought I could go three hours without any more Cannabis—in other words, I might not need the special room. She arranged for me to take the test at the teacher's desk in the front of the auditorium, so that I could stand up and move around without seeing anyone else's answers.

I took the first part, ate a quick lunch and smoked two more cigarettes in an area set aside for smoking. The first part of the exam hadn't seemed that hard. I was one of twelve people from R.L.R. taking it. They all thought it was hard. I got back to the class and told the proctor I thought I could do the same thing for the afternoon test. I made it through the three hours and walked out. Somehow, I felt like I had passed, even though I hadn't studied for anything since I was nineteen-years-old.

When the results arrived, I was one of only two from R.L.R who had passed. Three CPA's and others, with degrees ranging up to masters had failed. I took it as confirmation that Cannabis, so helpful to me physically, had not harmed me cognitively. I had absorbed and retained an enormous amount of material in a month's time, while smoking ten Cannabis cigarettes a day. My short-term memory seemed to be working just fine!

•

Throughout the summer of 1987, I immersed myself in my new profession. I spent Monday through Friday, 9:00 am. to 5:00 pm., plus several nights a week, talking to people I knew and didn't know about what I could do to help them make money. I opened many accounts and bought high-quality stocks.

When I buy a stock for a person, I put in what is called a "sell stop loss." The client decides how much he or she is willing to lose, and I put in a sell order at the lowest price, just in case the stock drops. The stock is then sold automatically when the price is passed.

October 19, 1987 came to be known as "Black Monday" as the market crashed. IBM, which closed Friday at $150 a share, opened Monday at $100, down 33%. People lost fortunes overnight. The decline had actually begun the previous week, and thanks to my sell-stop-loss strategy, my clients had gotten out with minimal losses. Those holding IBM, for example, had sold at $165 a share. I had saved my clients a fortune while smoking ten to twelve Cannabis cigarettes per day. I was too scared, however, to buy any stocks back on Monday afternoon when, it turned out, they were at their lowest prices.

As stock prices sank on Monday, my colleagues were acting as if this was the worst thing that could ever happen. When another broker asked why I seemed to be taking the crash in stride, I said, "I'm not on a stretcher getting ready to be wheeled into an operating room not knowing if I'll wake up." I guess my disorders had given me the benefit of perspective.

The sun did rise on Tuesday and the markets continued their rebound, so I called all my clients and got back in. Over the next several months, the market gained back what it lost, and life went on for most of us.

In late October 1987, my mother got into a small fender bender. My sister Susan picked her up and took her home. She sat in a chair not saying a word. When my other sister, Gayle, knocked on the door, my mother stood up and collapsed. They took her to the emergency room where she was diagnosed with brain cancer. She was completely out of it.

Six weeks later, on December 10th, 1987, I lost my mother, Thelma Rosenfeld, to brain cancer. She was one of my best friends, my physical therapist after each operation, and one of my biggest supporters in taking on Uncle Sam. I could always talk to her about anything. I'm glad she saw me win. She was the greatest. I will always miss her.

Reverse Insanity

One morning in March, 1988, I opened the *Sun-Sentinel* and on the front page of the local section saw a story about a woman arrested for growing marijuana to treat her glaucoma! Her name was Elvy Musikka. The story, which was accompanied by a photo of an attractive woman with thick glasses, portrayed her as a fiery person who insisted that she used marijuana as a medicine and would be totally blind without it.

My heart was pounding as I picked up the phone to tell Bob about this woman in my own neck of the woods who was using marijuana for the very same reason he did. As soon as Bob heard my voice, he said, "I know why you're calling. Do not contact her. We are planning to fight the arrest on a defense of 'medical necessity' and we want you to testify. You shouldn't have any contact with her until the day of the trial."

Bob started working on a protocol to make Elvy the third Federal patient. Her opthalmologist, Dr. Paul Palmberg, of Miami, was prepared to submit it.

Elvy's trial was held in mid-August in Fort Lauderdale. Bob flew down and stayed at our house during the proceedings. My first meeting with Elvy took place at the office of her lawyer, Norman Kent, the morning the trial began. She was excited to be having her day in court at last. An outspoken woman in her forties who spoke with a Spanish accent (her mother was Colombian, her father Finnish), it was obvious that she could hardly see.

Elvy had been born with congenital cataracts and endured multiple surgeries as a child. She developed glaucoma in her thirties. Although one doctor had suggested marijuana as an effective treatment, she opted for conventional treatment—pharmaceuticals that didn't slow her loss of sight, and then surgery on her right eye. When that didn't help, she underwent more surgery, resulting in total blindness in that eye. "I didn't lose my eyesight to glaucoma, I lost it to ignorance," Elvy says.

The prosecution's only witness was the arresting officer, a sympathetic figure who said he felt bad about having to arrest Elvy.

The first defense witness was Robert Randall, who explained how similar his own situation had been. He had been arrested for marijuana possession in Washington, D.C., and was acquitted after proving he needed it to prevent blindness. He went on to tell how the Federal Government grows and provides his Cannabis.

The next witness was Dr. Paul Palmberg, Elvy's eye specialist, whose medical credentials were impressive. (He was also a deacon of his church.) Dr. Palmberg testified that marijuana prevented Elvy's eyesight from getting worse. Failed surgery had already cost her the sight in one eye, and he would not recommend risking what little vision she had left in her other eye by undergoing more surgery. He was so convincing that Norman decided that my testimony would not be needed.

Elvy testified eloquently on her own behalf. She said, "Marijuana saved my sight. I don't think the law has the right to demand blindness from a citizen."

On that note the defense rested. Judge Mark Polen then ruled from the bench that Elvy's marijuana use was a matter of medical necessity. He characterized her defense as "a reverse insanity plea" —meaning she would be insane if, knowing what she knew, she didn't use marijuana for her glaucoma. "Not guilty" was the verdict! We went outside the courtroom and took part in a media circus.

Bob, Norman, Elvy, and I answered questions for so long that at last we invited the reporters back to our house. All afternoon we gave interview after interview explaining the Federal IND program. Dr. Palmberg had submitted a protocol on behalf of Elvy and now that she'd been found not guilty, we hoped the Federal Government would act quickly to make her a legal patient. That night Elvy's trial got not just local, but national coverage. She was a star.

•

Months went by with no action from the Federal government. Bob decided to hold another press conference in Ft. Lauderdale to demand that the FDA act on Elvy's application. Elvy arranged for the bank at which she once worked, Home Savings and Loan, to provide a conference room. (She had been forced to stop working when she lost her eyesight. If only her doctors had used Cannabis instead of surgeries, she would be working to this day.) It was another standing-room-only event.

Bob urged the media to investigate why the FDA had not responded to Elvy's application. I told my story and then Elvy spoke. She was at her most eloquent. Again the questions and interview requests were endless and we invited the reporters back to our house. Around 4:00 pm., our phone rang.

A woman introduced herself as the reporter from the Miami Herald. She said she had just been talking to an FDA official who told her that Elvy's protocol had been approved! I relayed the news and the room buzzed with joy. Bob called our contact at the FDA, and sure enough, it was true. Elvy was going to become the third Federal patient and the first woman in the program! Bob made a point of thanking the media for bringing Elvy's case to the attention of the American people. We went out that night and celebrated. Our ranks had increased by 50%!

About six weeks later, I drove Elvy thirty-five miles south to Miami's renowned Bascom Palmer Eye Center. Dr. Palmberg had asked me to accompany her to answer some questions about administering government-issued Cannabis. (I had been planning to drive her anyway.) As we drove up to the twelve-story building, I thought to myself, "I hope I never need to come here to be seen."

Elvy held onto my arm and steered us to her doctor's office on the fourth floor. Dr. Palmberg welcomed us and pulled out the canister containing her three-hundred government-issued joints. Based on my interaction with Dr. Goldman, I suggested that he take her intraocular pressure (IOP) before and after she smoked. He put a drop of anesthetic in her left eye, then gently placed an instrument over it to take a reading. Elvy's IOP registered forty, which is scary. Normal is around fourteen.

Now it was time for Elvy to medicate. Even though it would be legal, Dr. Palmberg thought it best we go from his office to the twelfth floor where construction was underway and there were no patients.

Amidst the scaffolding and plaster, he handed Elvy her first legal joint and I lit it for her. I also lit one of mine. Here were two of the three legal patients in all of the United States taking their medicine. It was a moment I will not forget. Elvy had the biggest smile on her face. I guess I did, too. She finished the cigarette and we went down and retook her pressures. They had dropped to eighteen! The doctor was shocked.

I suggested we break for an hour and re-take her pressures. We did—and they were down to fifteen. She smoked one more before lunch and Dr.

Palmberg found her pressures had dropped to thirteen, which is normal. He said, "I wouldn't believe how her pressures dropped from the use of Cannabis, if I hadn't seen it myself."

He checked her a last time to confirm that she was experiencing no adverse effects. I suggested we break for lunch. As we were standing in line in the cafeteria, Elvy started talking to a man with prosthetic arms. His name was John Yount and he worked for an agency that taught people how to deal with their blindness. Elvy had known him for several years. He seemed like a nice guy. Years later, John would introduce me to Shake-A-Leg, a sailing program for people with disabilities.

After lunch Elvy's pressures were measured at sixteen. We paid another visit to the twelfth floor and they came down to thirteen. Dr. Palmberg had seen enough to report that Cannabis was effective and safe in treating Elvy's glaucoma. He handed her the joint-filled can and said he would see her in a month. Before we got back to the car, we hugged each other with the realization we had made history. We each lit up our medicine and got in the car for the wonderful drive home.

A Mickey Mouse Detention

Two close friends from Virginia, Brenda and Mark Kozak, came down for a visit in July 1988 and we decided to spend a week-end at Disney World and Epcot amusement parks in Orlando. I had never been to either place.

On Saturday we went to Epcot, a very spacious park. Whenever I needed to take my medicine, I'd simply walk away from people and light up. It was no trouble at all.

The next day we went to Disney World, which was just the opposite, very compact. There appeared to be nowhere to get away from people so I decided to see how long I could go without smoking.

By 5:00 pm. in the afternoon my legs had tightened up to the point that I was suffering. We had just gotten out of a thirty minute show and ride that our friends really enjoyed and wanted to do again. I told them I needed to smoke and would meet them in thirty minutes.

They went back in and I looked for a place to take my medicine. I went behind some bushes lining the path and found myself standing in front of a building that seemed to house air conditioners. I lit up and had almost finished my first joint when a trap door opened and a girl who looked fourteen-years-old came out of a tunnel used by employees. She said, "You better put that out or you'll get arrested." I replied, "This is medical use approved by the Federal Government."

I was smoking my second when two guys in plainclothes stepped through the bushes and one said, "You're under arrest."

I said, "Gentleman, this is marijuana provided by the United States Federal Government, and I'm not breaking any law." They got on their walkie-talkies and repeated what I had said. "Bring him in," said a voice on the other end.

I pointed to the exit from which my wife and friends were due to emerge and asked if they could hold off for five minutes. They called headquarters again and were told, "No, bring him in now!"

I got to see parts of Disney World the public never sees. They took me to the corporate office, sat me down and walked out. There was an ashtray on the table, so I pulled out my medicine and lit up.

The head of security walked in and said, "What are you doing?"

I said, "I wasn't allowed to take my medicine out there, so I'll take it in here. I don't mind."

He said, "You're serious, aren't you?"

"Yes I'm serious," I told him. "I'm one of the two Federal patients (Elvy had not been approved yet) in the United States allowed to use medical marijuana, and I'm not breaking any laws." He had already sworn out a warrant for my arrest.

I told him that in my car I had a tin can with many more marijuana cigarettes, rolled and shipped by the Federal Government, with labels. I then pulled out the letter sent from the FDA to Orange County (the very same county that Disney World was in) when I was illegally arrested there in 1983.

When I didn't show up on time (I'm very punctual), Debbie knew I must have been arrested. She sheepishly walked up to a security guard and told him she thought her husband had been picked up by security and could he check. He asked why in the world she would think this. She told him about the marijuana. He didn't quite know what to say, but called and found out, yes, I was there. Security sent a cart to pick them up.

By now there were seven security people listening to my story. One of them was a good-old-boy from Tennessee, who I could tell was sympathetic. I said to him, "You believe me, don't you?" He replied, "Damn right I do. I'll help even things out for your troubles when I can."

•

About the same time, an Orange County policeman showed up with the arrest warrant. The head of security said, "Look, there's a problem. It turns out that he is a Federal patient and he's not breaking any law, apparently. I want to drop the charges."

"You can't drop the charges"

"Well, I'm the one who called you. I'm head of security here and I'm dropping the charges."

"You can't drop the charges. The only one that can drop the charges now is a judge."

"Then, get the judge on the phone," said the security chief.

But it was Sunday afternoon and no judge was available, so the officer said that I would have to go with him. I showed him the letter and said, "Officer, Orange County was worried about me furthering the case last time. I lived in Virginia then. I now live in Ft. Lauderdale."

I sat down and didn't say another word.

The Disney World staff was trying to be helpful. They took my wife and friends out to our car and got the tin can and different newspaper articles.

The head of security looked at them and was even more convinced: "This is real," he told the policeman. "You've got to drop the charges!" The officer said, "If I can't get a judge on the phone, he's got to come with me." He reached to take me by the arm but the security chief grabbed him and said, "You can't do this. You can't take him. Don't you see, the Federal Government allows him? This is real!"

I told the officer he could call the Portsmouth, Virginia Police Department. "I don't live there anymore, however, they do have a file on me." He wouldn't. He said, "This is Florida." I'd heard that line before.

The Disney people managed to keep him there for three hours until he finally got a judge on the phone, who was able to drop the charge. It was 8:30 pm. when he left.

The head of security turned to me and said, "Here are four three-day free passes. Reservations have been made for y'all at our nicest restaurant, on us. Is there anything else we can do to make up for this embarrassment?"

I said, "It doesn't take care of me taking my medicine."

He said, "How about this? We'll put your name in the computer so that if you're by the clinic, you can go in and take your medicine. If you're anywhere else in the park and you need to take your medicine, call security and they will come to you. There are many exits all around the park for employees. Security will let you out one of those exits near you. You can then walk fifty feet away and take your medicine, then just walk back in. How does that sound?"

I said, "That sounds good... One other thing I want: an address where I can send someone information about possibly adding a medical marijuana exhibition at Epcot." No problem!

The head of security apologized again and the good–old–boy said, "See, I told you I'd take care of you."

We went and had a great dinner. When we finished and were leaving, lo and behold, there was the clinic. So I thought, "Let's see if this works." I knocked on the door and a nurse answered. I told her that my name was in the computer and that I was authorized to take my medicine in the clinic.

She looked in the computer and said, "Oh yes, it's right here. What is it that you take?"

"Marijuana"

"Oh, that's interesting. We only have this room and the doctor's office, and he's not here."

So I used his office. It was a nondescript office with a desk and a bookshelf that had only two books. As I was lighting up, I noticed that one of the books was about medical marijuana written by a proponent, Dr. Norman Zinberg! I couldn't believe it. I asked the nurse for a pen and paper so I could leave him a note. I wrote that I was one of the two Federal patients in the country and "I am using your office to actually take legal marijuana."

We headed back to Ft. Lauderdale with unique memories of Mickey Mouse.

Finally, Our Day in Court

Though the suit was filed in 1972, it wasn't until 1987 that the DEA finally held hearings on whether marijuana belonged on Schedule 1. The case was heard by Chief Administrative Law Judge Francis Young. I was scheduled to be a witness for the plaintiff.

It was news to me, as it would be to most Americans, that when a government agency is challenged on a legal issue, the case is reviewed by an "administrative law judge" appointed by the agency itself. The ALJ does not have the power to decide how the agency should act; he or she can only recommend a course of action to the agency, which can then be accepted, rejected, or modified.

There were three major parties involved—NORML, the DEA, and ACT (the Alliance of Cannabis Therapeutics, Bob and Alice's group). ACT was represented pro bono, by Frank Stillwell of Steptoe and Johnson. Bob and Alice had started working with Steptoe in the summer of 1986, getting written statements from proponents of rescheduling. They had helped me draft mine, which of course described my bone disorders and how effective Cannabis had been as a treatment. Dr. Goldman also submitted an affidavit documenting how well Cannabis worked for me.

Once all the written testimony was in, witnesses were cross-examined. Our side cross-examined only one DEA witness, but the DEA cross-examined almost all thirty-seven of ours. We didn't mind, it gave us a public forum for our arguments.

I testified on the day the hearings got underway, November 18, 1987, in New Orleans. I knew how important my testimony was now that I was testifying as one of the two Federal patients. Lawyers for the DEA asked questions based on my written statement—which gave me an opportunity to reiterate how well Cannabis worked for me as a medicine. Judge Young asked no questions of his own, but listened carefully and took notes.

There would be two days of hearings in San Francisco, and eleven days in Washington, D.C. Then the judge began his review of the voluminous record.

•

On September 6, 1988, after reviewing the records for almost one year, Judge Francis L. Young issued a momentous recommendation on the rescheduling issue: marijuana should be moved to Schedule 2 so that doctors could prescribe it as they do morphine or cocaine.

The record showed, Young wrote, that marijuana "has a currently accepted medical use in treatment in the United States for spasticity resulting from multiple sclerosis and other causes. It would be unreasonable, arbitrary and capricious to find otherwise. The facts set out [in the hearings], uncontroverted by the Agency, establish beyond question that some doctors in the United States accept marijuana as helpful in such treatment for some patients. The record here shows that they constitute a significant minority of physicians. Nothing more can reasonably be required. That some doctors would have more studies and test results in hand before accepting marijuana's usefulness here is irrelevant.

"The same is true with respect to the hyperparathyroidism [it should have read hypoparathyriodism] from which Irvin Rosenfeld suffers. His disease is so rare, and so few physicians appear to be familiar with it, that acceptance by one doctor of marijuana as being useful in treating it ought to satisfy the requirement for a significant minority. The Agency points to no evidence of record tending to establish that marijuana is not accepted by doctors in connection with this most unusual ailment. Refusal to acknowledge acceptance by a significant minority, in light of the case history detailed in this record, would be unreasonable, arbitrary, and capricious."

My successful treatment had been a crucial piece of evidence that helped convince Judge Young to recommend moving marijuana to Schedule 2. "Marijuana is one of the safest therapeutically active substances know to man," he observed.

But the stall in the name of science continued. The DEA's politically appointed administrator, John C. Lawn did not act on Judge Young's recommendation until December 30, 1989. Then he simply rejected it, and while supplying no additional facts ordered that Cannabis remain on Schedule 1, as if it were a dangerous drug having no known medical use.

While we were not surprised by the DEA's decision, we were outraged. We had proved Cannabis was safe and effective. Why should a law enforcement agency have the right to decide a medical issue? It must be nice to not have to go along with a verdict if you don't like the outcome of the case.

The Alliance for Cannabis Therapeutics

In 1981, Bob and Alice formed an organization called the Alliance of Cannabis Therapeutics or ACT, of which I was a charter member. Our goal was to help other patients and their doctors file Compassionate Care Protocols, and to guide them through the government maze. Corrine Millet, a fifty-eight-year old grandmother with glaucoma (and severe arthritis), became the fourth member of our "club" when her protocol was approved in October 1989.

Corrine was a widow who lived in Fremont, Nebraska. Her husband had been a surgeon and she had access to the best care the medical establishment could provide. She underwent two operations and tried "every drop on the market," but was told by her ophthalmologist nothing could save her sight, she would be blind in three years.

Cannabis had been recommended by a family friend, but Corinne was afraid of heavy psychoactive effects. She finally decided "my sight means more to me than fear of a plant," and smoked a joint under the supervision of her general practitioner. The pressure on her optic nerve dropped almost immediately and she got an added benefit: relief from the inflammation and pain caused by arthritis. She did report a psychoactive effect, but said it was comparable to drinking one martini.

In March, 1990, George McMahon got the FDA approval to use Cannabis to treat muscle spasms, pain, and nausea caused by a rare hereditary disorder called "Nail–Patella Syndrome," which is characterized by skeletal abnormalities. George's mother had a mild form of the disease, but his sister (who didn't smoke Cannabis) would die at age forty-four. NPS is fatal by age forty to eight percent of those born with it, due to damage to the kidneys, liver and other internal organs. George had been born with mild deformities, including missing fingernails, double-jointed fingers, poorly jointed elbows, and small kneecaps. As he matured he developed numerous organ and skeletal problems that required surgery. The disorder caused bones to become brittle and break easily.

George had four operations on his right knee, surgery on his right wrist, surgery on his right elbow. He contracted hepatitis A and B from transfusions and required long stays in the hospital. Nevertheless, he held down blue-collar jobs in mining, construction, auto bodywork and aircraft repair. In 1979 he was hospitalized after a nail wound in his foot failed to heal. In 1983 he injured his back in a fall.

George is a tough man, physically and emotionally. He started smoking Cannabis on an occasional basis and found that it relieved his pain, which was otherwise constant. Like myself, George does not get high, rather, his muscles stop going into spasms and the pain leaves his body as he is able to relax. We seemed to have a lot in common, including some similar physical problems and the support of a loving family.

•

The mysterious, deadly Human Immunodeficiency Virus (HIV) had been spreading relentlessly throughout the 1980s. There were no medications to slow its progress. It destroyed appetite and led to emaciation—the infamous "wasting syndrome." Marijuana, which brings on "the munchies," is the only drug that induces appetite. If ever there was a condition for which Cannabis could provide relief, AIDS was it.

Bob and Alice had drafted a protocol for an AIDS patient from San Antonio Texas, Steve L. It was approved in January, but Steve only lived six more weeks. I never got to even talk to him. Bob thought he could take the protocol developed for Steve L. and help thousands of people with AIDS. He planned to work an alliance with some AIDS patients' groups.

I cautioned Bob about the political ramifications (At that time, it was political suicide to align with AIDS organizations. Thankfully, it's not that way anymore.) "We have so many people against us already, do we want to be identified in the public mind with IV drug users and gays who have unprotected sex? I feel for anyone who is ill, but..." Fortunately, Bob's compassion overrode my simplistic notion that we could "spin" reality itself.

•

Bob called in April to tell me about two AIDS patients who had contacted him for help after getting busted for growing several plants in Panama City, Florida. Their names were Kenny and Barbara Jenks. They had been virgins when they got married. Nine months later, Barbara fell ill. It was discovered she had AIDS. Kenny tested positive for the virus, too. Then, Bob revealed Kenny was a hemophiliac who had gotten tainted blood during a transfusion. And he challenged me: "What did they do wrong to get AIDS?"

I knew I deserved the implied rebuke. Here was a heterosexual couple who had never done illegal drugs, never been promiscuous, but had contracted AIDS nonetheless. What right did I have to "cherry pick" patients deserving of the best possible medicine? Kenny and Barbara Jenks would play an important role in opening my eyes—and many other people's, too.

•

On April 15, 1990, Elvy and I spoke at Florida State University in Tallahassee, the state capitol. The event was sponsored by the campus chapter of NORML. It was our first time out as advocates without Bob being present. We told our personal stories and called for Cannabis to be rescheduled so that doctors could prescribe it. About 100 students attended, along with local reporters. We were able to answer every question, got a standing ovation, and left convinced that we made a great team.

"A Doctor Who Cares"

One team that was not working out was me and my doctor, my old classmate who had become a respiratory specialist. Since he was not a doctor with expertise of my bone disorders, he was becoming less willing to understand and treat my conditions. He was not comfortable with my intake of Dilaudid and decided "I'm cutting you off everything." He added he was going to notify the government thinking somehow I was an addict!

Fortunately, a friend had given me the name of Dr. Juan Sanchez-Ramos of the Department of Neurology at the University of Miami, who I asked to take over my protocol. He agreed to do so, he said, not just for my sake (his expertise was more relevant than my previous doctor), but for his own. "You would be giving me a chance to study a patient using Cannabis legally. My other patients use it illegally."

"You have patients using Cannabis?" I asked.

"I have a handful of patients, some with Parkinson's and some with Huntington's disease who self-medicate and benefit tremendously from its use."

He inquired in detail about my experience with various medicines. I had been using Dilaudid for nineteen years. I appreciated the pain relief but disliked the side effects it brought on, including drowsiness, lethargy, and stomach problems. Dr. Sanchez-Ramos took a medical text from his bookcase and showed me how the pain in my ankle was the result of nerve damage—neuropathic pain, for which no conventional medicine would work well.

"Should I stop taking Dilaudid?" I asked.

He nodded: "I think we should try and wean you off."

"I can just stop," I told him. "I have always taken it for three weeks and stopped for a week, just to make sure I had no addiction."

He seemed skeptical. "I'm here if you need me," he said.

Somehow again, GOD had found me the right doctor.

•

Over the next several weeks forms were filed with the FDA and the DEA. Dr. Sanchez-Ramos had done research studies for the Feds before and his reputation was strong enough to negate any badmouthing I had received from my previous doctor. His applications to take over my protocol went through smoothly. The DEA inspected the area where the medicine was to be stored and signed off; Dr. Sanchez-Ramos got a Schedule 1 license and placed an order with NIDA. It arrived promptly and I drove down to Miami to pick up my medicine.

Dr. Sanchez-Ramos's smile of amazement reminded me of Dr. Goldman's when the first shipment arrived at his office. He was also amazed that I could stop using Dilaudid just like that.

I told him, "Doc, after our first visit I told Debbie all about you. And the second thing I told her was I was going to start playing softball again. I stopped playing sports nineteen years ago because I was afraid I would hurt myself and not realize it. That's what Dilaudid does, while it masks the pain, it makes you insensitive. That Sunday I found a neighborhood game and I have played every Sunday since. It was like riding a bike. Softball came right back to me. I remembered: I'm a pretty decent little ballplayer."

"Marijuana as Medicine"

That summer Kenny and Barbara went on trial for cultivation of marijuana. They were busted for two scrawny plants growing in their house
trailer. Their testimony was riveting. In the end, the judge found them guilty
of possession, fined them one dollar and sentenced them to community service, taking care of each other. While the judge thought he was being gentle,
it still made criminals of the Jenkses. He could have ruled it was medical
necessity as the judge had in Elvy's case. The verdict did not sit well with
them and they appealed. The case generated publicity worldwide. Morley
Safer, correspondent for "60 Minutes" saw the story while on assignment in
France. He thought it would make a good segment, spoke to his producers,
and got the go-ahead.

•

In late August, 1990, NORML sponsored a conference in Washington D.C. featuring the Federal patients—Robert Randall, Elvy Musikka,
George McMahon, Corrine Millet, and myself, the five American citizens
lucky enough to have the medicine we needed. It was the first time we had
all met.

The conference was organized by two members of the NORML board
from Virginia: Al Byrne, a retired U.S. Navy officer, and Mary Lynn Mathre,
R.N., an addiction specialist (who had been a Vietnam-era Navy nurse). Al
and Mary Lynn believed that healthcare professionals—-and the American people— would insist on access to medical marijuana when they understood that it was safe and useful, and that nobody was better suited to
carrying the message than the Federal patients. Not only were we living
proof that Cannabis was medicine, our image was very respectable. To put it
bluntly, we weren't hippies, we were "straight"—on ten joints a day.

Al and Mary Lynn arranged for the conference to be broadcast live on

C-Span in its entirety, which resulted in the NORML office being flooded with 40,000 phone calls in the month that followed. They also arranged for production of an eighteen-minute documentary, "Marijuana as Medicine," which told our stories as Federal patients.

I appreciated Al and Mary Lynn's emphasis on education, Central Casting couldn't have sent our movement two better spokespersons. Al is a lanky Vietnam combat veteran who, before that, had been a starting back for three years on Notre Dame's rugby team. Mary Lynn is a registered nurse who has written extensively about the medical use of Cannabis. She radiates such strength and kindness that if you were in a hospital bed and saw her coming towards you, you'd start feeling better already.

Another participant in the conference was Mae Nutt, a remarkable woman from Michigan whose twenty-two-year old son Keith had been diagnosed with testicular cancer. Chemotherapy made him so nauseous he wanted to stop the treatment. Mae learned from the mother of another patient that he prevented nausea by using Cannabis before his treatment. Mae then went to "the street" and got Keith Cannabis for his next treatment. Guess what? No nausea. Keith continued using Cannabis during his treatments. He did not survive, but it made his last days more pleasant and convinced Mae and her husband to get the word out that Cannabis has medical use.

We were still a small group—approximately three hundred people attended the NORML conference—but we felt that we were at the center of a national movement.

I especially enjoyed meeting the other Federal patients. We had a special bond that we knew would last a life time…however long that life might be.

•

In December 1990 I switched firms. Several of my best clients had been singing the praises of a New York brokerage firm, GKN Securities, and when they opened an office in Boca Raton, I went to work for them. The partners who ran the firm had no problems with my medical use of Cannabis but I was not authorized to name GKN when identifying myself to the media as a stockbroker. (This policy ended when the New York Times ran a front-page article on me in 1995.)

The partners feared that some people would assume my use of Cannabis made me less able to do my job. What colleagues and clients eventually come to understand is that my medical use of Cannabis does not alter my mind. The relief it brings makes it possible for me to do my job. I think people also appreciate that whatever intelligence and drive I apply to taking on the Federal Government successfully is the same intelligence and drive I apply to conducting my brokerage business.

•

As 1990 ended the FDA signed off on seven new Compassionate INDs, including the Jenkses', bringing the total to fifteen. But only five of us were actually getting cans of Cannabis. Being approved by the FDA and receiving Cannabis via the DEA are two very separate steps. The Jenkses' first shipment wouldn't arrive until February 19, 1991, after Bob and Alice had condemned the delay to the media.

The Alliance for Cannabis Therapeutics had decided to challenge the DEA's refusal to accept Judge Young's decision "In The Matter Of Rescheduling." A hearing was held in March, 1991, in the U.S. Court of Appeals, Washington D.C. ACT's lawyer (pro bono from Steptoe and Johnson) Tom Collier argued that Cannabis clearly has an "accepted medical use in treatment in the United States." Any other conclusion is, as Judge Young said, "unreasonable, arbitrary, and capricious."

Department of Justice attorneys argued only that the DEA administrator can decide if marijuana is medically useful. They cited regulations allowing the administrator to ignore the recommendations of the agency's chief judge.

One judge wondered why the DEA, a law enforcement agency, should decide if a drug is medically useful. Shouldn't doctors, patients, and health care professionals make such a decision?

Another judge asked, "If the FDA is approving marijuana for medical uses for glaucoma, AIDS, and cancer, then how can the DEA claim marijuana is medically useless?" It seemed like a blatant contradiction. The Justice Department attorneys didn't know how to respond. Every disease Cannabis proves useful in treating makes their position of total Prohibition less tenable. Now its value as an appetite stimulant for AIDS patients was impossible to deny.

The three-judge panel ordered the DEA to reconsider its decision to ignore Judge Young's rescheduling recommendation. "The agency acted unreasonably in evaluating the drug's possible effectiveness for cancer patients and many other seriously ill patients," the judges wrote. But our lawyers were concerned that the judges had focused more on the DEA administrator's authority to make the ultimate decision than on the factual basis for keeping Cannabis on Schedule 1. The case wasn't over, they cautioned.

•

In April 1991 Barbara Douglass of Lakeside, Iowa, had her protocol approved. Her malady was Multiple Sclerosis, a disease in which the body's own immune system destroys the protective sheath around nerve fibers, resulting in painful spasms, fatigue and incontinence. Marijuana reduced the intensity and severity of her spasms, and the pain associated with them.

Also that month Morley Safer and his crew from 60 Minutes showed up in Panama City to tape Kenny and Barbra Jenks. This rural area in the Florida panhandle was not used to seeing big-time TV production companies, so everyone turned out, including the local media. Kenny and Barbra were gravely ill, but proud to be publicizing the medical value of Cannabis.

Soon after the CBS crew left, the Florida Court of Appeals upheld the defense of "medical necessity" in the treatment of AIDS for Kenny and Barbra. The Appeals Court overturned the conviction and declared them "not guilty." This was the nation's first successful "medical necessity" defense involving the use of Cannabis in AIDS.

I called Kenny and Barbra and said, "Now I can associate with you'll since you'll are no longer criminals!!" They laughed, but to them, this was a very big deal, as it would have been to me.

Each successful step raised the question: what more would it take to make marijuana available to those who need to use it for medical purposes? Which legal case, which scientific study would be the turning point? How could we bring the politicians up to speed with the clinicians?

In May, 1991, the prestigious journal "Annals of Internal Medicine" published a survey to which 1,035 members of the American Society of Clinical Oncology had responded. Some forty-four percent acknowledged having recommended that patients smoke Cannabis, even though it was illegal, for the control of vomiting and nausea associated with chemotherapy. Nearly eighty percent of the oncologists surveyed thought Cannabis should be legally available by prescription.

The lead author, Dr. Mark Kleiman professor at Harvard's Kennedy School of Government, appeared on NBC's "Today" show, along with Dr. Herbert Kleber, Assistant Director of the Office of National Drug Control Policy (the Drug Czar's office). Kleber cited the IND program as proof that the government was acting with open-mindedness and compassion! It was no trouble for anyone to get Cannabis if they had a medical need, Kleber claimed: "Just have your doctor apply to the FDA and the waiting period should be less than a month."

Watching TV at the kitchen table with Debbie, I knew how far from the truth this statement was. The government was using me and my friends in the IND program as a fig leaf to cover up the cruelty of Prohibition! My conventional upbringing and political outlook—totally admiring and trusting of the U.S. government—had not prepared me for such dishonest behavior from its officials. I was shocked. And although I've heard many similar lies and distortions over the years, to this day I still feel a bit shocked when they come from our government's spokespersons. How can they just lie like that?

The Program in Jeopardy

B ob and Alice had started another organization, the Marijuana/AIDS Research Service (MARS), and sent out hundreds of fill-in-the-blank IND applications to AIDS organizations. With the protocols in hand, patients took Dr. Kleber at his word. By the end of May, the FDA was swamped with IND applications.

In June, 1991, Corrine, Bob, Kenny and Barbra experienced disruptions in their supply of Cannabis. I myself had some brief disruptions, but calls from Dr. Sanchez-Ramos to the FDA and NIDA always expedited delivery.

Bob assumed these supply disruptions were not coincidental and asked Steptoe & Johnson to intervene. Per Bob's book, the lawyers learned by phone the responsible bureaucrats were meeting at the upscale Breakers Resort in Palm Beach, Florida. Acting on a hunch, Bob called the Breakers and asked to speak to the representative from Unimed, the manufacturer of Marinol. The hotel clerk replied, "Which one?"

Bob had long suspected that Marinol—synthetic THC, named "Dronabinol" by the National Cancer Institute (NCI) chemists who developed it—would provide an excuse to keep marijuana illegal and maybe a way of substituting it for smoked Cannabis. The patent had been purchased from NCI by Unimed, a Buffalo, New York, company, which assigned the marketing rights to Roxane Laboratories of Columbus, Ohio. While Marinol was still in clinical trials in the early '80s, NIDA substituted it for the marijuana it had been providing to patients undergoing chemotherapy at four cancer centers. (Including Sloan Kettering in New York City where Senator Peter Babalas had been treated) The FDA approved Marinol as a treatment for nausea in 1986, and doctors began prescribing it to cancer patients.

But Bob kept hearing from patients they much preferred smoked marijuana to Marinol for several important reasons: It doesn't have to be swallowed. (Taking a pill is difficult, obviously, when you're nauseous.) Smoking has an immediate effect, whereas Marinol takes almost an hour to work. And patients could take just as many puffs as needed to achieve short-term relief, instead of having to endure an eight-hour downer.

Many people assume incorrectly that THC is the only active ingredient in marijuana. As of December, 2008, the DEA's website proclaims, "Medical marijuana already exists—it's called Marinol." But other compounds in the plant exert important modulating effects on THC. By keeping Cannabis on Schedule 1 and blocking research into its compounds, other than THC, the government is not only denying the American people access to a useful medicine but is denying plant scientists the opportunity to develop strains that could be even more effective in treating different conditions.

I often wonder which of the sixty-four different Cannabiniods work best for George's, and my medical problems compared to which ones works best for Elvy and Bob or Kenny and Barbra's conditions. We all know it works, but we all wondered if different strains would work better. Sadly, we will never know the answer to that question because of a blinded bureaucracy.

•

As of June, 1991, Kenny and Barbra's shipments of Cannabis had not resumed from NIDA and Bob was furious. Per his book, he called "60 Min-utes" producer Gail Isen, who said Morley Safer's segment on the Jenkses had been edited, but the date for airing it had not been set. Gail knew the story was powerful and had taken a liking to Kenny and Barbara. She was angered by the cut-off of their supply and called the FDA. She reached an assistant administrator who made excuses that vaguely blamed NIDA. Then Isen named specific FDA staffers who were blocking the Jenks shipment and put Morley Safer on the line. This was every bureaucrat's worst nightmare.

By that afternoon, the FDA had the problems miraculously solved. Again, I was thankful for the power the press has in a free society.

The next day, Bob got a call from Michael Isikoff of the *Washington Post*. Isikoff had heard that the FDA was planning on closing the Compassionate IND program. The FDA and the DEA were blaming NIDA for lack of supply. But was there another reason, he wondered, such as fear the pro-marijuana advocates were using the program as a wedge to promote full legalization?

According to Bob's book, Isikoff didn't realize the significance of the news he was relating. Since 1978, the Feds had promised medical Cannabis on a compassionate basis to anyone with a "legitimate" need. First, they made it extremely complicated to apply. When ACT finally made it easier to apply, and people were beginning to do so in significant numbers, the government threatened to close down the program.

Claiming a supply problem was ludicrous: marijuana grows like a weed. We all knew the real reason. Until now the IND program had been mere "window dressing," enabling the government to seem compassionate and scientific in its approach to medical Cannabis by supplying a few individuals. If the program began supplying AIDS patients, who were beginning to apply en masse, then the medical value of marijuana would become indisputable. President George Herbert Walker Bush was running for re-election with the strong support of the pharmaceutical industry. Dan Quayle, whose family had a large interest in Eli Lilly, was his Vice-President on the ticket. We know how much money is made by that industry as long as Cannabis is illegal. If the FDA were to approve marijuana use by thousands of AIDS patients, then Bush could hardly run on a "War on Drugs" platform.

•

Isikoff's call made clear to Bob our medical-marijuana movement was under very serious attack. The FDA was still acting as if everything was normal, still approving new INDs. But NIDA was disrupting supplies to previously approved patients, and the DEA was slow to inspect doctors' storage facilities.

On June 21, Isikoff's article appeared in the *Washington Post* under the headline, "Health and Human Services to Phase Out Marijuana Program." The subhead explained, accurately, "Officials Fear Sending Bad Signal by

Giving Drug to Seriously Ill." The story went on to explain that the program, which had been instituted under President Jimmy Carter in 1978, was at odds with the Bush Administration's "War on Drugs." James O. Mason, Chief of the Public Health Service was going to issue a new directive. Patients receiving marijuana from the government would continue to be supplied, but everyone else would be encouraged to try Marinol.

Bob and Alice arranged press conferences in Washington and several other cities. I was on the phone calling my media contacts and fellow patients. ACT provided the phone numbers, and people inundated the FDA, the DEA, the NIDA, Congressional offices, and the White House with calls and faxes. "Don't let compassion be the first casualty in a "War on Drugs," was our message. It must have registered, because Bob got word directly from the White House that the HHS directive was "being put on hold for now." It was those last two words that bothered him, he told me.

•

In late August, 1991, only four months after her IND had been approved, Barbara Douglass received her first shipment of Cannabis. She had contacted her Republican friends in Congress, Representative Fred Grandy and Senator Charles Grassley. It helps to have friends in high places. The average patient has no such help. I was happy for her…and sad for all the others.

In October Bob and Alice started a third organization, Paralyzed Americans for Legal Medical Marijuana (PALM), for which they drafted another fill-in-the-blank IND application. Two paralyzed patients' IND protocols had been approved, and they along with many others were still awaiting their supplies.

•

In mid-November a group called the Drug Policy Foundation held a conference in Washington attended by several hundred people. Bob seemed to know them all. I finally got to meet Kenny and Barbara Jenks, who had been fully vindicated when the Florida Supreme Court upheld their "medical necessity" defense. We got settled in the hotel and then met at the bar. Other than Bob, they had never met another Federal patient. We had lots to talk about.

When I invited them out for dinner, Barbra said she wasn't feeling well and just wanted to go back to their room. They invited me up. We all lit up with our own medicine. After our first cigarette, Barb looked like she was starting to feel better and became more talkative. Some time went by and we all lit another one. You could see with each puff, Barbra's color and mood improved. After she finished her second Cannabis cigarette, she turned to me and asked if my offer for dinner was still on. I said, "Of course, anywhere you want to go."

She didn't want to go out in the cold Washington night, so we ate at the steakhouse in the hotel. I watched Barb and Kenny looking over the menu. This was their first time in a big city and I knew the prices shocked them. I told them again dinner was on me, it was an honor to be with them. All I could think was: an hour and a half ago, Barb was too sick to even think about food, but after smoking two Cannabis cigarettes her nausea was gone and now her only problem was trying to decide which steak she wanted. I thought to myself how amazing Cannabis is.

We all ordered and started off with salads. Then our steaks arrived. Kenny and Barbra's eyes opened wide. I don't think they'd ever seen such big steaks. "Dig in," I said. It was such a pleasure watching her eat. We all did a number on our meal. Cannabis is a wonderful medicine.

After dinner we headed back to their room to smoke and talk some more. Barbra was not as well as Kenny. AIDS, they tell me, is harder on women for some reason. I looked at them and thought how unfair life can be. Kenny didn't ask to be a hemophiliac, nor did he ask to be infected with tainted blood. At least they had each other.

The next night was the banquet at which Kenny and Barbra were the guests of honor. They received the "Robert Randall Award for Citizens Achievement." Kenny spoke from his heart and thanked everyone. Besides a nice plaque, they received a check for $10,000 from the Drug Policy

Foundation. Barbra gave Kenny the plaque and she took the check. Smart girl! The next day we said our goodbyes and headed home. We would be lifelong friends.

Two weeks later on December 1, 1991, Morley Safer's segment on the Jenkses, "Smoking to Live," aired on "60 Minutes" and was seen by millions of viewers. Kenny and Barbra came across as a loving couple who never harmed anyone, but had been greatly harmed themselves. Also interviewed were the Jenkses' attorney, John Daniel, Dr. Ivan Silverberg from San Francisco, Harvard Medical School professor Lester Grinspoon, Bob Randall, and a doctor who provided the government's line. Kenny and Barb watched the show from Barb's hospital bed, as she had taken a turn for the worse.

I thought the show was brilliant and definitely educated a lot of people. I was so proud of the job Barbra and Kenny did.

•

On March 9, 1992 an HHS spokesperson announced that James O. Mason recommended permanent closure of the Compassionate IND program and the White House concurred. At the time there were twenty-eight patients with approved INDs who never received any medicine. With this decree, they never would. The thirteen patients receiving medical Cannabis from the Feds would be "grandfathered in," and continue to be supplied. Five had AIDS; three had glaucoma; Barbara Douglas had MS; George McMahon had Nail-Patella Syndrome; I had Multiple Congenital Cartilaginous Exostosis and a variant of Pseudo Pseudo Hypoparathyroidism; and two had chosen to remain anonymous.

HHS Secretary Louis Sullivan signed the order ending the Compassionate Care INDs on March 19, 1992. The government's pretense of compassion was dead. So was the pretense of sincere medical research. Despite its name, the FDA's "Investigational New Drug program" never analyzed or published data about how the patients fared on the drugs supposedly being studied.

On March 28, 1992, Barbra Jenks passed away with her husband and Alice O'Leary at her side. She was only twenty-five. I will always remember our dinner together in Washington and how enjoyable it was to see her eat. I called Kenny and gave him my condolences. We both agreed how wonderful she was and would miss her wry humor. Barbra, rest in peace.

Kenny continued to work with Bob and Alice thru MARS. I can only imagine how much he missed Barb. They were so good for each other, not just as wife and husband, but as allies fighting illness and ignorance. Kenny's health continued to decline. We were all worried.

International Incident

B rokers occasionally attend the annual meetings of companies in which our clients are heavily invested. I was called on to attend such a meeting in Vancouver, Canada, in September, 1992, for a company called "Gold Rush Casino and Mining." It would be my first trip outside the U.S. since I had become a Federal patient.

The FDA told me I would need to get permission to bring my Cannabis into any foreign country, so I phoned the Canadian Embassy in Washington, D.C. and explained my situation. They referred me to the Office of the Minister of Health. I eventually was put through to the chief medical officer, Dr. Ross Hossie. He seemed very nice and understanding, but refused to grant permission for me to come into Canada with my marijuana.

Dr. Hossie said the United States didn't let in Canadian citizens with medicine that was legal in Canada but not in the U.S., so why should he let me in with my medicine? I said, "So, I'm a pawn in the war between Canada and the U.S." He kind of snickered and said, "I guess so."

Dr. Sanchez-Ramos suggested I try Marinol, which was legal in Canada. He wrote me a prescription and directed me to take it in advance of my trip, to familiarize myself with its effects. On a Sunday morning—a few days before my flight to Vancouver— I got up and didn't smoke. I took one 10 mg capsule which was supposed to last four hours, according to the prescription. An hour later, feeling no relief, I took another. My muscles continued to tighten, so an hour later I took two more. One hour later, still with no response, I took another two. One hour later I still had no relief. I wasn't feeling anything from the pills, so I lit up. Marinol did absolutely nothing for me. I figured I was in for two and a half days of hell in Canada without my medicine.

•

Gold Rush Casino's vice-president, Kim Hart, picked me up at the airport at 2:00 am. When we got in the car he said, "We have one stop to make before you get to the hotel and I don't want to know anything about it." The statement seemed quite strange to me.

He drove into a residential neighborhood and pulled into a driveway. He turned to me and said, "Go in the house, he's waiting for you." I had no idea what was going on, but I trusted Kim so out I went. I knocked on the door and was told to come in by a man in his early forty's who said, "I've been waiting for you." He handed me a small container and said, "This is for you." I opened it up and it was full of sunflower seeds. I looked puzzled and he said, "Look in the bottom." There was a bag with about an eighth of an ounce of Cannabis and rolling papers. He said the cost would be fifty Canadian dollars, which I could give him tomorrow at the stockholders meeting. I thanked him and left. Kim then drove me to the hotel.

I checked in and quickly headed to my room so I could light up, as it had been a long time since I last medicated. I threw my suitcase down on the bed and went to the desk to roll a joint. The Cannabis was "Skunk Weed." I lit it up and it smelled to high heaven. It suddenly hit me that I was in a foreign country breaking the law. I got so paranoid I hastily put it out and decided I would return it to my anonymous provider when I saw him at the meeting.

In the morning, I got up and opened the curtains. My room was on the fifteenth floor, overlooking the Georgia Straits. I opened the window, lit the joint, and blew the smoke out. The wind took it drifting towards the sparkling, blue bay. My "paranoia" of the night before—thoughts of getting discovered, hassled, arrested, deported, humiliated, etc.—had not been caused by Cannabis itself but by smoking it illegally. Perhaps this principle applies to others, and the "paranoia" many people experience when they smoke marijuana illegally is simply a realistic fear of getting in trouble, not an inherent effect of compounds in the plant.

I went to the bank before the meeting and got some Canadian dollars to pay for my medicine. Having it sure made my visit better.

Clinton Raises Our Hopes

In July, 1992, I received a phone call from a friend of a friend of mine who was active in the Democratic Party. He wanted me to urge the medical-marijuana community to support Bill Clinton, the Arkansas governor who was running for President. He said that once Clinton was elected, he would nominate Dr. Joycelyn Elders as Surgeon General. She would cite the abundant anecdotal testimony about the medical value of Cannabis and propose that the Compassionate IND program be reopened so that serious studies could be undertaken.

According to him, Clinton and his top advisors were not in favor of medical Cannabis, but were willing to facilitate research into its potential and wanted the Democrats to be seen as the party of compassion. The pitch sounded good, but I had been fooled before. He gave me Dr. Elder's phone number and said that she'd be expecting my call in an hour.

An hour later I was on the line with Joycelyn Elders, explaining why the government was providing my Cannabis and how it affected my condition. I filled her in on the hearing conducted by Judge Francis Young and how his recommendation to move marijuana off Schedule 1 had been rejected. I told her that in the late '70s and early '80s more than thirty states had passed laws in their respective State Houses allowing patients access to medical Cannabis, but federal control of the supply made the state laws meaningless.

Dr. Elders asked me many questions, and I felt useful knowing most of the answers. She assured me that if Clinton won, his administration would follow the scenario laid out by my friend's friend. I eagerly agreed to promote Clinton within the medical-marijuana community.

It was not a hard sell. Even though many activists had libertarian leanings, President Bush's shut-down of the Compassionate IND program had handed the medical-marijuana issue to the Democrats. We were all happy and hopeful the night Bill Clinton was elected.

•

There was another significant vote that day, well below the national radar. In Santa Cruz, California, voters passed a measure permitting the medical use of marijuana. It was modeled after San Francisco's Proposition P, which had passed the previous year, enabling a charismatic organizer named Dennis Peron to openly operate a "Cannabis Buyers Club" in the Castro District, the epicenter of the AIDS epidemic.

•

November 20, 1992, was the tenth anniversary of my receiving Cannabis from the government. That night, Debbie and I went out to dinner and made a toast commemorating my good health that Cannabis had restored to me. I thought back about what had transpired since I became legal. I never thought with 1993 around the corner Cannabis would still be Schedule 1.

•

Would Bill Clinton—the first President from the generation that discovered marijuana for itself in the 1960s—finally end the Prohibition? Those of us who were contemporaries of the Clintons had high hopes (no pun intended) that the Compassionate Care IND Program would be restored. We were encouraged when Joycelyn Elders was appointed Surgeon General and Dr. Phillip Lee, a reputed liberal from the University of California at San Francisco, was named to head the Public Health Service—James Mason's old job. But we waited in vain for an announcement about the IND program being revived.

Per Bob's book, Bob and Alice tried to meet with White House officials, but were rebuffed. It seemed to us invisible interest groups were exerting pressure on the government to not allow any more INDs (because the more people who confirm that marijuana eases their symptoms, the more indefensible the "no-medical-value" line becomes). The pharmaceutical industry had been able to get Marinol approved by the FDA for appetite stimulation. Did they hope Marinol would appease the AIDS community and weaken the demand for medical marijuana?

•

The demand kept growing, as did media interest. On January 28, 1993 the Wall Street Journal printed a piece headed "Sometimes Marijuana Is the Best Medicine" by Doug Bandow, a Cato Institute fellow and former special assistant to President Reagan. He wrote about Kenny and Barbra Jenks and how they needed to smoke marijuana to live. He described Judge Francis Young's decision and the DEA's refusal to accept it. He criticized the Public Health Service for closing the Compassionate Care IND Program and called on President Clinton to reopen the program.

•

In March, Elvy and I spoke in Miami before the American Medical Student Association, which represented 48,000 med students and residents. AMSA delegates unanimously endorsed a statement calling on the new Attorney General, Janet Reno, to abide by the 1988 recommendation of Judge Young and move Cannabis to Schedule 2. They also unanimously passed a resolution asking President Clinton to reopen the Compassionate IND program. We were very proud with our results, as were Bob and Alice. Elvy and I agreed being around medical students gave one hope for the future!

On April 8, 1993, the *Miami Herald* ran a headline, "Medical Marijuana, A Renewed Push." The article described Elvy's, Kenny's, and my use of medical marijuana and how positive our results had been. It revealed that

Governor Lawton Chiles, then the governor of Florida, had told his "Red Ribbon Panel on AIDS" that marijuana reduces nausea, a side effect of chemotherapy, and stimulates appetite. Perhaps the Jenks case had helped educate the governor.

•

Kenny died On July 19, 1993. Alice and Bob had been there for him while I had stayed in close touch from my brokerage office. I could tell his health was waning... He died one day before Barbara would have been twenty-seven years old. Kenny was only thirty-one. Kenny and Barb were special people who never harmed anyone, but had been harmed by society and modern medicine. I loved and respected them. They are why this "War" on marijuana and the people who use it has to be ended.

•

The *Orlando Sentinel* ran a story in this period describing Chris Woiderski's plight as one of the twenty-eight patients who had been approved to get government Cannabis, only to be denied when the IND program was closed. Woiderski had been paralyzed in an accident and used marijuana to control his muscle spasms. He had been prescribed 490 pills per month; the pills made him groggy and damaged his kidneys. I could easily understand his plight.

•

The *New York Times* carried an article about a seventy-nine-year old woman who grew marijuana to relieve her son's multiple sclerosis. *NBC Nightly News* ran a story about Cannabis buyers clubs operating in several major cities such as San Francisco and Washington D.C. CNN, had a story about a rabbi who obtained Cannabis for cancer patients.

We kept hoping the intensifying publicity would convince the Clinton Administration to re-open the Compassionate IND program, but no action was taken. With Kenny's death the number of Federal patients had declined.

Was our government hoping we would just all die and vanish? To say I was disappointed in Clinton was an understatement. As far as I was concerned, the President had not upheld his promise.

•

In October, 1993, the United States Court of Appeals in Washington D.C. heard the case of the Alliance for Cannabis Therapeutics vs. the DEA. Steve Davidson of Steptoe and Johnson, representing ACT, argued that the DEA had acted arbitrarily in overruling Judge Young. We knew our chances were slim but felt we had to try.

•

In January 1994, came an announcement the federal ban against the use of marijuana for medical purposes would be reviewed by the Public Health Service. A PHS spokesman said while the ban would be reviewed, "there was no present plan to change it." PHS officials declined to spell out the timetable for the review, or details of how it would work.

The time I would have welcomed such an announcement had long passed. "They'll say anything and do nothing," I thought. I was becoming as cynical as Bob.

Skipper Irv

In early May 1994, I called John Yount, a friend and client whom Elvy introduced me to at Bascom Palmer Eye Center. John suffered a terrible accident when he was younger leaving him with no arms and one good leg and one bad leg. I asked him if he could do anything for activity. He replied, "I sail a boat." I asked him, "How the hell can you sail?" He told me, "I steer the boat with my one good leg. The boats are set up for all types of disabilities. They have a chair built into the back of the boat where paraplegics, quadriplegics or people with other disabilities can drive the boat holding a tiller extender. There is also a chair built into the front of the boat where a person can do the lines for the mainsail and the jib."

I told him I learned to sail when I was about ten-years-old before my bone disorder hit. John told me how to contact Shake-A-Leg, the Miami organization that ran the disabled sailing program. They were about to start a new beginners class and I promptly enrolled.

Debbie and I joined nine other students, including two quadriplegics— Dan Murphy and Karen Mitchell. This was my first time getting to know people confined to wheelchairs, quite a humbling experience. How lucky I was to still be walking! Three of the skippers were in chairs. If they could sail the boats, then I had to be able to.

The class started out with each of us describing ourselves, both able-bodied and disabled and why we wanted to learn to sail. I described my bone disorders and my use of medical Cannabis. "As long as it's legal and won't cause potential harm to others," a Shake-A-Leg officer had explained, "we will have no problems with your medicine." Everyone, including the volunteer skippers, were accepting and encouraging as I told my story.

After an hour learning about each other and a little about the boats, it was off to the docks. There they were, twenty-foot "Freedoms" that had no engines and did not look easy to handle.

I was paired with Karen Mitchell, one of the quadriplegics. Our skipper got us off the dock and showed us how to steer. When I took the tiller, it seemed easy. The skipper asked if I had ever sailed before. I told him of my limited experience. "Just like riding a bicycle," he said, "you never forget." I had to admit it felt perfectly natural.

As we came back in, the skipper told me to dock it. I watched another boat dock first and then I did it on my own. I realized I could sail these boats and it had not hurt me. I was hooked, and so was Karen. For her it was the freedom of leaving her wheelchair on the dock and doing something competitive and fun. For me, it was the quiet with no phones or CNBC blasting. I enjoyed the challenge of learning how to utilize the wind to get where you want to go.

After four beginner's classes, we were ready to train to become skippers. (Debbie, who had taken the early training with me, decided one skipper in the family was enough.) Karen and I passed the skippers class with flying colors and are both still involved with Shake-A-Leg and teaching physically, mentally, and economically challedged beginners how to sail. Karen and I raced together as a team for a while and even took first place in the 2000 Mid-Winters, Shake-A-Leg's biggest race of the year. Our team broke up when she decided to seriously pursue racing. While I still do some local racing, I was not as competitive when it came to racing as Karen. She has gone on to win many national and international races and even tried out to represent the United States in the 2008 Paralympics in Beijing.

Shake-A-Leg has given me so much more than I could ever give in return. I invite everyone to check out the website of this wonderful organization: **www.shakealegmiami.org**. You will not be sorry.

How Many Steps Will it Take?

In October 1994, my congressman, Harry Johnston, wrote a letter to Surgeon General Joycelyn Elders, asking her to re-open the Compassionate Care Protocols. She responded: "The Public Health Service (PHS) recently completed a review of the single patient IND process, which was used as a way of providing marijuana to patients with a variety of medical conditions. In considering whether to reopen the process, the current state of knowledge about therapeutic marijuana was carefully evaluated. This evaluation indicated that despite anecdotal claims that smoked marijuana is beneficial, sound scientific studies supporting these claims are lacking."

How disingenuous! The reason that no "sound scientific studies" confirm the benefits of smoked marijuana is that the government would not allow such studies to be conducted! I've been getting Federal Cannabis for almost twelve years and they haven't studied me at all, or any of the other IND patients. President Clinton had promised a more enlightened approach and now this crap.

Not giving up, Rep. Johnston wrote to other Administration officials: "It is my understanding that the Health and Human Services recently held a hearing into the possible beneficial effects of marijuana for patients who suffer from AIDS Wasting Syndrome. Given that the Food and Drug Administration has already approved this project and knowing of the beneficial effects that marijuana has for many patients of deadly diseases, I actively urge that this project be carried out as was originally planned.

"A constituent of mine, Irvin Rosenfeld, who is a long-time user of marijuana, originally brought this project to my attention. Mr. Rosenfeld, who continues to use marijuana under the Compassionate Care Protocol, has told me on numerous occasions of the benefits he receives by using this drug. I believe his situation is not unique and that further research into the beneficial effects of marijuana should be undertaken."

I admired Rep. Johnston's courage and appreciated his support. To my knowledge, none of his constituents objected to his pro-research stance. Unfortunately, the Clinton Administration, just like the Bush Administation, had no intentions of allowing any more patients to use marijuana legally.

•

In January 1995, the American Public Health Association came out with a policy statement on medical Cannabis. They encouraged research into the therapeutic properties of various cannabinoids and combinations of cannabinoids. They advocated research on alternative methods of delivery to decrease the potential harmful side effects related to smoking and most important they urged the Administrations and Congress to move expeditiously to make Cannabis available as a legal medicine where shown to be safe and effective, and to immediately allow access to therapeutic Cannabis through the Investigational New Drug Program.

I was elated such a large government agency was calling for the re-opening of the IND Program. However, I didn't hold my breath.

I had not been hearing much from Bob or Alice. I had a feeling something was wrong. Messages were left saying, "Nothing important, just checking in." This went on for several months. Finally in March, Bob called and told me he had been ill, but was on the road to recovery. "I need you to start helping me more with the public and media," he said. He and Alice had taught me well and I felt up to the task. At the time, I didn't realize how sick Bob was. Within the year he would reveal that he had AIDS.

•

In May 1995, I had an on-air confrontation with Wayne Roques, a retired DEA agent. We were doing a television show called "U Talk" in Miami. He recited the familiar Prohibitionist talking points: today's marijuana, grown in the U.S., was much stronger than the imported marijuana prevalent in the 1960s and '70s, and smoking it caused lung damage. I found it interesting that a retired DEA agent with no medical background believed he knew more than doctors and patients.

The medical reality is: the more potent the Cannabis, the less one has to smoke to alleviate pain, nausea, spasm, etc. Anyone concerned about lung damage should welcome the development of more potent Cannabis. I felt my understanding, which was based on my actual experience, trumped Roques's scare tactics. When the show was over, I walked away knowing I had made my points.

Each story, each interview, each radio or TV show in which someone speaks truthfully about marijuana gets us one step closer to ending Prohibition. Unfortunately, we just don't know how many steps it will take.

Patients Out of Time

Mary Lynn Mathre and Al Byrne left NORML and launched a new group called "Patients Out of Time" (POT) to educate healthcare professionals about Cannabis as medicine. "We need to explain the science, not argue the politics," is how Al summed up their strategy. The known Federal patients—Bob, myself, Elvy, George, Corinne, and Barbara—gladly agreed to speak at conferences and to the media on behalf of POT. (The name was chosen to emphasize the urgency of our situation.) George, Corinne and Barbara were on the original board of directors. I declined an invitation to be on the board. I had great respect for all involved, but I was more comfortable as a solo act.

In June 1995, the prestigious *Journal of the American Medical Association (JAMA)* published a comprehensive article, "Marihuana as Medicine: A Plea for Reclassification" by Lester Grinspoon, MD, and James B. Bakalar, JD. Dr. Grinspoon, a professor of psychiatry at Harvard Medical School, had recognized the anti-nausea and appetite-inducing properties of smoked marijuana when his son Danny used it while undergoing chemotherapy. Danny had been diagnosed with acute lymphocytic leukemia in July, 1967; he died in 1971.

Since then, Dr. Grinspoon had been trying to educate the medical establishment and the American public about the medical uses of marijuana. The article he and Bakalar published in *JAMA* provided a clear, compelling overview of a history that none of us had ever learned about in school.

Through the 1920s Cannabis was sold in tinctures made by Eli Lilly, Merck, Parke Davis and many other major drug companies. Most of the Cannabis was imported from India, but American farmers also grew some for medical use (as well as hemp for fiber, birdseed, and oil). Cannabis was widely prescribed as an appetite stimulant, muscle relaxant, analgesic, hypnotic, and anticonvulsant. Sir William Osler, known as "the father of modern medicine," considered it the best available remedy for migraine.

Medical use declined when alternatives such as injectable opiates, aspirin and barbiturates were introduced. The final blow was the Marihuana Tax Act of 1937, which was enacted over opposition from the American Medical Association. The law was aimed at preventing non-medical use, but it made Cannabis almost impossible to get for medical purposes.

There has never been a case of lethal overdose from marijuana, Grinspoon and Bakalar pointed out. Or as Judge Young put it, "Cannabis is the safest therapeutically active substance known to man." They urged physicians to acknowledge that the classification of marijuana as a dangerous drug with no known medical use is scientifically, legally, and morally wrong. Not every safe, effective drug is prescribed by every physician, they noted, but every physician should have the right to make prescribing decisions, and marijuana should be one of their options.

•

Soon after the JAMA article appeared, activist Jon Gettman submitted a petition to the DEA requesting "That proceedings be initiated to repeal the rules and regulations that place marijuana and tetrahydrocannabinols in Schedule 1 of the Controlled Substance Act." Gettman's petition was a continuation of the suit filed in the 1970s by NORML. The government had stalled on this issue successfully for more than twenty years! I was glad Jon made the request.

A different approach was being taken in California, where Dennis Peron and friends were drafting an initiative that would allow doctors to recommend marijuana for medical use. I contacted Dennis, whom I had first met at a NORML conference in Washington DC, and offered to help in any way I could. All he and his friends had to do was get about 750,000 signatures to get on the ballot. It seemed like a long shot.

No Big Deal

Debbie and I planned a trip back to Virginia in September, 1995. I called Delta Airlines, made our reservations and then asked for a medical supervisor to arrange a place to take my medicine during our layover in Atlanta. When ever I flew, I always let the airlines know that I'm a legal Federal Cannabis patient and would be carrying my medicine. I looked at the situation like a policeman carrying a gun on board. As long as they know it's legal there would be no problem.

When we got off the plane, two red-coat Delta Airline supervisors and a policeman met me and asked for my paperwork to prove I was a legal Federal patient. They took my papers and in only about eight minutes came back saying everything had been verified and I was led to a specific room at the airport set aside just for smokers. The policeman was there just in case anyone complained.

There were fifteen people smoking cigarettes under a cloud of smoke. The room had that smoky stench, but as we say in sailing, "Any port in a storm."

I didn't think anybody would notice my Cannabis. I finished the first one and was lighting up a second when I noticed two young women staring at me. I explained, "This is medical Cannabis supplied by the Federal Government. That policeman over there will confirm…" But they didn't have any problems with my smoking Cannabis, they were friendly and accepting. No one else even noticed. I smoked two cigarettes, thanked the officer and the Delta Reps and went to the gate to board the next flight. It was that easy.

•

On Sunday, October 22, 1995, the *Washington Post* ran a very informative feature story by Eugene L. Meyer: "Uncle Sam's Aunt Mary— In Which We Pay a Visit to a Far-Out Place: The U.S. Government Pot Plantation." Although the story concerned marijuana grown in Mississippi, it referred to the Federal patients as "The Acapulco Eight." Why is it that journalists cannot resist working jokes or puns into stories about marijuana? Could this reflect their understanding that it really isn't a dangerous drug after all?

A large picture of Bob taking his medicine was featured. There was also a photo of me medicating, a close-up of my tin can, and a picture of the gardener in charge of the five-acre plot on the Ole Miss campus where marijuana is grown for NIDA. The contractor, a Cairo-born pharmacologist named Mahmoud ElSohly, was quoted saying that Ole Miss students considered working on the farm one of the best jobs on campus. I'll bet they do, as it was an honor to be selected.

The marijuana grown in Mississippi is frozen for long periods, Meyer of the *Post* reported, so NIDA advises recipients to steam the cigarettes before smoking to restore moisture. I could have told him that steaming makes the paper soggy. The best method is to un-wrap the cigarettes, put the marijuana in a baggie with lettuce for eight to ten hours, and re-roll it. The marijuana absorbs the moisture and is not as harsh to smoke.

Our Breakthrough Year

Finally, 1996 was the year the term "medical marijuana" entered the national vocabulary. In January, CBS Evening News featured a report on medical Cannabis that started with me kissing Debbie goodbye as I left for work, and then showed me medicating in my car. "Rosenfeld, who contends he gets no high…" said correspondent John Roberts. He described my disorder and noted that all my friends, neighbors, co-workers and clients knew of my medical use. I was shown walking to my office as I explained I had tried many other medicines and that my case had been reviewed at many major medical centers, including the National Institutes of Health (NIH) Johns Hopkins, the Mayo Clinic, and Yale University School of Medicine.

•

I called for the IND program to be re-opened. As if addressing the authorities directly, I said, "Do something! What you have done now is totally taken away everyone's hope. There is no more hope, period. The government has shut the program down and is hoping the eight of us die."

My position was backed up by Dr. Grinspoon, who said that marijuana "can work when other drugs don't for diseases from glaucoma to multiple sclerosis."

The Prohibitionist line was asserted by Dr. Eric Voth, a Kansas addiction specialist: "It's a drug of abuse, not a medicine." Voth accused those who advocate medical use of having an ulterior motive: total legalization of marijuana.

Much of the CBS report focused on underground Cannabis buyers clubs that had sprung up in New York and San Francisco to serve people with AIDS. San Francisco authorities were said to be looking the other way, but in New York club operators had been busted. A New Yorker defended his civil disobedience: "We may need to break the laws until the system realizes the laws need to be changed—or not applied in the case of people who are ill."

The segment ended with a shot of me in front of my office and the narrator saying: "Rosenfeld agrees that some people may have an ulterior motive, but ultimately the choice should be between doctors and their patients." It was a powerful report, seen by millions.

•

In the spring of 1996, Congressman Harry Johnston announced he was not running for re-election and threw his support behind Robert Wexler. Needless to say I was quite upset he was not running again as he was my biggest supporter in the government.

As fate would have it, Roger Gladstone, one of the owners of GKN, the brokerage firm where I worked, was a large contributor to the Democratic Party and was helping Robert Wexler raise funds. He brought him to our office to give a speech. Since I knew he was coming, I went to all seventy employees and told them not to ask any questions so I could. Sure enough when he finished speaking he said, "I have time to take one question." I raised my hand and you could see Roger wince. I was called on and said the following: You have stated you intend to carry on with all the positions Congressman Harry Johnston had. In that case I am one of eight patients in the United States who receives medical Cannabis from the Federal Government and Congressman Johnston has been my biggest supporter. So I'm glad to know once elected you will become my newest biggest supporter.

He was elected, but it took me about a year to get him and his office behind me. Even though I was re-districted in the year 2000, he has continued fighting for me and the entire medical Cannabis issue. Thank you, Congressman Wexler and Congressman Johnston.

On another election issue, even though Dennis Peron's San Francisco Cannabis Buyers Club had some 7,000 members at the start of 1996, he and his allies were having trouble getting enough signatures to qualify a medical-marijuana initiative for the ballot in November. The deadline was April, and by January Dennis was on the verge of saying, "Wait till next time." Then came an offer of help from a New York-based reform organization called the Lindesmith Center (named after an American sociologist, Alfred Lindesmith, who believed that society should seek to reduce the harm associated with drug use instead of imprisoning users).

Now known as the Drug Policy Alliance, the Lindesmith Center was led by an articulate reformer named Ethan Nadelmann, who had the backing of philanthropist George Soros, among others. Nadelmann allocated approximately $1 million to hire a professional campaign consultant, Bill Zimmerman of Santa Monica, who in turn hired a signature-gathering firm, and by April was able to present the California Secretary of State with more than 800,000 signatures. These were verified, and the medical marijuana initiative was put on the ballot as "Proposition 215."

Since the start of the 1970s more than thirty states had passed some sort of legislation in favor of medical Cannabis, and yet not one patient had gained access under state law. Prop 215, as it came to be known, would allow patients to use marijuana, with a doctor's approval, to treat any condition for which it provided relief. Although the DEA could still arrest individual patients for possession, it was assumed that the Feds would only go after major distributors and "manufacturers" (growers), not patients growing their own medicine or being supplied by small-scale "caregivers."

I did what I could to support Prop 215 from my Boca Raton office. Reporters would call and I would answer their questions. My line was granting access to medical marijuana was really a Federal responsibility, but the people of California (and Arizona, which also had a reform measure on the ballot) had every right to allow it under state law.

In mid-June, Mary Lynn Mathre invited Barbara Douglass and me to represent Patients Out of Time in making a presentation about medical

Cannabis at the American Nurses Association meeting in Washington, D.C. Nurses are the real caregivers, as anyone who has spent time in hospitals knows. I know how important nurses have been in my life. Many nurses have observed patients on the wards using Cannabis to cope with pain, spasticity, and other problems. They tend to be tolerant.

I gave my usual presentation which was well received. Barbara got a knowing laugh when she introduced herself and said "...and I do inhale, because I have multiple sclerosis and marijuana works for me."

"Most nurses and most doctors tell us privately they know Cannabis works," according to Mary Lynn. "Our goal is for them to say it publicly."

I respected Patients Out of Time's approach and was feeling less like a solo act.

•

On July 1, 1996, during my regular three-month check-up, Dr. Sanchez-Ramos informed me that he had accepted a position as professor of Neurology at the University of South Florida in Tampa. He expected their Institutional Review Board (IRB) to approve our protocol. It would mean a 250-mile drive to pick up my medicine every five months. Fortunately, my nephew, Bobby Welsby, his wife, Michelle, and their lovely daughter, Kayla, lived nearby.

Three weeks later, Sanchez-Ramos called with the disturbing news that the head of the IRB decided not to approve a medical Cannabis protocol. He found a colleague in Miami—Dr. M.—who was willing to take over the protocol but not to store the Cannabis. That would be done by the pharmacy that took in Elvy's shipment. The new arrangements would require additional inspections by the DEA. "I'm glad we ordered six cans, so hopefully all this can be done before you need a refill," said Sanchez-Ramos.

While I was devastated by his not being able to transfer the protocol and keeping Dr. Sanchez-Ramos as my physician, at least he had found me another doctor.

My first appointment with Dr. M. went well, although his knowledge of medical Cannabis was minimal. "The only reason I'm taking over this protocol," he said, "is that I'm hoping Sanchez-Ramos doesn't like Tampa and comes back." He asked me not to divulge his name. I thanked him for coming to the rescue.

Over the next several weeks we sent off the paperwork to get Dr. M. a Schedule 1 license and to get the DEA to re-inspect Elvy's pharmacy. I figured this shouldn't take long since they have inspected it once a year since 1988 for the delivery of Elvy's medicine.

•

In October, Tom Brokaw did a story on NBC Nightly News about the ballot initiatives in California and Arizona. "Some of you would be surprised to learn there are people in this country who get their marijuana from the Federal Government," said Brokaw. "One of those patients is Florida stockbroker Irvin Rosenfeld." They showed the usual footage of me kissing Debbie goodbye, driving to work while medicating, and then in my office talking about my bone disorders and how much marijuana helped relieve the pain. I thought it was a very moving piece and was surprised when some reform advocates scolded me for allowing NBC to tape me smoking while driving.

As I had explained on the air, I do not get a euphoric effect from marijuana and my protocol allows me to operate an automobile as long as I am not impaired. (I certainly don't think people who are "intoxicated" on marijuana should drive or operate dangerous machinery.) I realized the movement had entered a new phase, and I would have to relate to activists who thought they knew best what the American people should and shouldn't be told about medical marijuana.

•

The ballot initiative made November 5, 1996 an historic day, the day on which California became the first state in the nation allowing medical use of Cannabis with a doctor's approval. Prop 215 passed with fifty-six percent of the vote. Prop 215 had been denounced by presidential candidates Bill Clinton and Bob Dole, California Governor Pete Wilson, Lt. Governor Gray Davis and Attorney General Dan Lungren, U.S. Senators Dianne Feinstein and Barbara Boxer, former Surgeon General C. Everett Koop, the police chiefs, officers, and sheriffs' lobbies, and 57 of the state's 58 district attorneys (the lone exception being DA Terence Hallinan of San Francisco). In voting "Yes," more than five million Californians were rejecting a lifetime of War-on-Drugs propaganda which was a million more than voted to re-elect President Clinton.

Prop 215 seemed like a pay-off for the work I had been doing all these years—talking to reporters, telling my story in any available forum, carrying the message that marijuana is a safe, effective, and in some cases, miraculous medicine. I may have been in Florida, but my heart was with my friends in California. I couldn't help wondering how the Feds would respond to their victory at the ballot box.

•

An ominous hint was provided Nov. 18 in a widely syndicated Associated Press story by Helen O'Neal that quoted Health and Human Services Secretary Donna Shalala saying, "Research shows that marijuana is harmful to one's brain, heart, lungs, and immune system. Any law premised on the notion that marijuana or these other illicit drugs are medically useful is suspect." This assessment was coming from the top "science" official in the U.S. Government.

O'Neal also quoted President Clinton's drug czar, Retired General Barry McCaffrey, who implicitly threatened California doctors: "We still have a federal law that says marijuana has no medical value, and it is against the law to grow it, distribute it, and prescribe it as a medicine."

O'Neal, who had interviewed me extensively, reported that a small group of patients were still receiving marijuana under the Federal IND program. She had asked an FDA spokesman to explain the obvious contradiction and printed his self-serving reply: "When we have a compassionate-use situation, out of feeling for the patient, we don't take that away. We just don't add to it." This was reassuring for me personally, but tragic for many thousands of others.

O'Neal's piece ended with a moving quote from Jackie Rickert of Wisconsin, who has a rare joint disorder called Ehlers-Danlos and was one of the twenty-eight heartbroken patients who had been approved but had not received any marijuana when the government closed the IND program: "Why should I have to break the law to get my medicine?"

·

A couple of weeks after the election, I flew to New York City to appear on Gordon Elliott's talk show. The theme was, "Medicinal Marijuana: Miracle or Hoax?" The opening shot was of me lighting up as Gordon said in his Aussie accent, "You're watching a man do something that you or I would be arrested for, lighting up a marijuana cigarette. Not only can he smoke marijuana for a debilitating bone disorder, but the Federal Government supplies it to him. And he smokes ten to fifteen per day with no euphoric effect!"

I explained why I don't get a euphoric effect and how the medicine relieves my inflammation and pain. "You speak very well for a man who is smoking a marijuana cigarette," said Gordon, as if he believed the stereotypical image of marijuana's effects. "This is my fourth one today," I said. "It's a medicine just like any other." I added that I tried to keep my distance from people when I smoked.

A member of the audience was concerned about giving the wrong message to students. My reply was, "Kids shouldn't use any marijuana, alcohol, or tobacco in their formative years, but this is a medicine. So, just because a substance can be abused, doesn't mean it should not be used as a medicine." I recalled how in high school I had spoken out against illegal drugs, including Cannabis.

Also on the show was a forty-year-old man with epilepsy named Alan Martinez, who had been arrested in Santa Rosa, California, for growing fewer than ten plants. Martinez said that using Cannabis made his seizures less severe, and that smoking a joint after a seizure helped him get over the inevitable headache. Martinez was accompanied by his lawyer, William Panzer of Oakland, who helped draft Prop 215. According to Panzer, Prop 215 was written to protect medical marijuana users from arrest and prosecution, but the state Attorney General was calling it "merely a defense people can use in court after they've been arrested."

Gordon's guests included former DEA agent Bob Strang, who was now in the drug-testing business. He argued that marijuana was a "gateway drug" that led young people to try other, harder drugs. He also cited the involvement of organized crime in marijuana distribution.

"Because it's illegal there's money to made," I put in. My timing must have been perfect because he seemed to slump in his chair.

Later in the show a woman in the audience asked, "What gave the DEA the right to practice medicine?" Strang reminded her about the Federal program through which patients such as myself obtained marijuana. I had to remind him the program stopped accepting patients in 1992.

In my appearances on talk shows and interviews with reporters, I've probably heard every argument proponents of Prohibition make. I can only hope I've had logical, accurate answers for each of them.

•

The Clinton Administration escalated its threats on Dec. 30 when Gen. McCaffrey, Attorney General Janet Reno, Health & Human Services Secretary Donna Shalala, and Alan Leshner of NIDA held a press conference to announce that doctors who recommended or prescribed marijuana to patients in Arizona and California could have their prescription-writing privileges revoked and be excluded from the Medicare and Medicaid programs.

The Federal officials stood in front of a big chart headed "Dr. Tod Mikuriya's (215 Medical Advisor) Medical Uses of Marijuana." Twenty-six conditions were listed. (Mikuriya was a Berkeley psychiatrist who had published an anthology of pre-Prohibition medical literature on Cannabis.) Gen. McCaffrey scoffed at the claim that one medicine could affect such a wide range of conditions. He called Prop 215 "a hoax" and declared, "This isn't medicine, this is a Cheech and Chong show."

•

The government didn't get the message California voters were sending about marijuana, but many Americans did. On the afternoon of McCaffrey's press conference, I was on "Talk Back Live" with Susan Rooks by phone from my office. One caller—Thomas, from Florida—seemed to sum up how most people felt about the medical-marijuana issue: "When my wife was dying from cancer, she had terrible reactions from the chemotherapy. Her oncologist told us Cannabis would help her and that you could buy it on the streets. I'm seventy years old, but I went to the streets and bought it and let my wife have some comfort before she died." Most people are practical and humane.

•

Despite the government's denial, the concept that marijuana was medically useful was slowly entering public awareness. The American people were learning, mainly through the media and word of mouth, some basic facts that we were never taught in school. "Cannabis," "marijuana," and "hemp" are names of the same plant. The Latin word "Cannabis" is used by doctors, botanists and other scientists. The slang term "marijuana" was popularized in the early 20th century by newspaper publisher William Randolph Hearst and other advocates of Prohibition to exploit prejudice against Mexicans. The old English word "hemp" refers nowadays to the strain of plant grown for fiber, seed, and oil.

Medicinal extracts made from the Cannabis plant had been available by prescription in the U.S. for more than seven decades until 1937 when Congress enacted Prohibition. Hemp remains illegal even though it contains only trace amounts of the psychoactive compound THC.

In addition to these basic facts, many Americans learned about the existence of the Federal Government's Investigational New Drug program through which a few citizens used marijuana legally. People began telling me, "I've heard of that program" when I described my unusual situation.

•

Unfortunately, my new doctor's Schedule 1 license had not shown up nor had the pharmacy heard from the DEA. I had been cutting back on the amount of Cannabis I was consuming each day. I didn't want to run out before we could re-order. First, I cut back to five a day, then four, then three... As I reduced my intake of Cannabis, my physical problems started appearing again: pain, then spasms and hemorrhages. My diminished quality of life was a stark reminder of what it meant to not have enough of a legal supply of medicine.

Other Federal patients had suffered when the government delayed their shipments of Cannabis on one pretext or another. Now it was my turn.

It wouldn't be until March of 1997 that the FDA processed the form and the DEA inspected the pharmacy so I could renew my supply. .

Public Puffer

Media interest reached a new peak in early 1997. An issue of *Newsweek* with Paula Jones on the cover included an item about the Federal IND program with a picture of me taking my medicine. It was captioned "Public Puffer." No mention was made of our supply disruptions.

Three weeks later *Newsweek* made "The War Over Weed" its main topic. The cover depicted a medical person in a white gown holding a joint in a hemostat (as if it were a roach clip). One of the pieces was by Marcus Conant, MD, a San Francisco AIDS specialist who was the lead plaintiff in a suit seeking to defend California doctors against the threats made by McCaffrey and Reno.

McCaffrey himself had a piece in that issue, claiming "There is no scientifically sound evidence that smoked marijuana is medically superior to currently available therapies." The Drug Czar's office had allocated $1 million to the Institute of Medicine to study the medical potential of marijuana. If there turned out to be beneficial compounds in the plant, McCaffrey wrote, they would be identified, isolated, and made available to doctors ASAP.

As Public Puffer, I think the discussion of marijuana as a treatment option should be between a doctor and a patient, not between doctor, patient, retired generals, politicians, police, etc. etc. Dr. Conant said it succinctly: "The government has no place in the examination room."

•

Among the spate of articles about medical marijuana that ran in the wake of Prop 215's passage, none was more influential than the Jan. 30 editorial in the prestigious *New England Journal of Medicine*. Editor-in-chief Jerome Kassirer, MD, derided U.S. government policy as "misguided," "hypocritical," "out of step with the public," and "inhumane." It skewered "the absolute power of bureaucrats whose decisions are based more on reflexive ideology and political correctness than on compassion." It called for moving marijuana from Schedule 1 to Schedule 2 so that doctors could prescribe it without fear of reprisal.

On the same day the *NEJM* editorial appeared—probably not coincidentally—the director of the National Institutes of Health, Harold Varmus called a special conference to resolve "the public health dilemma" raised by the passage of Prop 215. "I don't think anyone wants to settle issues like this by plebiscite," said Varmus, calling instead for "a way to listen to experts on these topics." The NIDA Director Alan Leshner was put in charge of the conference.

The NIH experts convened in Washington in February, 1997, and called for more studies into the safety and efficacy of Cannabis in treating numerous conditions. "More research is needed" is a truism—scientists can always learn more about why and how marijuana works in reducing certain symptoms. But more research is not needed with respect to the safety of marijuana. As Judge Francis Young pointed out after reviewing the medical literature, "Marijuana, in its natural form, is one of the safest therapeutically active substances known to man."

Not all doctors will agree on how to treat someone with a given medical condition. But there is sufficient data on marijuana's safety so that doctors who want to suggest it as a treatment should be allowed to do so.

In the Lion's Den

In late March of 1997 a Florida activist named Toni Latino phoned. She had heard about a one-day conference in Orlando to train people from all over the country to oppose medical marijuana initiatives. (There were rumors that the Lindesmith Center was considering an initiative in Florida.) The conference was a few weeks off. All the leading anti-drug organizations would be represented, led by the Partnership for a Drug-Free America. William Bennett, who had been Drug Czar in the 1980s, would be the main speaker. She suggested we get credentials and attend along with some fellow activists.

I told her it was a great idea, but if I went, it would be by myself. I would not acknowledge that I knew anyone else. I only wanted to be responsible for me, myself, and I.

Then it occurred to me: why not try to become one of the speakers? If they would let me speak at the conference, they would know exactly how to combat medical Cannabis.

Toni provided a phone number and I called to request credentials. I was asked why I wanted to attend. I answered, "Since I work for GKN Securities, I need to know how to go against medical marijuana." That was satisfactory.

Then I called the organizer of the conference and asked if I could be one of the speakers.

"What would you speak on?" I was asked.

"This conference is to teach people how to go against medical marijuana, isn't it?"

"Yes."

"I'm the second-longest surviving patient receiving medical marijuana from the Federal Government, so if you allow me to speak, you all will know how to go against us."

He said there was no way he would allow me to speak and he wanted to know how I got credentials. I told him I worked for GKN Securities. He asked, "What type of Security Company is that?" I replied, "Stocks and bonds."

He slammed the phone down. I proceeded to call the four major television stations and the Orlando Sentinel and told them who I was and that I had asked to speak only to be told that not only would I not be allowed to speak, but my credentials would be pulled for the conference. I knew exactly what they were going to do next. They all called the head of the conference and asked why he wouldn't let me speak, since I would have provided valuable intelligence about medical marijuana. He blew up, I was told.

Each did a story exposing the bias of the conference. Needless to say, because of the media attention, my credentials were not pulled.

Sometimes political work is actually fun. I decided to call my own press conference at the hotel where the conference was being held. I put together a release—"They may not let me speak, but they can't keep me from speaking!"—and faxed it to the media and to the head of the conference.

The conference was on Saturday, April 12, 1997. Intending to get there early, I hit the road at 4:30 am. for the two-hundred-mile drive to Orlando. The last time I made a long drive to speak on medical Cannabis had been fifteen years ago when I told my story to the FDA doctors' panel. Now my status had changed, I was a Federal patient. The Cannabis I was carrying was legal. I was still the same person, only a lot healthier. "Too legit to quit!"

I got to the Adam's Mark Hotel, which was part of a mall where the conference was to be held, around 8:00 am., two hours before the conference started. As I was pulling into the parking lot, about twenty uniformed police officers turned to look at me. The closest parking spot was a handicapped spot, which was empty. I pulled in and about eight officers started walking towards me. I got out of my Explorer, smoking my medicine, and walked to the passenger side to put on my dress shirt, tie and to grab my coat.

I greeted the officers and said, "I heard the governor's going to be here."

"He's not coming," I was told.

"It seems like a lot of police for no governor." I continued taking my medicine and changing my shirt. I tied my tie, put my Cannabis cigarette out, put the roach in my roach bag in my shirt pocket, put my coat on and started walking to the entrance.

Two officers walked in front of me, two behind, two to my right, two to my left. I was sandwiched in. I wondered what they thought I was going to do. I walked into the hotel lobby where another twenty or so uniformed officers turned to stare at me. I asked the officer with the most stripes where the conference was. She pointed to the escalator and off I went to the second floor with my new entourage.

There were tables set up with envelopes in alphabetical order for the attendees. Sure enough, my name was on one. I picked up my package, put on my nametag, and headed into the auditorium. The room, which seated a thousand people, was empty. There were three aisles with a microphone stand halfway down each one. I headed down the left hand aisle and I sat down right beside the microphone. My bodyguards sat all around me. I felt like a chess piece. The quiet was deafening. (Now I knew what that meant.)

Little by little, the room filled up. The chairman welcomed everyone and while looking at me said, "Anyone getting out of line will be escorted out and risk arrest."

The first speaker was William (Bill) Bennett, an overweight man whose gambling addiction had not yet come to public attention. Bennett's theme was that people who didn't "just say no" to marijuana are immoral, because its use is illegal. (As Drug Czar, Bennett had urged prosecutors to go after illicit drug users—not just dealers. He also ordered public hospitals to drug-test pregnant women, which resulted in many poor women losing custody of their kids.)

As soon as Bennett finished, I got up and stood behind the microphone. About ten people formed a line behind me. He first called on the questioner at the right-aisle microphone. Then he called on the questioner in the middle-aisle. Then he went back to the right side, and so on. He was not going to call on me. I just stood there not making a move. The police were tensed, I could feel they were ready to pounce. Once the people behind me realized that for whatever reason Bill Bennett was ignoring our aisle, they moved to the other microphones.

One by one, people asked their questions and made their comments—everyone but me. I stood there looking directly at Bill Bennett, who would not look my way.

When everyone had asked their questions the chairman announced that Bill was going to hold a private press conference in a smaller room. I got up with my escorts in tow and tried to get into the press conference. I was denied entry. So I waited outside for the reporters to emerge.

Fifteen minutes later, out walked all the reporters and camerapersons. I raised my voice and announced that I was Irvin Rosenfeld and would be holding a press conference later. They all stopped and came over. Someone asked if I could hold my press conference then and there. I asked one of my police guards to please find the head of security for the hotel.

The head of security came over and asked what he could do. Along the hallway were eleven rooms with the lights on and nobody in any of them. I asked if I could use one of the rooms to hold my press conference. He said "No."

I asked him why and he said, "All the rooms are being used."

A reporter cracked, "I didn't realize how many ghosts there were in this hotel."

"What about 1:00 pm.?"

He replied, "They're already booked."

Meanwhile, the heads of the conference had showed up. The head of security said I could hold a press conference at a location just beyond the mall. Through a window he pointed toward it. It was a distance of about five football fields. Not the kind of walk I would normally do.

The leaders of the conference and the police had these smug looks, as if to say, "We got you."

I said, "Fine, that's what we will do." The reporters and cameramen looked at me skeptically and I said, "Let's go."

Down the escalator I went, followed by the media, the conference organizers, and the cops. I walked to my car—the car parked closest to the hotel—unlocked the door, took off my sport coat, took out my medicine and lit up. It had been almost three hours since I last medicated and I was hurting.

I stood there taking my medicine and just started talking to the reporters. The cameramen started filming. The heads of the conference started yelling I was not allowed to hold a press conference on the hotel grounds. I said, "I'm just talking to some people while I take my medicine. Do you have a problem with me taking my medicine, which is prescribed by the United States Federal Government?" The media loved it.

The conference people insisted the police to do something. With cameras going, the police said I had every right to take my medicine. The power of the media can turn a lion into a lamb.

For the next forty minutes I smoked two joints, talking the whole time. I pointed out why I should have been allowed to speak at the conference and why medical Cannabis was not a stalking horse for full legalization. It wasn't a press conference, I was just educating some new friends—including some cops and some prohibitionist bureaucrats—about medical Cannabis.

Upon finishing the second joint, I announced that I was now ready to take that long walk to hold my press conference, at which point I would be glad to answer all questions. The media had gotten all the material they needed, of course. It turned out to be one of the best press conferences I never had!

•

I went back into the hotel and had lunch. My police escort stayed outside the restaurant. I was actually starting to feel sorry for them. You could see a change on their faces. They had heard what I said, and they knew I was right, but right or wrong, they had a job to do.

After lunch I went back outside and took more medicine. Now the police just stayed by the front door and talked amongst themselves. After smoking two more, I went back into the conference.

I went into the room and lo and behold, the same seats were open. My escorts and I sat down, but I didn't feel as much tension.

When the panel finished, people seated in my section went to the other microphones to ask their questions. I guess they expected me to try and ask another question. I sat in my chair thinking that I had made a difference.

•

The last panel included an AIDS specialist who was against the medical use of marijuana because he thought it compromised the immune system. An activist in the audience, an AIDS patient named Greg Scott, credited Cannabis with saving his life by restoring his appetite. He stood up to yell at the doctor and was told to sit down. The doctor continued and Greg did it again. He was told to sit down or be escorted out and arrested. Guess what happened a few minutes later? Greg was arrested and taken to the same Orange County Jail that I had visited in 1983.

That was the reason I wanted to be on my own at the conference.

The doctor finished and it was time for questions. I stood up and was the only one in my line. They started taking questions from the right aisle, then the middle, then back to the right, then back to the middle. The woman at the mike pointed towards me and asked, "Why won't you let him ask a question?"

God was around again.

Now the panel was stuck and the head of the conference begrudgingly said to me, "You have one minute to ask your question."

I said, "My name is Irvin Rosenfeld and I am the second longest Federal medical marijuana patient in the United States, having been supplied by Uncle Sam for fifteen years and my question is this. Being one of six patients in the country using medical marijuana, I want to ask the following. As a stockbroker handling millions of dollars on a daily basis, all while using ten to twelve Cannabis cigarettes, from which I get no high, my question is this. Since all these organizations spent all this effort and expense to teach and educate people how to go against medical marijuana, I would think these organizations would want to put on as complete a conference as possible. Since I contacted the head of this conference almost a month ago telling him my credentials, my question is this: Why wouldn't you allow me to speak on the subject of medical marijuana so everyone here would know exactly how to go against us?"

The head of the conference responded, "We weren't going to let you speak and we shouldn't even have let you in." You could see steam coming out of his ears.

As I was walking out at the end of the conference, the woman who supported my right to ask a question came over and said, "I really wish they would have let you speak. I'm president or the United States PTA and I have one question for you. What do you say to the kids?"

I thanked her and said, "Your question is easy to answer. Start telling kids from the beginning that Cannabis is a medicine and only a doctor can recommend it just like any other medicine. My nieces and nephews grew up with me and were against drugs and cigarettes, but Cannabis was their uncle's medicine and today they are all successful and not using marijuana. All the neighbor's kids were also anti-drug and anti-cigarettes, but Cannabis was Irvin's medicine. Kids are not dumb and shouldn't be treated that way." She liked my answer. I thanked her for her courage and said goodbye.

I walked out of the hotel about ten steps and realized the police were staying at the door. I yelled back to them, "Stay well" and walked to my car. I took off my tie and coat, changed to a short sleeve shirt, lit up and drove off. I had survived in the lion's den.

Media Messaging

On April 15, 1997, the Arizona Legislature gutted Prop 200, the medical-marijuana measure approved by the voters. The lawmakers mandated that Arizona doctors could prescribe marijuana only after the FDA had approved it. (California's constitution prevents the legislature from weakening a law enacted by popular initiative—but the voters of Arizona had no such protection.)

•

In May, I participated in a segment for ABC's "Discovery News," that showed me taking my medicine outside my office. Reporter George Strait said the government had shut down the IND program. The NIDA director Alan Leshner defended the government's decision on the grounds that "more research is needed." Jerome Kassirer M.D., editor of the New England Journal of Medicine, explained the Federal Government made research almost impossible by refusing to provide marijuana to scientists who wanted to study it. Strait accurately noted, "This caused a catch-22."

Marinol was described as an alternative to marijuana. I said it didn't work for me.

•

The various media in which I carried my message ranged from the South Florida entertainment guide "Boca Raton" (which awarded me "Best Smoke in Boca") to the Jewish Times, which described my upbringing in Portsmouth and how my disorder played a role in my beliefs. Author Lois Solomon wrote: "Mr. Rosenfeld realizes he is privileged to get Cannabis while other seriously ill patients must pursue illegal avenues to obtain it. That's why he speaks out about legalizing marijuana for medical use whenever he is invited.

"Something I did learn from my Jewish education," he said, "Was to speak out for what I believed in. Without marijuana, I'd be dead. Doctors should have the right to prescribe marijuana for medical use."

•

Finally, on May 9, 1997, I got a call from Bascom Palmer pharmacy saying that my medicine had arrived. It took almost ten months for the DEA to re-inspect the pharmacy, which was already taking in Cannabis for Elvy, to allow the same pharmacy to take in mine. It could have taken just one day, one week, or one month, if they had wanted it to. I drove down to Miami and picked it up. I was as happy as could be, knowing I could now get my physical condition back to where it had been. Amen.

•

The July 1997 issue of "George," a magazine published by John F. Kennedy, Jr., ran a story about "Uncle Sam's Pot Farm." Writer David Saltonstall got the usual runaround when he asked Federal officials why no more compassionate-use protocols were being approved. "'We just do what we're told,' said Sheryl Massaro, a NIDA spokesperson. 'If we are told to provide marijuana to eight people, then that's what we do.' She deferred to the FDA, which granted the Compassionate IND waivers that made it possible for a few people to benefit from the program. 'It's really not an FDA question,' countered FDA spokesman Don McLearn, who said it was the U.S. Public Health Service that decided back in 1992—due to a sudden surge from AIDS patients to close the program to all but the remaining eight. When pressed he added, 'Technically, these [eight] are research subjects,' a convenient feint also picked up by McCaffrey's office. 'The general had no objection to research,' said McCaffrey's spokesman Bob Weiner. 'Those are people who are being researched.'"(YEA, RIGHT!!)

The same implicit question was asked in every story: Why is our government fighting a war against its own citizens? The New York Times Sunday Magazine July 20, 1997, carried a long feature story by Michael Pollan about

California's Cannabis buyers' clubs, which had begun to spring up in Oakland and other Bay Area cities.

•

Activists in Florida were interested in getting a medical-marijuana initiative on the ballot in Florida, and of course, I lent them my support. There was no illusion that we would succeed, as we had no organization or resources. We could however use the premise to educate. Our goal was public education.

In early September, Toni Latino of the Coalition Advocating Medical Marijuana held a press conference to kick off a signature drive. "Sick people," she said, "should have the option of using marijuana without fear of prosecution."

The Miami Herald ran a story about the signature drive along with a picture of Elvy and me taking our medicine in front of the Broward County Sheriff's Office. Reporter Juan Rodriguez described Greg Scott, who was diagnosed with AIDS in 1990, and was ready to give up after dropping from 175 to 130 pounds and watching purple lesions spread over his body. He began using marijuana, regained his strength, and stopped getting scared looks when he rode the bus. "In order to survive I had to break the law," Scott told the Herald. "Marijuana saved my life."

The Florida Medical Association weighed in by calling for more studies on marijuana as medicine.

•

In November, episodes of the hit CBS show *Murphy Brown* dealt with cancer. The character played by Candice Bergen was stricken with cancer and chemotherapy made her nauseous. When no other medicine worked, a friend went to the streets and bought some marijuana for Murphy Brown. The shows were riveting and were viewed by tens of millions of people. The local CBS affiliate did a story with me to show a real person legally using the medicine.

Nov. 20, 1997, Debbie and I celebrated. It had been 15 years since I received my first legal joint. I had not taken any other pain medicines for seven years. I was sailing and playing softball. I figured I had saved more than $150,000 dollars not having to buy marijuana on the street, at prices tremendously inflated by Prohibition. As for the relief from the anxiety— knowing my medicine would always be available- and I was in no legal jeopardy when I used it—priceless.

A Stall in the Name of Science

The Clinton Administration's threat to California doctors had been deemed illegal, but it sought another way to curtail the movement. On January 9, 1998, in Federal court in San Francisco, the U.S. Department of Justice filed a civil suit to close six Cannabis buyers clubs, including Dennis Peron's San Francisco club.

By seeking a civil injunction from a judge instead of charging the club owners criminally, the Feds could avoid a jury trial on the clubs' right to operate. I wasn't surprised by their undemocratic tactic. I already felt betrayed by Clinton's unwillingness to open the IND program to new patients.

The Administration had also changed its "Public Relations" strategy. A year ago the Drug Czar had been dismissing medical marijuana as a "Cheech and Chong show." The new line was that "more research is needed" to identify any potentially beneficial compounds in the plant and develop them into synthetic pharmaceutical drugs. The Drug Czar's office had allocated $1 million for the Institute of Medicine to conduct an 18-month "comprehensive review" of "the health effects and potential medical use of marijuana."

The IOM study was conducted by Stanley J. Watson, Jr. a research psychiatrist from the University of Michigan; and John A. Benson, Jr., a silver-haired, bow-tie-wearing professor emeritus from Oregon Health Sciences University. In addition to reviewing the medical literature, they held hearings in three cities. Barbara Douglass and I testified in New Orleans on

January 18. (George, Elvy, and Bob would testify in Washington, D.C.) We told our stories and answered all their questions.

In 1998, one was still allowed to smoke in buildings. So, during the two days of hearings, I took my medicine whenever I needed to, including in the hearing room. I sat in the back by myself and lit up. I wasn't trying to show off, rather to show the opposition that here I was smoking Government marijuana, and I was as clear-headed as they were. During breaks, I made it a point to speak to the scientists and doctors who opposed us, so they could see how lucid I was.

During a break on the second day, Dr. Thomas Klein, a researcher in Medical Microbiology & Immunology at the University of South Florida, came over and said he noticed how much marijuana I'd been smoking, and it didn't seem to affect my cognitition. He was against marijuana, for his studies showed it compromised the immune system. He asked if I would be willing to give him a blood sample to check my antibody levels. I consented, and on my next trip to Tampa stopped at his office to provide a blood sample. Guess what? My immune system turned out to be normal.

Another study of my condition by Dr. Sanchez-Ramos would show decreasing muscle spasms and improving pain-scale scores over the five years I'd been his patient.

I just wish the government would study me. What are they afraid of? The sad part is...we know.

•

Debbie and I had planned several trips to Portsmouth that spring for various family occasions. USAir had the best flights from Ft. Lauderdale, so I called and made reservations. I talked with their medical supervisor about getting a room in which to take my medicine during the hour-and-a-half layover in Charlotte. She asked me to fax her my paperwork.

As it turned out, she had problems getting the permission. Our first trip was to attend the wedding of my niece, Sherri Welsby. We were to leave Ft. Lauderdale the evening of April 2, 1998, and be going through Charlotte around 10:00 pm. I still wasn't sure if I had permission to take my medicine. That morning I got a call from a reporter named Bob Knowles at WBTV, a CBS affiliate in Charlotte wanting to know why I wasn't on the 10:00 am. flight. I told him I would be coming through Charlotte at 10:00 pm. and asked how he knew about my travel plans.

"You have no idea the uproar you have caused this city the last three weeks," he said. "The District Attorney's office, the police department, and the airport authorities have all been going back and forth about whether to allow you to smoke marijuana at the airport. I knew about you from one of my sources in the police department. After extensive discussions, you will be allowed to smoke during your layover. In fact, the manager of the airport will be in a cart at your gate to personally take you to the infirmary. What I was hoping was that you would allow me to go with you and do an interview while you are here."

I said I'd be glad to do an interview. "To me, taking my medicine is no big deal. Hopefully, with more stories from reporters like you, one day it will be no big deal for anyone."

When I got home, I told Debbie to dress as if a camera crew was going to shoot our arrival.

Sure enough, when we landed there was a cart with a driver and the airport manager and reporter Knowles and his cameraman. The other passengers and people at the gate were trying to figure out why a camera crew was present. We walked over to the cart, introduced ourselves, and were driven off as the reporter and his cameraman scurried to keep up.

At the airport infirmary there was a police officer waiting with the keys. We walked in and the manager turned on an industrial smoke eater. Then he left me with the reporter and cameraman, saying he'd be back in forty minutes. Debbie sat outside and waited.

The reporter was friendly as he told me about the debate I'd triggered among Charlotte's politicians. He asked the usual questions and kept the camera rolling while I sucked down two Cannabis cigarettes as fast as I could. He seemed amazed that I was just as coherent at the end of the interview as I was at the beginning.

He asked one question that bothered me: "How do you feel that they made taking your medicine the highest medical priority, and if anybody else needed to use this facility, they would have to wait until you finished?" I said, "I'm appalled to think if someone needed medical attention they would make them wait until I'm done. After all, this is just smoke."

The cart and policeman showed up right on time. We said our goodbyes and off we went to board the plane and take our seats. My legs felt so much better.

The segment on WBTV was called "Flying High." Debbie and I saw a tape of it. We laughed when the anchor commented, "He should have been passed out on the tarmac after smoking two joints. He was sober as a judge." I always wonder if such comments are made from personal experience.

Our next trip on USAir—April 25, for my cousin Aaron Barham's Bar Mitzvah—did not go as well. When we landed, no cart was waiting. We called and one finally arrived. We got to the infirmary and no police officer was waiting to open up. We called and they finally showed. I barely had time to smoke one. Why was I treated better on the previous trip? That time, a reporter had been on hand and the authorities knew whatever happened would be publicized. The power of the media.

"Boy, I'm Good!"

Near our house in Ft. Lauderdale is the entrance to an expressway I took everyday when I worked in Boca Raton. You had to slow down and throw money in a basket, wait for a light to turn green, and go. A lot of people used to run it.

On the morning of June 22, 1998, just like every morning, I got in my car, started it up, lit up my medicine and headed for work. I approached the tollbooth, rolled down my window, threw in my quarter, waited for the light to turn green, and took off. As I accelerated, I saw a motorcycle cop waiting against the building to catch people running the toll. He flipped his lights on immediately and took after me. I knew the light turned green so I knew why he was stopping me. I immediately pulled over and he pulled behind me. I started to get out of my Explorer when he yelled, "Get back in your truck and keep your arms and legs where I can see 'em."

Okay...

He came over with his gun drawn. I had never had a policeman point a gun at me before. He said, "Get out of your car slowly, go to the back of your vehicle, and lean against the back of it." Which I did. While keeping his gun and eye on me, he also looked inside to see if he can find the joint.

He saw the joint in the ashtray, reached in and grabbed it still keeping his gun pointed at me. "Boy, I'm good," he said with great satisfaction. "I smelled that when you rolled down your window. You're under arrest."

I said, "Officer, you are good. But no sir, I'm not under arrest."

He said, "What do you mean?"

I asked permission to stand up straight.

He said, "Keep your arms up in the air."

I stood up keeping my arms in the air and said, "I'm one of the Federal patients. The marijuana I'm smoking is provided by the Federal Government."

He said, "What proof do you have?"

I said, "In my front pocket"—I wasn't going to reach for it- is a baggie with my prescription and another twelve joints. May I get it?"

He said, "Very slowly."

So, very slowly I reached into my front pocket and pulled out the baggie and handed it to him. Now he was trying to read the prescription while keeping the gun on me. "This looks pretty official," he said, finally putting his gun into his holster.

"It is," I assured him.

"What other proof do you have?"

"In the back of my truck I have an empty tin can that the Federal Government ships the Cannabis in and I have numerous newspaper articles that describe my Federal program. May I get them?"

"Go ahead," I was told.

He looked at the canister with the Federal Government labels and looked at the *Newsweek* story and at last said, "But you can't drive with this."

I said, "Yes sir, I can." I got out a copy of my protocol and showed him the part that said I'm allowed to operate dangerous machinery as long as I'm not intoxicated. I asked, "Am I intoxicated?"

"No," he conceded.

I said, "Exactly, that's why I can drive."

I gave him my business card, which showed where I worked and he wrote down my home address from my driver's license, because he still suspected somehow I was breaking a law.

When he finished writing everything down, he asked, "How many people in the country get that?"

"Only eight."

He said, "Damn, I wish I was that lucky in Lotto."

He let me go, still not quite believing I could drive while smoking marijuana. I've always wondered how he described our encounter to his Highway Patrol colleagues.

•

Medical marijuana initiatives were on the ballots in several states and the District of Columbia in November, 1998. Congressman Bob Barr of Georgia—fearing that Washington residents would pass Initiative 59, as the medical-marijuana measure was known— introduced a resolution forbidding the D.C. Board of Elections from counting the vote thereby not certifying it! President Clinton signed the legislation from Congress denying the right of hundreds of thousands of District of Columbia voters to vote pursuant to law because the subject was medical marijuana. The Clinton Justice Department then defended this denial of the right to vote in court.

The Drug Czar's office orchestrated the opposition campaign nationally. Barbara Bush appeared in TV ads saying, "Now is not the time to send the message to our young people that marijuana is 'medicine.' It is not. It is a dangerous, illegal drug." Ex-Presidents Gerald Ford, Jimmy Carter and George Bush all issued statements denouncing the new state initiatives. Gen. McCaffrey published a nationally syndicated op-ed stating, "If components of marijuana other than THC are found to be medically valuable, the current scientific process will approve those components for safe use."

Having claimed for years that the marijuana plant had no beneficial effects whatsoever, the drug warriors were now promising to deliver us the "good" parts of the plant without the "bad," that being smoking the natural plant.

On Nov. 3, Washington D.C. residents got to vote on Initiative 59 because ballots had been printed before Congress prohibited the certification of the results, but the votes were not tallied—the first time in American history that a vote had been voided in that way. An exit poll showed Initiative 59 winning by a 69-31 margin.

In Arizona, a proposition to override the 1996 vote allowing medical use of all schedule I drugs, lost by a 57-43 margin.

In the states, Oregon, Washington, Colorado, Alaska, and Nevada, medical marijuana measures passed by substantial majorities. And in California, Attorney General Dan Lungren, who led the campaign against Prop 215 in 1996, lost his bid to become governor.

"Cannabinoids"

In 1999 America had a new problem to worry about—"Y2K," which was supposed to bring about crashing computer systems and chaos. My main worry was still how to get Cannabis available to everyone who needed it. Education was still my most valuable tactic.

On January 31, 1999 a documentary aired on PBS that had been produced at WUSF, the University of South Florida station called, "Smoking Medicine: Medical Marijuana," which was written and produced by Martha

Bone. It was another telling of my story and Elvy's, another recitation of facts to overcome mis-education: "Marijuana or hemp is the popular name for the plant Cannabis sativa. Marijuana's usage as an intoxicant, painkiller, and a productive fiber has been documented in China and India since before the time of Christ... George Washington and Thomas Jefferson grew hemp... the Declaration of Independence was written on hemp paper... Prohibition was suspended and hemp was grown for fiber during World War II."

The documentary featured my doctor, Juan Sanchez-Ramos, and researcher Thomas Klein, whom I had met at the Institute of Medicine hearing in New Orleans, describing why marijuana works as medicine. Compounds in the plant called "cannabinoids" activate certain receptors in our bodies. Although these were dubbed "cannabinoid receptors," scientists assumed normally they are activated by neurotransmitters made in the body. Sure enough, research in many labs resulted in the discovery of at least two compounds made in the body that activate the cannabinoid receptors.

The documentary, which won a regional Emmy, ended with a close-up of a cartoon I had clipped from the Wall St. Journal and given to the producer. Two men in suits are sitting at desks under a sign that says "FDA." One is saying to the other, "Say, if laughter is the best medicine, shouldn't we be regulating it?" I thought that cartoon said it all.

•

On March 17, 1999 the Institute of Medicine (IOM) released its long-awaited report on the medical potential of marijuana. It contained a diplomatic mix of positive and negative findings. The IOM team

• confirmed that marijuana has been effective in treating chronic pain, nausea from cancer chemotherapy, and lack of appetite and wasting in AIDS patients.

• strongly advocated research into and development of cannabinoid drugs.

• debunked the notions marijuana is addictive and its use leads to heroin and cocaine use. In other words it is not a gateway drug.

• noted marijuana has a lower potential for abuse than alcohol or tobacco, and is safer than many commonly used drugs.

However, the report contained strong warnings about the dangers of smoking, and advised against using marijuana in the treatment of Parkinson's or Huntington's diseases, seizures, migraines, glaucoma, and many other ailments for which patients and doctors contend it provides relief.

White House spokesman Joe Lockhart summarized the official response: "What we found out is there may be some chemical compounds in marijuana that are useful in pain relief or anti-nausea, but smoking marijuana is a crude delivery system. So I think what this calls for is further research."

•

In conjunction with its news story on the IOM Report, the *New York Times* ran a piece by Sheryl Gay Stolberg about the IND program—"For a Very Few Patients, U.S. Provides Free Marijuana"—with a picture of me taking my medicine. The hook was the IOM Report called into question whether the government should be providing marijuana to only a chosen few now that it had been deemed beneficial for certain conditions, including pain, nausea, and the severe weight loss associated with AIDS.

The IOM Report was contradictory, Stolberg pointed out. It said the benefits of marijuana are negated by the toxicity of the smoke, but recommended it be given under close supervision to patients who don't respond to other therapies. Stolberg also noted the contradiction inherent in the government's closed-to-new-patients "compassionate-use" program.

"The government hopes the program will eventually become extinct through attrition," is how Stolberg summarized the Justice Department attitude. In other words, the government was waiting for us to die off.

Stolberg reported on a lawsuit filed in federal court in Philadelphia by one-hundred-sixty-five patients seeking access to marijuana from the FDA. She quoted Lawrence Hirsch, the lawyer for the patients: "The compassionate access program is an acknowledgement by the Government that marijuana has medicinal value. It's fundamentally unfair for the Government to supply marijuana for medical necessity to eight people in the U.S., when the rest of the potential candidates for therapeutic Cannabis are excluded."

Stolberg told the story of Ladd Huffman, an MS patient from Iowa who had applied for the compassionate use program, also with Bob Randall's help, at the same time as Barbara Douglass "The program was shut down before his final paperwork had been approved. (He didn't have the political connections Barbara did) A spokesman for the Department of Health and Human Services said the department determined marijuana was no longer necessary, because of the advent of the drug Marinol, a capsule containing synthetic THC, which is the most psycho-active ingredient in marijuana.

"Mr. Huffman says Marinol does not work. 'With these capsules, you take them and about an hour later you get so stoned you can hardly function,' he said. But, having been sentenced to two years' probation for a previous marijuana offense, he's afraid to smoke the drug again.

"As for Mr. Rosenfeld, he has pangs of conscience, knowing people like Mr. Huffman have been prosecuted for buying a drug he gets courtesy of the taxpayers.

"'I'm not against the Government. I appreciate what they do for me.'"

And I sincerely wished they would do it for everyone in need.

•

On May 21, 1999 the U.S. Department of Health and Human Services issued an "Announcement of Services Guidance on Procedures for the Provision of Marijuana for Medical Research." It stated "the single-patient IND process would not produce useful scientific information, and we do not foresee that they would be supported under this program." Neither the FDA, the NIDA, nor any other agency ever tried to assess what effects Cannabis was having on the small group of us being supplied by the government. No wonder HHS concluded the program didn't produce useful scientific information!

In June 1999, I had a trip involving an hour-and-a-half layover in New Orleans. I called Southwest Airlines to arrange a place to take my medicine, and was told I could use a special room at the airport in New Orleans that had been set aside for smokers.

As I was about to board the flight, I asked a stewardess how to find the smoking room when I got to New Orleans. She said it was "in the bar."

"They don't have a closed off room for smoking?"

"No."

I told the stewardess my dilemma and she said she would work on getting me a room while we were in flight.

When I got off the plane I was approached by a man in plain clothes, not much bigger than me, and two men in uniforms, but not police uniforms. The man in plain clothes asked,

"Are you Irvin Rosenfeld?"

"Yes."

"Then tell me why I shouldn't arrest you."

I said, "Excuse me?"

He said, "You're asking to smoke marijuana here?"

"Yes, it's my medicine."

Again, "Tell me why I shouldn't arrest you. I'm a police officer."

I said "Okay," and took out my prescription and started explaining everything.

The two men in uniform were with the Federal Aviation Authority and the Port Authority. The detective kept saying things like, "I really should just arrest you."

I said, "I don't think your city attorney would like to have a lawsuit to deal with."

He took all my paperwork and off he went.

About ten minutes later he returned and said, "Okay, I've verified everything and it appears it is legal, but we don't have a room where we can take you to smoke." (Again verification was done quickly)

He then looked at the others and said, "It's up to you two." The Port Authority guy said, "I don't have any objections." And the FAA guy went, "I don't have any objections."

So the policeman said, "I know where to take you." We walked about twenty steps to a locked door. He worked the keypad and we entered a stairwell which led to the tarmac. This was where the airport workers smoked.

While I smoked two Cannabis cigarettes, I had an opportunity to answer all their questions. They actually were very nice. The last comment from the officer was, "You know, this was really unusual."

I thanked them for taking the ten minutes to verify my paperwork and off I went on my connection feeling much better.

Other places I've been taken to smoke at airports include a broom closet and the tarmac itself.

Who's Fleecing Who?

In July 1999, I got a call from Frederica Whitfield of NBC Evening News, asking me if I would participate in a news story she was producing for their "Fleecing of America" segment. Their angle would be the government was wasting money by spending $250,000 a year to supply eight people with medical Cannabis. Knowing they were going to do the story with or without me, I agreed to take part.

Whitfield flew down from New York and, with a crew from the local affiliate, spent a day taping me driving to work, medicating, functioning without impairment, etc. I had ample opportunity to share what I knew about Cannabis, including some facts about how inexpensively it could be produced. Bob Randall had learned through the Freedom of Information Act the government spent ninety cents per ounce on the Cannabis it provided him, and that 2/3 of the cost went towards security measures. The bottom line was government Cannabis cost about a penny per gram! If the American people were being fleeced, it wasn't by the Federal patients. I also pointed out the farm was capable of growing Cannabis for thousands of patients if the government would allow it.

The day Whitfield's story was supposed to run she called to apologize.

She said she tried unsuccessfully to get it pulled knowing that the story was not correct journalism. I thanked her for her efforts, then called family and friends to tell them to watch.

The show began and there was no reference to the government growing marijuana for a small group of patients. We kept watching, but the story never ran. The next day I called to ask what happened. Frederica said at the last minute she convinced the decision makers at NBC that to air the story as a "Fleecing of America" piece was misleading, and they agreed to pull it.

"So you won," I said.

She said, "Yes I did... In more ways than one."

•

On November 2, 1999, 61% of Maine voters supported a medical-marijuana initiative that removed criminal penalties on the use, possession and cultivation of marijuana by patients who possess an oral or written "professional opinion" from their physician that he or she "might benefit from the medicinal use of marijuana." Approved disorders included epilepsy and other disorders by seizures; glaucoma; multiple sclerosis and other disorders characterized by muscle spasticity; and nausea or vomiting as a result of AIDS or cancer chemotherapy.

Maine was the fifth state to pass a law that legalized medical Cannabis. Each state brings us that much closer.

PART THREE:

IT TAKES A MOVEMENT

Patients Out of Time's
First Clinical Conference

Midnight came and went and the world didn't come to a halt as the year 2000 began. What a great relief. Now all we had to worry about was life itself.

Problems had been anticipated in the market. When none materialized, stocks took off. I worked, sailed, played softball, and took my medicine. It was nice having a normal daily routine. I had now been at GKN Securities for nine years and was happy there. Everyone at the firm was used to my medicine and had no problems with it.

In March the markets started what would be a three-year drop. I saw the handwriting on the wall and started divesting growth stocks for my clients and buying income issues with good dividends. (I'd had to do that in the late 1980s. It was the old story of flight to quality.) Clients would have to be happy with a lower return.

•

In April 2000 Patients Out of Time organized the first-ever "National Clinical Conference on Cannabis Therapeutics" at the University of Iowa. The speakers included not just the five Federal patients, but Janet Joy, the author of the Institute of Medicine Report; Geoffrey Guy, the founder of a British pharmaceutical company licensed by the government to grow Cannabis and produce plant extracts for research; neurologists Denis Petro and Ethan Russo; UCLA pulmonologist Donald Tashkin; my doctor, Juan Sanchez-Ramos; Tod Mikuriya, the Berkeley psychiatrist who had helped draft Prop 215; research psychologist Rick Musty; historian Michael Aldrich; Mae Nutt; and Mary Lynn Mathre.

The conference was co-sponsored by the College of Nursing and the College of Medicine at the University of Iowa. Continuing medical education credits were awarded to doctors, nurses and pharmacists who attended. Melanie Dreher, Dean of the College of Nursing, hosted and spoke at the conference. Dreher had studied the health status of Jamaican babies and children whose mothers used Cannabis during pregnancy. The "exposed" babies seemed slightly better off. By age five no differences could be detected.

Arriving in Des Moines I had run into Bob at the airport. We were booked at the "Iowa House," which we both imagined to be a quaint hotel on or near campus. But it turned out to be the student union and we would be staying in dorm rooms. When we checked in, some students said the main cafeteria just closed, but there was a snack bar. Bob and I were not happy. We put our luggage in our rooms and proceeded to the snack bar.

We sat down and shared our disappointment about not being in a decent hotel. The students around us were very friendly, as was the student who took our order and brought us our burgers. As we ate and talked to the students, we started feeling differently about the place. In fact, we started to think it was kind of neat not being in a regular hotel. It was encouraging being around unprejudiced, lively young people. It had been a long time since we'd gone to college.

•

The Patients Out of Time conference created a new model for challenging marijuana Prohibition: the on-campus symposium. George and Barbara, being from Iowa, were especially proud of their state university for providing the venue.

Al and Mary Lynn said they wanted to make the conference a bi-annual event and I told them to count me in because Al, Mary Lynn and all involved had done a top notch job. By the time I left, I felt that the Iowa House was one of the best places I ever stayed. They even arranged for it to snow on Saturday morning. It didn't seem that cold outside, but it was snowing as I stepped outside. The campus looked beautiful covered in white.

On June 14, 2000, Governor Ben Cayetano of Hawaii signed a bill removing criminal penalties on the use, possession and cultivation of marijuana by patients who possess a signed statement from their physician affirming that he or she suffers from a debilitating condition and that the "potential benefits of medical use of marijuana would likely outweigh the health risks." The law established a mandatory, confidential state-run patient registry that issues identification cards to qualified patients.

Chalk up another one!

Millenium Ends, Prohibition Continues

During the last weekend of June of 2000, I flew to St. Louis, Missouri, to attend a cook-out with two of my clients—men who hunt and fish around the world, and then, once a year, host an extravagant cook-out for a small group of friends.

I made my reservation with TWA to fly out of Fort Lauderdale airport.

I was in line at the gate waiting to get my boarding pass. It was 11:00 am. Four counters down, I saw a police officer in full uniform with a police dog on a twenty-five foot leash. The dog was sniffing all the passengers in line and their luggage. He was obviously well trained; the officer didn't say a word. I was thinking, "This will be interesting."

He came to my line and sniffed the two people in front of me and their bags. Then he sniffed my bag. Then he sniffed me. No reaction. He and the policeman headed away. "Officer," I called out, "is your dog trained for bombs or drugs?"

He replied, "For drugs."

I said, "Officer, I'm one of the eight Federal medical marijuana patients and in my bag is a tin canister with about five ounces of Cannabis and a baggie with fifteen rolled joints and another baggie with roaches in it. Put your dog back on my bag."

He ordered the dog back on my bag and again the dog sniffed without reacting. He sniffed me again and locked on my wallet in my front pocket. The officer still twenty-five feet from me said, "You've got drugs in your pocket."

I said, "Officer, I have residue all over me, but all my medicine is in my bag, put the dog back on my bag."

The officer walked up to me and looked astonished "You reek of marijuana!" I said, "I just smoked two driving here. But all my Cannabis is in my bag, put your dog back on the bag." The dog sniffed my carry-on bag again with no interest. The dog then turned to me and again locked in on my wallet. That's when I said, "Officer, I think you need to re-train your dog."

He ordered the dog off me, turned and walked away without saying a word. He never asked for any identification or looked into my bag. The people who overheard our exchange were just as surprised as I was that he didn't even look in my bag or have me prove I was a Federal patient. I think it never occurred to him his dog wasn't infallible.

By the way, the cookout was wonderful.

•

In July 2000, I got a call from Jeff Jones, the director of the Oakland Cannabis Buyers' Co-operative. The OCBC had opened as a dispensary when Prop 215 passed in 1996. It was one of six clubs the Federal Department of Justice sought to close by a civil suit.

In November 1998, ordered not to sell Cannabis by a Federal judge, the OCBC reinvented itself as a center that issued identification cards for patients. (Dispensaries would honor these cards and doctors would be spared phone calls to verify the patient's status.) The OCBC also sold hemp products, publications, and accessories such as vaporizers, which heat Cannabis to a point below combustion so users can inhale the active ingredients without the harmful tars and benzene present in smoke.

Jones appealed the order preventing the OCBC from selling Cannabis, and obtained a stay from the 9th Circuit. Now he was calling to tell me the Justice Department was taking its case against the OCBC to the U.S. Supreme Court. He believed as a dispensary his Co-Op would qualify as a "medical necessary" facility under Federal law. This would be the first case involving medical Cannabis to be heard by the highest court in the land. I told Jeff I was very proud of him. He knew his chance of winning was a long shot. "My winning was also a long shot," I reminded him.

I gladly agreed to work with the OCBC attorney, Rob Raich, on a "friend-of-the-court" brief supporting the right to dispense medical Cannabis to qualified patients.

•

In November two more states passed medical marijuana laws—Colorado and Nevada. In Colorado, fifty-four percent of the voters approved a measure decriminalizing the use, possession and cultivation of marijuana by patients who possess written documentation from a physician affirming that they suffer from a debilitating condition and "might benefit from the medical use of marijuana."

Patients could possess two ounces of usable marijuana, and could grow up to six plants. The law established a state-run registry to issue identification cards to qualifying patients.

In Nevada, sixty-five percent of the voters passed a similar measure in a repeat of the 1998 vote (as required by Nevada law).

Legislators added a preamble: "The state of Nevada as a sovereign state has the duty to carry out the will of the people of this state and regulate the health, medical practices and well-being of those people in a manner that respects their personal decisions concerning the relief of suffering through the medical use of marijuana." A separate provision required the Nevada School of Medicine to "aggressively" seek federal permission to establish a state-run medical marijuana distribution program.

Two more!! I like winning. We now had eight states.

•

The millennium ended with the U.S. Supreme Court declaring George W. Bush the winner over Al Gore in the presidential election. I didn't believe Bush would be helpful in my cause. It was his father who shut the IND program down in 1992.

I think Gore might have won if he had come out in support of allowing doctors to recommend marijuana, a position that 75% of Americans agree with, according to a Time Magazine poll. Instead, when asked where he stood by a reporter in New Hampshire, Gore said, "Right now, the science does not show me or the experts whose judgment I trust that it is the proper medication for pain and there are not better alternatives available in every situation."

When politicians say "More research is needed," they really are saying "More Prohibition is needed."

•

The new millennium also began with the U.S. Department of Health and Human Services re-stating its commitment to prohibition. On January 17, 2001, responding at long last to activist Jon Gettman's 1995 petition to reschedule marijuana, HHS recommended it "continue to be subject to control under Schedule 1." Officially the DEA and the HHS claimed marijuana·has a high potential for abuse similar to other Schedule I substances like heroin and relative to other substances scheduled under the Controlled Substances Act. The DEA asserted marijuana can only be placed in Schedule I, regardless of its abuse potential, because it does not have an accepted medical use in the United States.

It has no official medical use because the government wants it that way. It is all a crock of shit. I'm medical proof Cannabis works as a medicine.

Last Visit With Bob

In early March 2001, I got a call from Bob Randall asking me to drive over to Sarasota to see him. I was elated and jumped at the opportunity. Bob looked all right but I sensed Alice was worried. We had a glorious afternoon talking about recent events... until Bob told me he didn't know how much longer he would live.

Bob explained his arrangement with Steptoe and Johnson, the prestigious

Washington law firm that had represented him and our cause, pro bono, since 1978. When he died, Bob said, I should tell them his last wish was that the firm continue working, through me, to legalize marijuana use by those in medical need. I was stunned by his declaration. I couldn't look at Alice, or I would have broken down.

Bob was worried once he died the government would try to withdraw the compassionate care protocols because he was the only patient with a lawsuit against them. "If Steptoe and Johnson would represent you in court," Bob said, "and you were to win, then the other patients would also win."

The rest of the afternoon was a blur. After his news, I'm not sure what small talk we shared. The drive home was somber. I couldn't and didn't want to think about being without Bob.

I never saw my old friend and ally again.

Supporting the OCBC

On Monday, March 26 2001, I held a well-attended press conference at my brokerage firm to discuss the Supreme Court case involving the Oakland Cannabis Buyers' Co-op. I would be leaving for Washington that night and would attend oral arguments before the Justices on Wednesday, the 28th. I distributed copies of an amicus brief supporting the OCBC's right to sell marijuana to patients who used it as a matter of medical necessity.

Lawyers working for the Drug Policy Alliance, Dan Abrahamson and Judy Appel, had drafted the brief on behalf of me, the American Public Health Association, the California Nurses' Association, and the Lymphoma Foundation of America. Additional "friends of the court" included Elvy, Barbara and George. We were responding to a brief filed by the Drug-Free America Foundation asserting using marijuana as medicine has no scientific basis, and for every medical condition there is a conventional therapy that works better. (It also linked medical marijuana to a "homosexual agenda.")

The points made in our brief were documented with ample citations of the scientific and medical literature: "The U.S. Institute of Medicine and the British House of Lords independently confirm Cannabis is medically appropriate for some patients... Cannabis provides essential relief from pain, nausea, anorexia, muscle spasticity, and seizures... The side effects of medicinal Cannabis are often less severe than those of conventional medications... For many seriously ill patients, Marinol does not offer a satisfactory treatment alternative."

Our briefs pointed out 'alternative options' are not available for patients who need Cannabis. "Few patients will be able to participate in controlled clinical trials involving herbal Cannabis... The Federal Government refuses to provide herbal Cannabis for controlled clinical trials involving single patients... Pharmaceutical-quality non-smoked Cannabis medicines are years away from developing and marketing... The prospect of rescheduling herbal Cannabis is remote and uncertain."

•

The day before the Supreme Court hearing, I was scheduled to take part in "Case Day" at Langley High School in McLean, Virginia. Every year Langley students are assigned to research a Supreme Court case and study the issues from each side's perspective. A day or so before oral arguments at the Supreme Court, an elaborate, unscripted mock trial is held in the school auditorium, presided over by local legal authorities playing the part of Supreme Court Justices, who then issue a ruling. The Langley students who argue the case get to attend the actual oral arguments. (In recent years they have had seats reserved courtesy of Justice Antonin Scalia, parent of a Langley alumnus.)

"Case Day" in 2001 was devoted to U.S. v. Oakland Cannabis Buyers' Co-operative. The student who invited me said I would be testifying between 11:00 am. and 12:00 pm. on Tuesday morning. He mentioned that C-SPAN would be covering the trial. I told her I'd arrive in Washington Monday night to be rested and ready.

Delta Disaster

I made reservations on Delta Airlines. I had flown on Delta many times with my medicine ever since becoming legal, and never a problem. As always, I reserved an aisle seat so I could stand whenever I needed to without bothering anyone. I then asked to speak to a supervisor and explained I would be traveling with Cannabis, but would not need a room in which to smoke unless my return flight was delayed for several hours—in which case I should have a contact at the airport in Washington who understood my situation and could make the necessary arrangements.

I was told to fax all my information to Delta and they would get back to me with the name of someone to contact, if necessary, at National Airport. About ten days before I was supposed to leave, it dawned on me I hadn't heard back from Delta. I called and got a supervisor who said, "I'll call you right back," but didn't. Then I got busy and totally forgot about it.

On the day I was supposed to leave I realized I still hadn't heard from Delta, so I called and explained my status to another supervisor. She asked me to fax her all the relevant paperwork. I sent a copy of my protocol, a copy of my prescription, a letter from my doctor, and the letter from the Federal Government that said I was not breaking any Federal law by possessing Cannabis. I called and verified she had gotten the material, but she never called me back.

This happened to me once before. That time, while at the gate waiting to board the plane, I was called up to the counter and told, "Your contact is Mr. Smith."

I drove to the airport in Ft. Lauderdale, checked in two bags with Delta sky caps, and parked my Explorer. I walked into the airport with my carry-on bag, which held my Cannabis. (I had been instructed by the DEA, the FDA, and the NIDA to never check it through.) I was two hours early, as usual, because you never know what can happen going through airport security with a canister of Cannabis. Nothing did. I found my gate and was reading when, about forty-five minutes before departure, I heard an announcement telling me to report to the ticket counter.

"I'm Mr. Rosenfeld," I told an agent. Alongside him stood two supervisors, one of whom said, "Mr. Rosenfeld, Delta Airlines is not going to allow you to fly to Washington National today." I looked around in hopes of seeing Hector Baldadi, the head of security for Delta, who helped me in the past. I thought maybe he had seen my name and was playing a joke on me, but he wasn't there. I said, "Excuse me? Delta Airlines is not going to allow me fly to Washington today? Why?"

The supervisor replied, "It has come to our attention you are carrying marijuana." I said, "It has come to your attention I'm carrying marijuana because I told you so. What does that have to do with it?"

"We just talked to the lawyers for Delta Airlines, and they said because you don't have permission from the states we're flying over, allowing you to carry marijuana, unless you can prove to us you're leaving your marijuana here in Ft. Lauderdale, we're not going to allow you to fly to Washington today."

"This is a Federal program," I explained. "I don't need permission from any state." I said if I could speak to the lawyers for Delta, I could straighten things out.

They replied, "No, you may not." I told them I had flown with Delta for over 18 years with their knowledge I was carrying my Cannabis. I unzipped my bag, took out the tin can and showed them the label. I said, "Look, this is Government marijuana. I am legally allowed to fly with my Federal prescription. My prescription is just like any other and is allowed nationwide."

They said, "Sorry."

At that point, I realized they were serious and I asked to speak to Hector Baldadi. "Hector no longer works for us," I was informed.

I said, "Let me ask you a question: How would an average passenger know the name of your head of security if he hadn't helped me in the past? Please get the attorneys on the phone."

"No, we will not. Unless you can prove to us you are leaving your marijuana here, we are not going to let you board." Meaning they were going to search me.

So again I showed them the letters and everything else I had to prove I was allowed to possess and travel with my medicine. Everyone nearby could hear what we were saying and I was getting embarrassed. It was like when the police arrested me in Orlando —there's nothing you can do, they're in complete control. It was so frustrating! All you can do is say, "Yes sir," "No sir," and try to plead your case.

•

When I realized they weren't going to let me board, I said, "Call the police." They looked at me like I was going to cause trouble. Since I had been standing all this time, my legs were giving out, so I went and sat down. An officer from the Broward County Sheriff's Department showed up minutes later and went directly to the counter. I could hear him being told, "We don't need you, he does."

The officer came over and said, "What can I help you with?" I pulled out my baggie with twelve joints in it and said, "Sir, I am one of the patients who receive medical marijuana from the Federal Government..." He said, "Isn't there another person down here who gets it, also?" I was thinking, "Thank you God." I said, "Yes, Elvy Musikka lives in Hollywood. She has glaucoma."

The Supreme Court had given us a booklet with all the amicus briefs filed in connection with the OCBC case, which I pulled out of my bag and showed him. "Here's mine, Irv Rosenfeld... and here's Elvy's."

He said, "So what's the problem?"

I said, "Come with me to the counter."

We went to the counter and faced the two supervisors and the gate agent. I said, "May I board this flight?"

"No you may not."

"Why?"

"Because you are carrying marijuana and you do not have permission from each state that we're flying over."

The deputy said, "Excuse me, I'm familiar with this gentleman's program. It is a Federal program, so he doesn't need permission from each state."

"The lawyers for Delta say he does."

Again I asked, "May I please speak to the attorneys for Delta Airlines?"

"No you may not.

"Will you allow the police officer to speak to the lawyers?"

"No we will not."

The policeman turned to me and said, "I can't get you on the plane. What would you like me to do?"

I said, "I'm going to have to sue them. Right now it's the word of two supervisors and a gate agent against me. It would look better if I had a police report saying why they would not allow me to board." He agreed to write one.

While he was calling the Bascom-Palmer pharmacy to verify my prescription, I pleaded again with the Delta staffers to let me board the plane. I showed them my can with the Federal label, letters from the DEA—to no avail. I had to get to D.C. I was supposed to meet the media and a client later that evening. Finally I asked which other airlines were flying to D.C. I was told, "We're not going to help you, go to a pay phone." The policeman said, "My God, give him a break, he's disabled."

So they checked and told me Air Tran had a flight to Dulles airport leaving in two and a half hours, with seats available. It would cost $450 for a last-minute ticket versus the $245 I had paid Delta. I asked if they could make the arrangements and was told "No, you're going to have to do that yourself." They wrote down the information and told me to go to a pay phone. I asked, "What about my refund from Delta?" They replied, "Oh yeah, I guess we need to get you a refund."

The Sheriff's Deputy, whose name was Bailey, waited with me while they arranged my refund and retrieved the two bags I had checked. I looked at them and said, "I'm disabled. How am I going to get three bags back to my car, drive to another concourse, and carry three bags in? I won't be able to check bags at the curb because I don't have a ticket."

They said, "That's not our concern!"

Officer Bailey offered to help me back to my car. He grabbed one bag and I grabbed two. We went downstairs to a pay phone where I called Air Tran and made my reservation. We got back to my car and I thanked the officer for his efforts on my behalf. He said I could get a copy of his police report in two days, and wished me good luck.

I drove to the airport's other building, found a parking place and struggled to get my three bags to the Air Tran counter. I was furious. I wondered what else could go wrong.

I didn't have to wait long for the answer. At the counter, I was told Air Tran's flights had been delayed three to four hours all day, and most likely there would be no flight to Dulles that night. In fact, the agent said, "I'm going to make reservations for you now at a hotel in Atlanta for the night and hopefully you can take an early morning flight out and get to Dulles on Tuesday.

I was seething. I was supposed to be on a two-hour non-stop flight direct to D.C., and now this.

I checked my bags and started the wait. I called the student in Virginia who invited me to Langley High and explained to her what happened. She felt terrible. I told her I'd make it if I could.

We didn't fly out of Ft. Lauderdale till one o'clock in the morning. I was so frustrated I wanted to kill! By that time I should have kept my appointments in Washington and been in bed at the hotel.

I finally got to Atlanta at 3:30 am., and took a cab to the motel. I had to be back at the airport by 7:00 am. to catch a 9:00 am. flight that would get me to Dulles by 11:00 am.

•

As it turned out, we landed around 11:15 am. and by the time I got my luggage it was 11:45am.—too late for me to go to the school. So I took a cab to my next scheduled appointment, an interview at the Cox Broadcasting studio.

I walked in and the producer said, "What are you doing here? We figured you'd be running late from the high school." I told him why I never made it to the high school and the guy started smiling! I glared at him. "What are you smiling about?" He said, "Cox Broadcasting owns 90 TV stations and newspapers around the country, including WSB, the number-one rated station in Atlanta, Georgia, home of Delta Airlines! Lead story tonight: 'Disabled Person Refused Right to Fly With a Legal Prescription.'"

Now I was smiling. They wanted to give the story to two newspapers owned by Cox, one being the *Palm Beach Post,* whose reporter had been in my office on Monday covering my press conference.

So I did the interviews and that night my ordeal was the lead story on WSB, less than 24 hours after what Delta put me through. Also it was a front-page story the next day in the Atlanta Journal Constitution and the Palm Beach Post. Thinking about all the Delta executives watching the news on TV and picking up the morning paper and seeing their company trashed made me happy. I don't think the powers' to be at Delta Airlines expected this "free publicity"!

Civics Lessons

In the late afternoon a few of the students picked me up and we drove to a cookout at their teacher's home. The judges had ruled 8-0 against the OCBC. I was told there might be a judge or two at the cookout who might have some questions for me. I said, "That's fine."

It was a set-up. I walked in to find the teacher and all eight judges ready to hear what I had to say. "It's about time you got here," I was told. "Now sit down and we will start the questioning." The teacher added, "You didn't think you would get away without testifying, did you?"

The questions started coming from all directions—the students, the teacher, and the judges, boom, boom, boom, for more than two hours. I was impressed by everyone's understanding of the medical marijuana issue, especially the students'. They knew all about the Compassionate Care Protocols and the relevant medical studies. They asked about the ramifications if the OCBC lost. They didn't have preconceived opinions, for or against. When we had finished, several judges said it was a shame I hadn't been able to appear at the school, it might have changed the final vote. I thought that was a great compliment.

The burgers and hot dogs were tasty and the company was wonderful. Those high school students were brilliant and I told them how lucky they were to have such a knowledgeable teacher. Everyone got to see me take my medicine and not turn into a zombie.

•

The next day I went to the Supreme Court. On a beam above the main entrance is inscribed "Equal Justice Under Law"—a fine ideal, but does our country live up to it? Does the law itself treat marijuana and prescription drug users equally? Obviously not... yet.

A long line of people hoping to attend the trial had formed and I felt fortunate to have a reserved seat. What a privilege to sit in that historic courtroom, observe the Justices behind the long, high mahogany bench, and listen to a discussion of the issue to which I had devoted so many years, energy and effort. Whatever the outcome, our movement succeeded in raising public awareness. Millions of Americans who started smoking marijuana in the 1960s, '70s, and '80s had no idea it was once legally prescribed as medicine. Now the historical truth was known to many. The California Medical Association, which opposed Prop 215 in 1996, had filed an amicus brief in support of the OCBC. I felt we had won a victory just getting to the Supreme Court.

Each side had half an hour to address the Justices, who could cut in with questions. Arguing for the OCBC was Gerald F. Uelmen, a University of Santa Clara law professor who had been part of O.J. Simpson's defense team. The tone of the questions indicated to some experienced observers the government would prevail. When Uelmen said California had created a "limited exception" to the Controlled Substances Act, Justice Anthony Kennedy put in, "It doesn't sound limited at all." Allowing the OCBC to provide marijuana to some patients, Kennedy added, would mean a "huge rewriting" of the Controlled Substances Act—which was the job of Congress, not the courts.

A politically realistic note was provided by Justice David Souder, who asked the government's lawyer, "Isn't the real concern behind this that with the passage of the California proposition and the popularity within the California population that that necessarily entails, it will be very, very difficult for the government ever to get a criminal conviction in a jury trial?"

After an hour the courtroom drama was over. Outside, microphones had been set up on the broad courthouse steps for the lawyers and major players to make their statements. The anti-Cannabis speakers went first and we listened respectfully. When we spoke, however, they tried to shout us down. During my turn at the mike, I heard people screaming that I represented the devil. I ignored them and had my say.

•

It had been three and a half hours since I had taken my medicine and my legs were getting tight, so I walked across the plaza and lit up away from the crowd. I thought I was by myself. Next thing I knew, two uniformed policemen came over and one took my arm as if to lead me back into the Courthouse. I said, "Excuse me gentlemen, I'm a Federal patient and I'm allowed to take my medicine wherever I am."

They said, "That hasn't been decided yet."

"It has for me and six other Federal patients," I said, taking out a bag containing Cannabis from my pocket. "The Federal Government gives us this to use. This is my prescription."

One officer examined my documents while the other held on to my arm. I asked, "If you have a problem with me taking my medicine here, where can I take it?"

The validity of my prescription was acknowledged. "If you go down the steps," I was told, "you will be on the sidewalk, and we have no jurisdiction." So I broke away and went down the steps. I hadn't come to Washington to push the envelope. I wasn't trying to say, "Look at me, I can smoke marijuana. Ha. Ha."

I spent the rest of the afternoon doing interviews and visiting with friends. I flew home the next day on Air Tran with no problems.

•

It took four months to find an attorney willing to file a suit against Delta. Because I was suing under the Americans with Disabilities Act, there would be no monetary victory; my goal was simply to establish I'd been wronged and I had every right to bring my Federal prescription into any state I needed, no matter the mode of transportation. Attorney Christopher Sharp of Fort Lauderdale agreed to pursue the matter.

The Missoula Chronic Cannabis Use Study

Although the U.S. Government often took credit for the existence of a "Compassionate Investigational New Drug program" through which our tiny group of citizens received marijuana, the program existed in name only, and the name was misleading. The Food & Drug Administration never actually investigated whether the individuals getting Cannabis from the National Institute on Drug Abuse were benefiting from its use or being harmed. Any investigation into how the "new drug" (which had been used as medicine for at least 5,000 years) affected us was left up to us, the patients, and our physicians, whose findings might not have the same impact as government scientists'. And of course, none of us had the resources to pay for all the extensive tests that would be involved.

Ethan Russo, MD, a neurologist in private practice and an adjunct faculty member of the Department of Pharmacology at the University of Montana and the Department of Medicine at the University of Washington Medical

School, proposed doing a rigorous study of how the surviving IND patients were faring. Al Byrne and Mary Lynn Mathre, through POT, helped raise funds and made arrangements with the patients to be studied. George, Elvy and I flew to Missoula; Barbara Douglass was tested by an associate of Dr. Russo's, Kristin A. Kirlin, at home in Iowa. Bob was too sick to be involved. The other surviving members of the program had maintained their anonymity over the years.

We arrived in mid-June and checked into a Red Lion Inn. For the next two days we were "put through the wringer" by Russo, Mathre, and colleagues at the office of Montana Neurobehavioral Specialists and St. Patrick Hospital. It seemed as if we were given every test known to modern medicine: MRI brain scans, pulmonary function tests, chest X-ray, neuropsychological tests, hormone and immunological assays, EKG, memorization, brain-wave testing, etc. It's amazing given how many millions of Americans have used Cannabis over the years, the long-term effects have been rigorously studied in only the four of us, and not by the government who keeps stonewalling more research is needed.

The Missoula Chronic Clinical Cannabis Use Study, as it was formally called, showed long-term, heavy use of Cannabis had not caused us any harm! The findings were normal for almost all the tests, showing only minor changes in pulmonary functions and mild effects on short-term memory loss, due to the use of their medicine during testing. Memory testing is usually done at different times following the use of Cannabis and studies find short-term mild memory lose diminishes over time. However these patients needed their medicine all day.

•

The study also confirmed the "clinical effectiveness" of Cannabis in treating our various illnesses — glaucoma (Elvy), chronic musculoskeletal pain (me), spasm and nausea (George), and spasticity of multiple sclerosis (Barbara).

The study, as written up by Russo with co-authors Mary Lynn Mathre, Al Byrne, Robert Velin, Paul J. Bach, Juan Sanchez-Ramos, and Kristin A

Kirlin, can be seen at:

www.medicalCannabis.com/PDF/Chronic_Cannabis.pdf

Here are the "Conclusions and Recommendations of the Missoula Chronic Clinical Cannabis Use Study:"

1. Cannabis smoking, even of a crude, low-grade product, provides effective symptomatic relief of pain, muscle spasms, and intraocular pressure elevations in selected patients failing other modes of treatment.

2. These clinical Cannabis patients are able to reduce or eliminate other prescription medicines and their accompanying side effects.

3. Clinical Cannabis provides an improved quality of life in these patients.

4. The side effect profile of the NIDA Cannabis in chronic usage suggests some mild pulmonary risk. However no cancer has ever been detected unlike lung cancer due to cigarette smoking.

5. No malignant deterioration has been observed.

6. No consistent or attributable neuropsychological or neurological deterioration has been observed.'

7. No endocrine, hematological or immunological sequelae have been observed.

8. Improvements in a clinical Cannabis program would include a ready and consistent supply of sterilized, potent, organically grown unfertilized female flowering top material, thoroughly cleaned of extraneous inert fibrous matter.

9. It is the authors' opinion the Compassionate IND program should be reopened and extended to other patients in need of clinical Cannabis.

10. Failing that, local, state and federal laws might be amended to provide regulated and monitored Cannabis to suitable candidates.

•

The authors noted, "All four patients are stable with respect to their chronic conditions, and are taking many fewer standard pharmaceuticals than previously." The reduced need for other drugs is an under-publicized aspect of medical Cannabis use that may explain why the pharmaceutical industry is so opposed to it.

Life Goes On

On May 15, 2001, the Supreme Court ruled in the Oakland Cannabis Buyers' Co-operative case that Federal law bars the distribution of marijuana even to people who need it to alleviate symptoms of serious illness. Clarence Thomas wrote the opinion, which noted the only people allowed to use marijuana in the U.S. were those with a Federal exemption, meaning those of us on the IND program. There was no minority opinion because the Justices voted 8-0.

The ruling was a setback for the medical Cannabis movement in California and would encourage law enforcement to crack down on distributors, even though it in no way invalidated Prop 215, or any other state medical-marijuana law. The court merely rejected one possible justification— "medical necessity"—for distributing marijuana in violation of the Controlled Substance Act. The Court merely said a club or Co-Op distributing marijuana to ill patients could not plead "medical necessity" defense in Federal court. Police and prosecutors who wanted to enforce Prohibition read headlines like "Supreme Court Rules Against Medical Marijuana" and feel less restrained by state laws.

Jeff Jones compared the ruling to the Supreme Court's pro-slavery decision in the infamous Dred Scott case. OCBC attorney Robert Raich said he would be raising other issues in Federal court. "This isn't the Court's last ruling on medical Cannabis," Raich said, "It's the first."

Editorial writers across the country expressed disappointment in the Supreme Court ruling. "Medical Marijuana: Don't Hold Your Breath Waiting For Fairness" was the headline on a piece by Philip Terzian of the *Providence Journal*. The *Ft. Lauderdale Sun-Sentinel* accompanied it with an appropriate cartoon. In the first panel a woman is saying, "I was diagnosed with cancer, went through chemo, lost all my hair, threw up all day, and was withering away until I tried marijuana." Next panel is a Supreme Court Justice calling the woman "Pothead!" How true.

•

On June 2, 2001, we lost Robert Randall. He was only fifty-two, much too young. The cause of death was "AIDS-related complications." The pro-tease inhibitors that now make it possible for people with AIDS to survive for decades hadn't come along in time for Bob. Ironically, widespread use of "drug cocktails" by people with HIV has provided a new impetus for using medical Cannabis: it stops the nausea that the life-saving drugs can bring on.

Bob had been my political organizer. He played the same role for Elvy, Corinne, George, Barbara, and almost everyone else in the IND program. He not only helped us draft our protocols and overcome the Federal bu-reaucracy, but he educated us about the so-called "War on Drugs", which is really a war on certain people who use certain drugs. Although he was less active towards the end, I considered him my leader and mentor till the day he died. I know many others felt the same.

Goodbye, dear friend. Rest well. You have earned it.

•

Now, I was the longest-surviving Federal IND patient. Would I be up to playing a leadership role? No one could replace Bob and I didn't expect to. But, he had asked me to call Steptoe and Johnson...

I got a secretary on the phone and asked if she knew who Robert Randall was. She responded, "What do you mean 'was?'" I told her Bob died three days ago. She was a private secretary for one of the partners in the firm and had known Bob since 1978. I explained his request that Steptoe and Johnson add me as a client so the firm would stay involved in the defense of the IND program. She said she would ask the decision makers.

I called back the following Monday and was asked to sign release forms so the firm could conduct a background check on me. It must have been a thorough one because I was told it would take two weeks and it took almost six. I was assigned two attorneys—Steve Davidson, who had worked on Bob's case for many years and was now a partner, and a newcomer to the issue, Andy Hefty. I called Andy and introduced myself. He asked a lot of basic questions which I was able to answer. I got the feeling he was more comfortable after our conversation. I informed him at that time about my situation with Delta Airlines. I told him about my local attorney and what we had planned. I wanted to make sure Steptoe knew about my upcoming lawsuit and that they had no problems with what I was doing.

A few days later, I was able to talk to Steve for a few minutes. We mostly talked about Bob and Alice. While I didn't have the resume of Bob, Steve said my accomplishments were impressive and he and Andy would be proud to represent me. He told me then to go forward with the lawsuit against Delta Airlines. I knew I was in good hands!

•

In early August, my attorney Christopher Sharp and I worked on our plan against Delta. Our first step was to hold a press conference we hoped would induce Delta to acknowledge they had denied my rights. I wanted an apology, a pledge I would never again be barred from flying, and I wanted Delta to donate $10,000 in plane tickets to Shake-A-Leg, so disabled sailors could travel to events. I thought these demands were reasonable, and offered Delta the consolation of good publicity.

I invited all video and print media in South Florida and Atlanta—my home base and Delta's—- to the press conference at Sharp's law office in Ft. Lauderdale August 15. It was well attended. We got our points across. At the end I went outside to take my medicine and be videoed doing so. A manager of the building came over and told me I had to put it out. He had no grounds, but I wasn't looking for another lawsuit, so I complied. When you're fighting for your rights there's a time to advance and a time to retreat. Besides, the camera operators already had the footage they needed.

The press conference generated a lot of coverage. "This is no different than if they told a diabetic, 'You can't bring your insulin on the plane,'" was Christopher Sharp's most picked-up sound bite. He was also quoted saying, "It's important to stand up to this invidious discrimination. If Delta would issue an apology, Rosenfeld would go back to flying on its planes." We told Delta they had thirty days to respond, or we were prepared to file suit in Federal Court.

•

Meanwhile, the stock markets had been shaky all year. It seemed as if every morning the markets would be up in pre-markets, only to be down by the time I drove the fifty minutes to work.

On September 11, 2001, I got up around 6:00 am. and sure enough, the markets were up before the opening, which was at 9:30 am. I started my normal daily routine of smoking two Cannabis cigarettes while watching the business shows. I took a shower and left for the office around 7:35 am. Traffic was a little worse than usual, so I didn't get to work until 8:30 am. I went to my office, turned on CNBC and the futures were still up. I thought, "Great, maybe we will have an up day."

As I was printing up my daily reports, it was announced that a small plane had hit the World Trade Center. Soon we saw video and it was obvious it hadn't been a small plane. Immediately the futures started dropping. Everyone knows what happened next. The World Trade Center and the Pentagon were attacked by terrorists using hijacked airplanes as their weapons. The markets never opened that day or for the next three days.

•

Because of 9/11, we decided not to file suit on September 15, 2001. However, since Delta never responded to our offer, Chris and I decided the only way to get their attention was to file our suit.

On December 5, 2001 the suit was filed. We ended up filing the suit under the Air Carriers Access Act which covered any complaints a person has with an airline. Under that Act, we could sue for actual and punitive damages which made Chris happy. He might get paid after all. Maybe my problem seemed trivial given the destruction and death of 9/11, but I decided not to let the terrorists prevent me from standing up for my rights. Life goes on and so must we.

Option Strategies

G KN Securities was sold to a company that I and some other brokers didn't want to work for. My old manager of ten years, Marty Schaffer, left to head an office for a firm called Meyers & Associates. They were opening an office a few minutes from my home in Ft. Lauderdale. He offered me a position and I accepted.

On my first day, as I was taking my medicine in my car at a handicapped spot in the parking lot, a security guard came over and asked what I was doing. I explained and he was amazed. He said I should let the building manager know. I found her office and told her my medical situation. She had no problems with my using Cannabis.

The next morning the guard showed up again and said, "My boss doesn't believe what I told him about you. He said marijuana is not legal federally. He's going to be here tomorrow morning so you can prove it to him." I advised the guard to bet his boss a hundred dollars and said I would see them both tomorrow.

The next day, sure enough, as I was taking my medicine in my car, the security guard came over. He was accompanied by his boss, a man in dress pants and shirt. The boss looked over my paperwork and realized, to his astonishment, I was legitimate.

I told him who I was working for and our conversation turned to the market. "I only do currency options," he remarked. I had done options forever but didn't know anything about currency options. He had a tip for me: "I follow the recommendations from a publication called 'Currency Option

Hotline,' written by Meyer Eisner from Boca. I'll give you his phone number." He gave me the number and off he went... $100 lighter! The security guard was all smiles.

That day I called Meyer Eisner. We talked about the markets and different option strategies along with our personal stories. Meyer suggested we meet for lunch, which we did later that week. I told him about my disorders and how I had taken on the Federal Government to become a medical Cannabis recipient. He had been a competitive wrestler in school and now was a weight lifter, even though he had medical problems. We got along well and respected each other's accomplishments.

Meyer and his partner write three different option newsletters, "Oil and Gas Option Hotline," "Gold and Silver Option Hotline," and "Currency Option Hotline." People pay $5,000 a year to get their weekly recommendations. The newsletters list brokers from around the world who can do the trades. I was flattered when Meyer said he would add my name to the list. "Anyone that can take on the Federal Government and win is a winner, and I only work with winners." Then he explained how currency options differed from regular options.

To this day, my clients and I owe a huge debt of gratitude to Meyer Eisner, for we have made a lot of money on his recommendations,—and the parking lot attendant who facilitated our introduction.

•

In late January, 2002, the *Journal of Cannabis Therapeutics* published the paper that Ethan Russo and colleagues had written evaluating the effects of long-term, heavy marijuana smoking on the four Federal patients. The bottom line was none of us had been harmed and we each had been helped; Cannabis "demonstrated clinical effectiveness in these patients in treating glaucoma, chronic musculoskeletal pain, spasm nausea, and spasticity of multiple sclerosis." Russo, et al recommended improvements in the IND program, and called for reopening it to patients in need.

Everyone involved hoped a paper in a peer-reviewed journal, backed by

Haworth Press, a leading scientific publisher, would attract media attention. But this one didn't. The media giveth, and the media taketh away.

The end of February, Shake-A-Leg's Annual Mid-Winter Regatta took place. Some of the nation's top disabled sailors attend. It is always good to see all my friends from around the country. I discovered over the years that many disabled sailors used medical Cannnabis, so while I was able to openly take my medicine, my friends had to hide their use of medical Cannabis for fear they would be arrested. It just wasn't fair.

•

On March 26, 2002, I spoke at the University of Central Florida. This engagement was special to me, for this was the first time Debbie had come with me. While she knew my story backwards and forwards, she had never seen how an audience responded to my telling it.

I spoke to a class taught by Michael E. Dunn on "Psychobiological Aspects of Drug Use." I discussed the Supreme Court case and the state initiatives being organized by the Drug Policy Alliance and other reform groups. I said "The fight is really in Congress," and explained why. I predicted if marijuana was legalized, the pharmaceutical industry, among other powerful interests, would suffer—which might explain their commitment to Prohibition. The hour-and-half went well, with students asking engaging questions.

The next day the student newspaper, "The Central Florida Future," ran a front-page story by Jason Irsay with pictures of me taking my medicine and holding up the can in which the government sent it to me. The headline read, "Speaker: Marijuana Should Be Legalized." They forgot to add "for medical use."

Debbie was quoted saying while she didn't like the smoke, she had witnessed firsthand the effectiveness of Cannabis for me. This was an accurate summary of her attitude,

Meanwhile, the owner of my new firm didn't live up to expectations. In April, my old manager resigned and we brokers were left alone to do our own business with little support from our main office in New York. I was doing well, thanks to my new business of currency options. The stock markets were still doing poorly, which was blamed on 9/11. I did a lot of exchange-traded closed-end funds (ETF) on the New York Stock Exchange paying nine to ten percent per year and a lot of options.

POT in Portland

In early May, 2002, I flew to Portland, Oregon to take part in Patients Out of Time's second national conference. It was a very politically supportive environment. Voters had passed an initiative in 1998 establishing the Oregon Medical Marijuana Program (OMMP). The state Department of Health, which administered the program, was co-sponsoring the conference, along with the Oregon Nurses Association. Sandee Burbank, founder of Mothers Against Misuse and Abuse (MAMA) was the local host.

The official in charge of OMMP, Grant Higginson, MD, described how it worked. At the time, 3,003 patients were enrolled and 628 doctors had approved their Cannabis use. The patients' average age was forty-six; most were men; pain was the most common condition.

Patients Out of Time conferences include cram courses in what scientists have learned about the body's response to Cannabis, in other words, why it works as medicine. Here's a brief intro:

Our bodies make chemical messengers that certain compounds in the Cannabis plant—"cannabinoids"—resemble. When the plant cannabinoids are inhaled or ingested, they activate the same receptors that the body's own chemical messengers normally activate.

The plant compounds were identified and named first. When the body's similar compounds were identified in the 1990s, they were named "endocannabinoids"—"endo" being short for "endogenous," which means "within the body." The names imply the plant came first, but in fact, animals developed their chemical messenger systems many millions of years before the Cannabis plant evolved.

The discovery of the human body's own endocannabinoid receptor system was very similar to the discovery of our "endogenous morphine" system. Compounds in the poppy plant activate receptors that normally respond to our body's own opioids. These are called "endorphins," which is short for "endogenous morphines."

Among those explaining the science in Portland was Esther Fride, PhD, an Israeli researcher. Dr. Fride said the cannabinoids and opioid systems interact. In laboratory studies, animals given cannabinoids use about half the amount of opioids they would otherwise require to achieve pain relief. So it's no coincidence that Cannabis users typically cut their use of Vicodin, etc., by fifty percent.

Fride's lab showed that if the cannabinoid receptor is blocked by an "antagonist" drug, newborn rats will not suckle and will fail to thrive. From birth, the cannabinoid system controls appetite, which is why marijuana brings on "the munchies."

Pharmaceutical companies are trying to develop synthetic drugs that have the medical benefits of Cannabis without the psychoactive effects. Dr. Sumner Burstein of the University of Massachusetts discussed his tests of a modified THC molecule that has potent anti-pain and anti-inflammatory effects on mice. Although my experience suggests heavy, everyday use reduces or eliminates the psychoactive effects of smoked Cannabis, I understand why many people would prefer a drug that has no such effects at all.

•

Donald Abrams, MD, a cancer and HIV specialist at the University of California San Francisco, told a story that I could relate to involving a long-term government stall. Dr. Abrams spent years trying to get approval for a study of whether smoking marijuana led to increased appetite and weight gain in AIDS patients. His original plan was to import Cannabis from Holland. The FDA helped him draft his protocol in 1993, but the DEA—after many months of silence—said he would have to get the Cannabis through the NIDA. He applied to the NIDA but "didn't hear back from them... I had trouble getting through to them..."

Finally, after the NIDA rejected his proposal and the NIH wouldn't give him a grant, Abrams revised his study to include a search for harmful effects. Does marijuana damage the immune system when taken by patients using protease inhibitors? By adding this question to those he hoped to answer, Abrams got government approval—and the NIDA Cannabis— to conduct his study. In the end, his data would show that smoking Cannabis stimulates appetite, leads to weight gain, and has no negative effect on the immune system of persons with AIDS who are on protease inhibitors.

•

Other speakers included Dr. Audra Stinchcomb of the University of Kentucky, who described her attempts to design a patch that delivers cannabinoids through the skin—an alternative to smoking—and Ethan Russo, who reported on the Missoula study. We, the patients involved, took part in a panel. Patients from Oregon and California who used Cannabis under state law also told their stories.

It felt good to be in a place where others could use marijuana as medicine. Relief of pain should be a right, not a special privilege.

•

Summer came with not a lot of activity on the Cannabis front. I worked, sailed, and played softball (until I cracked my left tibia reaching for a foul ball) which kept me "riding the pines" for five months). Even though I could barely walk, the people at Shake-A-Leg had very little sympathy for me. After all, a lot of them can't walk at all, so I had to keep sailing or be called a wimp. That's why Shake-A-Leg is so wonderful. No matter how bad you think life gets, just look around.

•

In the middle of September I attended a stockholders meeting in Las Vegas. I got to the airport two hours early for my flight home. Near my gate was a room where people could smoke cigarettes, so I went to the back of the room to medicate. There were about twenty people in the room, including seven employees. I didn't think anyone took notice, but I was wrong. I was just about finished with my second cigarette when in walked a woman employee with two guards that looked like teenagers carrying M-16's (this was after 9/11) pointing at me. She saw me smoking Cannabis and instead of saying something to me, she went and got the guards.

They came over to me and one said, "What's the stuff?" I pulled out my baggie and said, "This is medical Cannabis supplied by the Federal Government. I have Multiple Congenital Cartilaginous Exostosis and a variant of the syndrome Pseudo Pseudo Hypoparathyroidism."

The response was, "Oh." And they turned around to walk out. The woman was furious. "Aren't you going to arrest him?" One of the kids replied, "It looks official to me," and kept walking.

On the flight back to Ft. Lauderdale, I thought about the incident. Here I was minding my own business, taking my medicine, not bothering anyone, but yet somebody wanted me arrested just because I was smoking something different then what they were smoking. Maybe we should make cigarettes illegal and see how they like it. Why do people try to legislate what a person can do for their health, or lack of it?

•

That fall there was a push in the Virginia House to repeal the medical Cannabis bill I had helped pass in 1979. My friend Lennice Werth notified me of the intent. I joined Lennice, her group Virginians Against Drug Violence and a disabled Air Force vet named Michael Krawitz in opposing the repeal. I made numerous calls from my brokerage firm to politicians. I reminded them about Senator Babalas and what Cannabis meant to him. We put on a great campaign, and in the end, we kept our measure on the books. Even though I didn't live in Virginia anymore, the bill and its history had a big place in my heart.

Conant v. Drug Czar et al

On October 29, 2002, our movement won its most important legal victory to date. In a case originally called Conant v. McCaffrey, a panel of judges from the Ninth Circuit Court of Appeals upheld an injunction preventing the Federal Government from punishing California doctors for discussing marijuana as a treatment option with their patients.

The case stemmed from that infamous press conference at which Drug Czar McCaffrey and other Federal officials had threatened to revoke the prescription-writing licenses of doctors who recommended Cannabis. Within weeks, a lawsuit had been filed by the Drug Policy Alliance and the ACLU, with AIDS specialist Marcus Conant, MD, as lead plaintiff. In March, 1997, a Federal judge, Fern Smith (a Reagan appointee), enjoined the Drug Czar and the government from acting on their threats. Judge Smith saw it as a matter of free speech—doctors and patients have a First Amendment right to discuss Cannabis. In September 2000, another Federal judge made the injunction permanent!

•

The Bush Administration appealed to the Ninth Circuit. George, Elvy, and I were among those filing amicus briefs on behalf of Dr. Conant (whose co-plaintiffs included California patients). Judge Alex Kozinski was sufficiently impressed to include our personal statements in his concurring opinion, which concluded: "In the thirty years Mr. Rosenfeld has used herbal Cannabis as a medicine, he has experienced no adverse side effects (including no 'high'), has been able to discontinue his prescription medications, and has worked successfully for the past thirteen years as a stockbroker handling multi-million dollar accounts. Mr. Rosenfeld and his physicians believe but for herbal Cannabis, Mr. Rosenfeld might not be alive, or, at the very least, would be bed-ridden."

It felt great to be involved in the Conant case. California's medical marijuana law could not have been implemented if the Federal Government had been allowed to intrude between doctor and patient.

•

November marked my twentieth anniversary as a Federal patient. An Associated Press story by Adrian Sainz quoted Debbie recalling my condition without Cannabis: "He would scream out in the middle of the night and I would wake up, and he'd be dragging himself on the floor." She said Cannabis "had given us a better life together."

•

On December 12 2002, I flew to New York City where I testified before a committee hearing on a state medical Cannabis bill sponsored by Assemblyman Richard Gottfried. The bill would allow licensed MDs to "authorize marijuana for a patient with a life-threatening, degenerative or permanently debilitating condition."

•

Also in December, my suit against Delta Airlines was stopped dead in its tracks when the 11th. U.S. Circuit Court of Appeals in Atlanta ruled on a separate case that complaints must be handled administratively by the Department of Transportation because Congress didn't authorize lawsuits under the Air Carrier Access Act. To say I was pissed was an understatement. Oh well.

Since the case now had to be filed in Washington D.C., I asked Steptoe and Johnson to represent me in dealing with the DOT. They initially agreed, but then I got a call from Andy Hefty, who said, "I've got good news and bad news for you. Which do you want first?" I asked for the bad. "Steptoe cannot represent you against Delta because we represent all the airlines and that would be a conflict of interest." The good news was they considered my case important, and arranged for Sheila Bedi of Georgetown Law Center to represent me, pro bono.

•

Between December and January, I assisted Sheila in everyway I could to prepare the filing to the DOT. We sent our request to the DOT to file suit in early February. Finally, on March 26, 2003, the Department of Transportation filed my complaint against Delta Airlines. This was almost two years to the day when I was so wronged by Delta. Even though I could not win a monetary judgment, I still needed to win or else any airline could keep me from flying with my Federal prescription.

It wasn't until March 26, 2004 that the DOT came back with their decision which basically agreed with the DEA stance that I have every right to bring my "Schedule 1, Investigational New Drug" onto a plane and I do not need permission from any state as it is a Federal prescription. However, the DEA also made clear my prescription is for an experimental new drug, not a medicine!

The DOT also stated because there are less than 10 of these people in the United States who use Federal Cannabis, it serves no purpose to fine Delta for their actions. They slapped Delta on the wrist and said don't do it again.

I appealed the verdict, but to no avail. I eventually won a small moral victory: On appeal, the DOT ordered Delta to pay me the difference between their fare and what I had to pay Air Tran, plus the added cab fares. After many additional calls and letters from Sheila Bedi, Delta sent me a check c/o Georgetown Law School, in the amount of $387.65. To this day I carry the receipt in my briefcase.

The So-Called Patriot Act

A nyway, back to April 2003. The NORML annual conference was going to be held in San Francisco late that month. I called American Airlines and made reservations on flights connecting through their hub at Dallas–Ft. Worth. I was put through to a supervisor and explained my need to take medical Cannabis during the layover. American had accommodated me in the past and I wasn't expecting a problem.

A few days later another supervisor called back to say that American could no longer arrange a room for me. I would have to make arrangements with the police department at the Dallas–Ft. Worth airport. He provided me the number.

I called and a sergeant answered. I told him my story and asked if the police could get me an isolated place to take my medicine at the airport. He was unresponsive. I asked, "Do you understand what I need?" He replied, "You want a room to smoke your dope." I said, "No, officer, I want a room to take my Federally prescribed medical Cannabis."

"Now that I know what flight you will be on," said the sergeant, "I'm going to arrest you for possession as soon as you get off the plane." Knowing I was talking to an uneducated cop and was not going to get anywhere with him, I said, "Since Federal law supercedes state law, shouldn't we notify the district attorney's office of your intentions?" After some stalling—he actually said he didn't know what county the plane would land in—he gave me the name and phone number of the Dallas County DA. His parting words were, "I'll see ya later."

I called the office of Dallas DA Bill Hill and left a message on his voice mail. About an hour later, I got a return call from the DA himself. He knew the sergeant threatened to arrest me. "After he arrests you, I will prosecute you," said Mr. Hill, to my surprise and dismay.

I said, "Sir, I can understand the sergeant's ignorance of the law, but you should know better. I'm under a Federal law and Federal law supersedes state law."

"You will be in Texas," he said.

"When did Texas secede from the United States?" I asked.

Now I was worried. I thought for a few minutes and decided to call the U.S. Attorney General's Office. I called and started telling my story. I was transferred to a lawyer and started anew, but again I was told I was talking to the wrong person. This happened over and over. I would get about three minutes into it and be told, "Sorry, I'm not the right person. Let me switch you to so-and-so." I estimate ten people at the Department of Justice heard part of my story before I reached a gentleman named Tim Estep.

I started telling my story and he didn't stop me. When I finished the short version, he started asking questions about the program that indicated he was familiar with it. After I answered them he said, "Okay, I believe you are one of the patients. You and I both know they cannot legally arrest you."

I said, "We know that, but the DA in Dallas County said he didn't care about Federal law, I would be in Texas."

Agent Estep said, "Most of the airport is in Tarrant County and I'm friends with the DA there. Do you have an attorney who could contact my friend on your behalf? I don't want you contacting him yourself."

I told him about my arrangement with Steptoe and Johnson. He gave me the name and email address of the reasonable DA, Mike Parrish, chief of the felony division. I called Andy Hefty and brought him up to speed. He then called Parrish on my behalf, and followed up with a letter asking Parrish to notify authorities at the airport and Dallas County of my medical use. Andy stated I would not be allowed to take my medicine inside the airport. He also sent a letter to the airport's Director of Public Safety.

I thanked Andy for his help and thought all was well. However, a couple of days later I got a phone call from an American Airlines supervisor saying because of my use of medical Cannabis, I would need to get a letter from one of my doctors saying I was coherent enough to follow instructions. I told him I had been flying with American for more than twenty-one years and never had a problem. Why now? I dropped the name of a supervisor who helped me in the past, and he said, "I know, I've talked to her. But we still need you to get a letter."

I told the supervisor I didn't think their request was legal and they would be hearing from my attorney. Next I called Shelia Bedi at Georgetown Law School, who had filed suit against Delta on my behalf with the Department of Transportation. After she stopped laughing, she agreed American's request was illegal and said she would help.

She got through to American Airline's lead attorney and explained their request for a letter from my doctor violated the Americans with Disabilities Act. She was told the request was valid under the new "Patriot Act." Sheila asked "How does the 'Patriot Act' allow you to make this request?" When the attorney couldn't cite a relevant section of the new law, Sheila said, "We will get you letters from two of his physicians, and as soon as Irvin gets back from California, we are going to file suit against you."

Sheila called to report what transpired. I told her I would get the letters, but added, "Since they are letting me fly, do we really have to file suit against them?" She said, "Since we are doing Delta Airlines for you, you will do American for us."

Just what I needed, another lawsuit.

I contacted Drs. Sanchez-Ramos and Russo and got letters from them stating I was not impaired by Cannabis and would be able to understand any and all instructions and be able to carry them out. Sheila forwarded these to American Airlines, and I then got an apologetic call from the supervisor who had been helpful in the past. She said I had been approved to travel. She had done everything in her power to prevent me from being made to jump through these absurd, insulting hoops.

•

On April 11, 2003, I spoke at the campus of University of Florida in Gainesville, sponsored by the NORML chapter. It's always rewarding speaking to students who are striving to make a difference. Six days later I flew out to the conference in San Francisco, where District Attorney Terence Hallinan gave the opening talk. I always feel at ease in settings where other people can use medical Cannabis. Activists from states where Prohibition is strictly enforced are amazed at the sight of sick people getting relief by taking their medicine outside the hotel, or in rooms where smoking is permitted. To the Californians it has ceased to be a big deal.

NORML conferences usually draw between four and five hundred people. Activists from all over the country report on the situation in their states, and share strategic ideas. At the 2003 meeting Ed Rosenthal, an Oakland-based writer and friend, described his conviction on cultivation charges in Federal court. Ed had been growing "clones"—cuttings from Cannabis plants that would grow into mature plants—for sale by California dispensaries. Legally, each clone was considered a plant. And because the prosecution was under Federal law, the jury was not allowed to take into account the plants were intended for medical use under state law.

The keynote speech was by travel writer Rick Steves, whose books and TV shows on PBS are familiar to millions of readers and viewers. Steves said "Most of Europe prefers to deal with marijuana as a health issue rather than a criminal one. Europe has learned you can't legislate personal morality. It's futile. It's counter-productive. Most Europeans believe society has to make a choice. You can tolerate alternative lifestyles, or you can build more prisons. In Europe they'd rather tolerate alternative lifestyles."

On May 22, 2003, Maryland passed a medical Cannabis bill allowing defendants possessing less than one ounce who can prove they used marijuana out of medical necessity and with a doctor's recommendation can use an affirmative defense in court against criminal charges of possession and/or cultivation. Meaning, plead guilty for medical use and you pay a $100.00 fine. Not the best law but, none-the-less, another state, another victory!

In September, we started back our monthly meetings with the South Florida Stock and Bond Club. We meet once a month from September thru May. As I was speaking to other members, Arthur Lenowitz, who had been badly hobbled by arthritis, came in walking with a normal gait. "Arthur, you look great," I told him. He said, "I'm on a new diet." I said, "I'm not talking about your weight, I'm talking about your walking." He explained he was on a diet that minimized the symptoms of arthritis. It involved giving up vegetables in the Nightshade family—tomatoes, white potatoes, peppers, and eggplant—and products containing Nightshades. It sounded simple, and Arthur's "anecdotal evidence" was very convincing. I have been on a no-Nightshades diet ever since, and I am convinced it eases my arthritis. I highly recommend anyone with arthritis try it….along with Cannabis.

•

In late September, I had another trip to California with a three-hour layover in Dallas. This time I left a message for the District Attorney's office in Tarrant County requesting a place to medicate. I soon got a call from Captain Rick Smith of the airport's police department. He said, "Irvin, I know you and have helped you in the past. But I've been informed by the district attorney of Tarrant County, not only can I not get you a room, but if we see you smoking your marijuana anywhere outside, we are to arrest you. You would then have to post bail, get an attorney, come to court, and in the end, you will win because Federal law DOES supersede state law. Then you would sue Tarrant County for false arrest, which you would win. Neither you or I need all that trouble, so please do us both a favor and not light up while you're here."

I was pissed and told him so. I also told him, "Captain Smith, if you know me, then you know I stand up for what I believe in. The national publicity would give this area a black eye. But y'all aren't worth it. I'm not about to waste my time on stupidity." So I didn't take my medicine during the layover.

•

One day in October my sales assistant was online playing a MSN game called "You Know It" when a question came up: "Irvin Rosenfeld sued Delta Air Lines because they kicked him off a plane for carrying this drug, which he used to relieve pain from a bone disease: A) Percodan B) Marijuana C) Tobacco D) Morphine." She called me into her office and we both had a good laugh. I was now famous enough to be trivia.

Newbridge Securities

On November 18, 2003, I changed brokerage firms and started working for Newbridge Securities in Fort Lauderdale. The firm was owned by two brokers I used to work with at GKN. They knew I didn't like moving around and assured me I could work at Newbridge for the rest of my career.

I was immediately happy with my move. I had complete support and my business flourished. The one negative was the company attorney and office manager did not know me or how I handled talking publicly about medical Cannabis. So my two friends asked me for the time being, to only identify myself publicly as a stockbroker from Ft. Lauderdale. I agreed, knowing once they saw me in action they would come around.

Since there were State and Federal law enforcement offices in the complex, Newbridge sent a letter notifying them of my employment and my use of legal marijuana. In response, our attorney received a letter from management stating I would only be allowed to take my medicine in the privacy of my own vehicle. When I read the letter, I realized there was more educating to be done. Even though I had two Supreme Court orders stating as a Federal patient I could take my medicine wherever smoking was allowed, I knew I had no choice but to comply. I'm always being hassled about my medicine, but thank God I have it.

The attorney informed me Newbridge was negotiating with management to rent more space and didn't want me to rock the boat. I got a handicapped parking spot close to the front door so I would not have to walk far to get to my car. They failed to realize the smell would travel to the area where people smoked cigarettes outside the door. So, being relegated to my auto didn't conceal my Federal-patient status for long. After a while I became just one of the gang (although occasionally someone would tell me they were amazed I could smoke so much and still work so efficiently). It was great starting the new year in a workplace I enjoyed going to everyday.

•

In early February, 2004, I got a call from Joshua Kessler, who worked for the company that produced "Penn and Teller: Bullshit" on Showtime. I had never seen the show. Kessler said they take a subject and reveal why it's "Bullshit." They were planning to do one on the "War on Drugs" and wanted me to be involved.

"We want to fly you to D.C.," Kessler said, "and show you smoking marijuana in a hotel room as we ask you questions and then on Capitol Hill and in front of the White House. What do you think?"

My first thought was, "Is this a setup? Do they want me to take my medicine in D.C. hoping a scene would take place with the police?" I asked for more details—what did they think the show could achieve and how did I fit in? "

The "War on Drugs" is ridiculous, and a total waste," said Kessler. "Nothing shows its absurdity more than the fact you are given a drug by the Federal Government that others are arrested for having. You are a professional and your medicine allows you to be a productive member of society, not a criminal. That's what we want to show."

This was an offer I couldn't refuse. I flew to Washington and was interviewed and filmed on Capitol Hill. I looked at the famous building where Congress made our laws, took a puff of my medicine, and said, "The Federal Government has been giving me this medicine for over 21 years and they don't even want to know how well it works."

We then went across to Pennsylvania Avenue and repeated the process with the White House in the background. There was one policeman there and he could have cared less I was smoking Cannabis. The taping went well and I had to admit I got a very special feeling taking my medicine with a backdrop of the White House.

I developed a routine at Newbridge Securities. If I had time after lunch—if the market could spare me for forty-five minutes, I would get in my car, drive to the back of the parking lot and park in the shade of some trees. This enabled me to get as far away from people as possible. I close my eyes to get myself into a biofeedback state, I put on sunglasses and listen to music at low volume while taking my medicine. That's how I try to get myself out of pain.

One day in late March, as I was in my car taking my medicine with my eyes closed, I heard a sudden pounding on all four windows. I opened my eyes and saw a man about 6 feet 7 waving a gold badge. "Get out of the car slowly," he said, "you're under arrest." I looked up at him and said, "I'll get out of the car slowly, but no, I'm not under arrest."

I got out of the car and there were eight men in plain clothes. One said, "Do you know who we are?" I said "No, I don't," although I had a pretty good idea. When they said, "The DEA," I said, "Well then you should be familiar with my medical-marijuana program, because the DEA oversees it."

"We don't know of any medical-marijuana program the DEA oversees."

"Well then you should be re-educated."

Of course they demanded to see proof. I pulled out a baggie with my prescription. One of the agents was nasty—the smallest one. He took the baggie and walked away with it to call the pharmacy. I got my tin can out from the car and a Fed Ex envelope with all my papers in it. I pulled out a copy of my protocol to show the agents, along with the *New York Times* article by Cheryl Stolberg. One of them said, "You could have made this up."

So then I got out *Newsweek* and turned to an article about me. "Do you think I made up the entire *Newsweek?*"

The nasty agent came back. I learned later he had called Serafin Gonzalez, the head pharmacist at Bascom Palmer, who had vouched for me and explained the program was real. But he was still suspicious: "If you're really overseen by the DEA, you should have some agents' names."

I said, "As a matter of fact, I do. I have the names of two agents in Washington. I've never met them, but I had their names and phone numbers from previous correspondences." They phoned Washington and got answering machines.

Then the nasty one had a thought: "Wait a minute! If this is real, your doctor has to have a schedule 1 license."

I said, "Very good."

He asked me my doctor's name and how to spell it. I told him and he made a phone call to confirm that a Schedule 1 license had been issued to him.

Even that wasn't enough to let a disabled man smoke medical Cannabis in the privacy of his car. "Who else do you know in the government?"

"Well, I have the phone number of an attorney with the FDA."

"What's his name?"

I said, "Her name..." They called and sure enough, got an answering machine.

Suddenly I remembered—just a few days earlier I had given a long phone interview to Tim Estep, the DEA agent in Washington who had helped me deal with the Dallas Airport! I don't know why I hadn't thought of it before. And I had his number on the folding rolodex I keep in my wallet.

The nasty agent called Tim Estep, walking away so I couldn't hear the conversation. Then he came back and said, "I have one question for you and you better get it right. What did you help this agent with last Sunday?"

"I helped him write his Master's thesis on medical marijuana," I said.

"Yeah, Tim," he said into his phone, "It is him... It is legal? They do supply patients with marijuana?"

Finally the investigation was complete. I asked, "Why did you do this to me today when I've been smoking my medicine here for four months?" I was told a visiting DEA agent had come downstairs and spotted me in my car. He called upstairs and said, "You dumb fucks, you're so stupid you got somebody smoking pot next to your own parking lot."

I asked how many agents worked in the office and was told, "That's classified."

I said, "It doesn't matter how many. Anytime you want, I'll come up there and educate all of them."

They told me not to park near their designated spots in the future.

"Where else can I park and be out of the sun?" I asked. I knew I had lost my place in the shade.

Back in my office I called Tim Estep. "There were eight agents out there," I told him. "Not one of them had heard of the Compassionate IND program."

He said, "That bothers me, too. Let me make a call and I'll get back to you." Next day he called and said, "Irvin, you're not going to believe this. Since the day your program was shut down, they stopped teaching DEA agents about it. So agents hired after 1992 would have no idea that such a program ever existed."

Intentional miseducation on the part of the government? Not that hard to believe.

A Sad Honor

I was back in Washington in April for the NORML annual conference. Whenever this event is held in the spring, the organizers plan it to fall on or close to April 20—4/20. The huge community that has developed in the fight against marijuana Prohibition has given special significance to the number 420 for reasons nobody can explain with certainty. Some say 4:20 was the time of day students at a high school in Mill Valley, California, used to meet at a nearby fountain to smoke marijuana in the afternoon. Others say it was police code for a marijuana bust in New Jersey or Connecticut. Or could it be the face of a clock at 4:20 resembles a person smoking a joint? Whatever the origin, placing special significance on 420 has become an in-joke shared by millions of Americans.

At the conference, NORML gave me its Peter McWilliams Memorial Award for advancing the cause of medical marijuana. McWilliams, whom I never met, was a man whose determination I could identify with. He had been a prolific author and the founder of a small publishing company, Prelude Press. Five of his books had made the New York Times bestseller list. In 1996 he was diagnosed with AIDS and non-Hodgkins lymphoma. At the time he was not a marijuana user.

"The chemotherapy and radiation for the cancer and combination therapy for the AIDS caused extreme nausea," he wrote in a memoir. "If you can't keep the life-saving pills in the system, they do no good. After trying all the prescription anti-nausea medications my doctors had to offer, I turned to medical marijuana. It ended the nausea within minutes and I was able to continue treatment. The cancer went into remission. My AIDS viral load dropped from 12,500 to undetectable. I told myself if I lived, I would devote my life to getting medical marijuana to all the sick people who needed it."

Being in California, he was able to take his campaign beyond the realm of public education. He financed a young friend, Todd McCormick, to grow different strains of Cannabis which would be made available to medical users—the idea being some strains would be more effective than others in treating certain conditions. McWilliams calculated that high-quality medical Cannabis could be grown for $28 an ounce. A libertarian, he wrote "The difference between $28 an ounce and $500 an ounce is what Milton Friedman calls 'the Drug-War tariff.'"

The DEA raided the large old house in Bel Air he had rented for the grow site. The raiders not only took the crop but came to McWilliams' house and seized computers containing all his business records and books-in-progress. A grand jury indicted him. The DEA agents arrested him and hauled him off to jail, where he went without AIDS medications for nine days. The conditions of his release prevented him from using medical marijuana. He appealed, citing California law, but a Federal judge ruled "We are not empowered to grant what amounts to a license to violate Federal law. Marijuana is classified as a Schedule 1 controlled substance. As such, Congress determined it has no currently accepted medical use."

McWilliams' last request was for placement in the Federal IND program. But no new patients were being admitted. He and Todd McCormick, were convicted on Federal charges of cultivation and conspiracy. While awaiting sentencing, unable to use marijuana to control his terrible nausea, McWilliams choked to death on his own vomit. McCormick went to Federal prison for more than four years.

Todd is a friend of mine and a patient, just like me.

•

One day of the NORML gathering in D.C. was devoted to calling on members of Congress. The *Washington Post* ran an article previewing our lobbying effort headed, "A Different Kind of Joint Session." Journalists wouldn't make such light-hearted puns—the top editors wouldn't let them— if they didn't all know marijuana is harmless. However, I think they make puns because they don't understand the seriousness of the medical issue and consider marijuana only a recreational get high drug. We somehow have to distinguish marijuana from medical Cannabis. The story noted that Capitol Police recently busted an intern for bringing a baggie of pot and a bong into the Cannon House Office Building..."But they will have to look the other way when stockbroker Irvin Rosenfeld brings his stash onto the same territory..." The *Post* quoted an attorney for the Capitol Police saying I could use marijuana legally but nobody else could.

•

While I was in Washington, Showtime aired the 30-minute Penn and Teller segment on the "War on Drugs." It ended with me taking my medicine in front of the White House and commenting on the government's hypocritical claim to be compassionate saying, "The Federal Government has supplied my medicine for over twenty-one years and they don't even want to know how well it works." Later in the year the segment was nominated for an Emmy, but lost. I thought it was extremely well done and deserved to win—but of course, I'm biased.

Continuing Medical Education

During the third week of May, Debbie and I flew to Roanoke, Virginia. First, we visited my nephew Dr. Gary Bennett, his wife Anita, and their beautiful daughter, Taylor. Gary grew up seeing me take my medicine, so he didn't start off prejudiced against Cannabis. He went to medical school and became a family practitioner. He has a way of explaining to a patient what is wrong with them so they understand what needs to be done. He's a competent physician who uses all his knowledge of medicine to treat his patients. I hope one day he will have the right to prescribe medical Cannabis if he sees fit.

Then it was off to Charlottesville for the third biennial Patients Out of Time conference. Virginia is Mary Lynn Mathre and Al Byrne's home, and they arranged for sponsorship from the University of Virginia School of Medicine and the Pain Management Center. In this they had help from Dr. John Rowlingson, the pain specialist who years ago doubted my claim Cannabis worked for me. Not many people are capable of changing their outlook, but Dr. Rowlingson did just that as the evidence Cannabis relieves pain mounted over the years.

The UVA School of Law co-sponsored the conference (thanks to Richard Bonnie, the attorney who helped me get a hearing before the FDA panel), along with the School of Nursing and the Virginia Nurses Association. Virginia is conservative, politically, and acceptance of the conference on Cannabis therapeutics was a testament to years of educational work by many activists. I admit to feeling some home-state pride.

The highlight for me was getting to meet Raphael Mechoulam, the Israeli researcher who is the "grand old man" of the cannnabinoid field. In the early 1960s Mechoulam and a colleague at the Weizman Institute in Israel, Yehiel Gaoni, isolated and identified the chemical structures of delta-9 THC and many other compounds in the Cannabis plant. They coined the term "cannabinoid" to describe them.

Mechoulam then spent many years trying to figure out how THC worked—its "mechanism of action" at the cellular level. In 1988 Allyn Howlett, a researcher at the University of St. Louis and a graduate student, Bill Devane, identified a cannabinoid receptor in the brain.

Mechoulam and other scientists realized the receptor didn't exist to respond to a compound in a plant, and began looking for compound(s) in the brain that activated it. With Devane, who had come to work in his lab, Mechoulam spent two years overcoming tremendous technical problems. Eventually they isolated a compound Devane proposed naming "anandamide," after the Sanskrit word for "supreme joy." Mechoulam says he "looked for a suitable Hebrew equivalent, but nothing came to my mind. There are lots of synonyms for 'sorrow' in Hebrew, but considerably less for 'joy.'"

What I will always remember about Dr. Mechoulam is how nice and down to earth he is. Of course I told him about my bone disorder and how I didn't get a high from the medicine. He said, "Maybe your cannabinoid system is defective, or maybe your body is using it differently. Just be happy it works." That was my sentiment exactly!

•

One speaker, a California doctor named Tom O'Connell, presented his study on 622 of his patients. O'Connell is a thoracic surgeon and former Army officer who came out of retirement to start a Cannabis-oriented practice in Oakland. His patients have no regular doctor, or are reluctant to ask their regular doctors for approval to use Cannabis, or have doctors unwilling to issue approvals. They find O'Connell and a small but growing group of pro-Cannabis doctors through the Internet and word of mouth.

He said the majority of his patients use Cannabis for anxiety, stress and depression—although many emphasize their physical problems when he takes their history, assuming their psychological problems won't entitle them to an approval. Many people remain ashamed about their "mental illness" or "psychological conditions." Somehow emotional pain is not "real pain." Emotional handicaps that can prevent one from working or enjoying life are not judged to be "real" as "physical" handicaps. This is a problem for our society, and for the persons who suffer from them. Many don't feel entitled to treatment of their conditions the way they would if they had a physical disorder. O'Connell called for wider recognition that stress and depression are prevalent in our society, even among young, able-bodied people. Strong drugs like Prozac and Xanax are widely prescribed, so why shouldn't Cannabis, with its benign side-effects, be an option as well? [As a side note, I find it interesting that Dr. Grinspoon, a psychiatrist, was so clear about the medicinal value of Cannabis for physical and physiological conditions, and that Dr. O'Connell, a surgeon, was so sensitive to the medicinal value of Cannabis for treating emotional illnesses.]

I wondered what Bob Randall would have made of Dr. O'Connell's practice. Bob always distinguished medical use of Cannabis from recreational use, and the patients he tried to organize had severe physical noticeable problems. Neither he nor I had much knowledge of the use of Cannabis for stress related disorders. Bob's immediate goal was getting people into the Federal IND program. His longer-range goal was re-scheduling. Bob said many times he did not appreciate Dennis Peron's famous line, "In a country where they give Prozac to shy teenagers, all marijuana use is medical." I doubt he would have appreciated O'Connell's variation on it either: "all chronic marijuana use is medical."

•

Among the conference attendees was Susan Henry, a producer of the Montel Williams Show on Fox. She told me they were considering doing a show on medical Cannabis and might want me to take part. Montel has a personal interest on the subject, she said. He is a Multiple Sclerosis patient and can use Cannabis legally in California for pain relief, but is unprotected in New York. After announcing that he's breaking the law every day, he had not been fired or arrested.

In May, 2004, Vermont legislators approved a narrow medical marijuana bill allowing only patients suffering from AIDS, cancer, and multiple sclerosis to possess up to 12 plants or 2.5 ounces of cultivated marijuana. Governor James Douglas (R) allowed it to pass into law unsigned. Vermont became the eleventh state to pass a medical Cannabis law.

Tenacious

On Wednesday evenings during daylight savings time, we skippers have "beer can races" at Shake-A-Leg—friendly events in which people who want to learn how to sail volunteer as crew, and others just go along for the ride. The racing is fun, but we all want to win.

On the last Wednesday in May, I skippered a Freedom 20. I had four people on board, including a pleasant chap from England. I explained my Cannabis use and asked if it would bother anyone if I lit up. No one had a problem.

As we were sailing out to the race course, my companions introduced themselves. Grahme, who was British, said he was the cook aboard "Tenacious," as if we should know what that meant. I said, "What is 'Tenacious?'"

He explained the British ship was the largest wooden sailing ship in the world, 213 feet long—and one of only two tall ships set up for people with disabilities. It was equipped with lifts (elevators) so wheelchairs can be moved from one deck to another. The crew had been in Miami for two weeks and would be starting the Tall Ship race on Monday, racing from Miami to Jacksonville, then Charleston, Baltimore, Boston, and ending in Nova Scotia before heading back to their home port in Portsmouth, England.

Grahme said twelve people from Shake-A-Leg were going on the first and second legs as "voyage passengers." Tenacious had five full-time crew members, four part-time, and the rest of the crew was made up of the voyage passengers. There was to be a cookout on Saturday for Shake-A-Leg members and all the passengers flying in from the United Kingdom who would be sailing to Charleston.

This sounded very tempting, but I thought, "Oh, my medicine." I asked Graham if he thought my medical Cannabis use would keep me from being a voyage passenger from Miami to Jacksonville. He said, "You are allowed to bring on board any prescription, so it wouldn't be a problem. But the passengers learn to work together and don't change until every two ports of call." This meant those who sailed from Miami were committed to Charleston. Grahme suggested I talk to a Captain Fisher, who was racing on one of the other boats. I found it hard to believe my Cannabis wasn't going to be a problem.

We won two out of the three races and headed back to the dock. Grahme introduced me to Captain Fisher, a distinguished-looking middle-aged man. I explained I had been away and not down at SAL for a few weeks, hadn't known about Tenacious, and would like to be considered as a passenger. "But before you answer," I went on, "I have two concerns…" I explained my bone disorders and that I was prescribed Cannabis by the United States Government. I showed him my prescription and he said, "So what's the problem? Everyone is allowed to bring on board all prescriptions." This sure was a different attitude than I was used to. "What's your second concern?"

I said, "I can only sail to Jacksonville because of my work." He replied, "Normally we don't like anyone leaving early because it can hinder the group you're assigned to. But I will make an exception for you. You need to get Shake-A-Leg's approval, have them fax you the forms, fill them out ASAP and fax them to the Jubilee Sailing Trust Foundation in England for final approval. You need to do this quickly. You board Saturday."

I thanked him profusely and drove home hoping I could pull it off. The next day, I called Harry Horgan at SAL, he sent me the forms, and I filled them out and faxed them to England. The approval came the next day! I had no idea what I was in for.

On Saturday Debbie and I drove down to Port of Miami with the gear I would need for the week. When we saw Tenacious, we were awed by its size and magnificence. It is a three-masted square-rigged sailing ship—a "barque"- that had been finished in 2002 but looked right out of the 18th century.

I asked the mate on duty for permission to board. I felt like a real sailor going to sea. I was shown where my bunk was and stowed my gear. By nightfall there would be a total of twenty-nine voyage passengers. I met the rest of the crew as I walked around the ship, and looked forward to meeting the rest of the passengers.

Captain Fisher welcomed everyone and introduced the crew. He told us what we would be expected to do. Everything on Tenacious was done by hand, or hands as the case may be (as opposed to machinery). The only way the sails got set was by climbing the mast, going out on the braces (booms) and lowering them. Everyone was crew and would be assigned duties. Our twenty-nine passengers included six people in wheelchairs, one with two artificial legs, and my racing partner, Victor Brown, who was ninety-five percent blind and me. The rest were able-bodied. There were sixteen men and thirteen women, with an average age fifty.

We each were assigned a watch and met our watch leader. It was his or her responsibility to make sure that we were where we needed to be, and on time. My group consisted of me, Karen Mitchell, the guy with two artificial legs, and four others who were able-bodied.

The cookout ended. I kissed Debbie goodbye and said, "I will see you in a week." We all settled in and started getting to know each other.

Before turning in for the night, I rolled enough medicine for the next day and gave the ship's nurse the rest to lock away. That worked well for the entire week.

The next day-and-a-half we were given a crash course on all facets of the ship. Our duties included sailing and cleaning the ship and working in the kitchen. Every morning from 9:00 am., to 10:00 am. was "happy hour." Unless you were on kitchen duty, everyone was assigned an area to clean. It was called "happy hour" because everyone was happy to finish.

On Monday morning we got our first and only lesson on climbing the mast, which was 124 feet 8 inches above the deck. Just think about having to climb 125 feet, and then walk out twenty-five feet on the braces (booms) and either dropping the sails or pulling them up. There were five different levels of braces going up the main. We were fitted with harnesses which could hook up to safety lines once you got to the first level at twenty-five feet. You had to climb the outside riggings to get there.

One by one, each person climbed. Some stopped at the first level, while others climbed all the way to the top. Even Victor made it to the first level. I was not planning on trying. Besides having tumors everywhere, which would make climbing difficult to say the least, I am not fond of heights. However, the nurse thought I should try. Not wanting to act like a wimp, I gave it a go. I started climbing outside on the riggings thinking a real sailor should be able to do this. I got up about fifteen feet when I started pulling muscles in my left leg. I was never so happy to have muscle spasms. I yelled down to the nurse what was happening and told her I could make it back down. I got to the deck and she saw the muscles pulling. She asked me if there was anything she could do? I said, "Let me just sit down and start smoking." After about two joints (forty-minutes) I was able to get up and walk. That was the only duty on the ship I was excused from. Oh well, I was still a real sailor.

At 2:00 pm., with Captain Fisher at the helm, we left the dock to start the race. As we got to the ocean, we set the sails and made ready for the start. We saw our competition, which included two smaller ships and a ship about our size which was the pride of the Mexican Navy with an able-bodied crew of 125.

I was on watch as the race was about to start. The Captain called me over and said, "Take the wheel and keep it steady." I took the wheel as ordered and all the spectator boats from Shake-A-Leg yelled good luck. There I was guiding a 213-foot ship as the gun went off to start the race. I had goose bumps all over. That's what I call a real "high!"

I had watch on Wednesday from 4:00 am., to 8:00 am. I reported for duty and was told to take the wheel and keep it on course. I was then left alone. I looked at the sky and saw more stars than I ever had. I thanked God again for my health and good fortune.

We crossed the finish line on Wednesday evening outside of Jacksonville in first place. That's right, we won. Not bad for a bunch of inexperienced sailors and gimps.

On Thursday, we sailed into the harbor and docked the ship. The city threw a big party that night for all the sailors. Besides our four ships, another four had arrived to race the next leg, including the U.S.S. Eagle, pride of the U.S. Coast Guard. It was docked right behind us. I wondered if my smoke was being carried over to them.

All too soon the week was coming to an end. On Saturday, I was again on duty from 4:00 am., to 8:00 am. Since the ship was docked, there wasn't a lot to do. The weather was hot and sticky with no breeze. The harbor was still and quiet. At 7:00 am. I was told to raise the flags. I raised the British flag first and than figured it would be appropriate to be smoking my medicine as I raised the American flag. So I lit up, and just as I started raising the flag, loud speakers all around our ship started blaring out the Star Spangled Banner—as played by Jimi Hendrix- at top volume. Our head engineer had arranged everything and that's why my watch had duty again at that time. The entire harbor reverberated as I raised the American flag on a British ship, smoking a joint, with the U.S.S. Eagle docked right in front of us. It was one of those moments one will never forget.

I had never worked so hard in my life, nor had I ever enjoyed a week more. When I asked for permission to leave the ship I was almost in tears. The ship, the people, the camaraderie, the sailing—what a time! I will be back.

If anyone would like to sail on Tenacious, go to www.jst.org.uk and tell them Irvin Rosenfeld from Shake-A-Leg Miami sent you.

Montel

Also in May, I heard from Susan Henry, Senior Producer of the Montel Williams Show saying they were planning a show on Medical Cannabis sometime in the future and wanted me to participate, which I agreed to do. It wasn't until early September that they sent a camera crew to tape me at work with the usual scenes. I flew to New York the night of September 8, and went to the studio the next day. Montel and his producers had gone all-out to present a complete overview of the medical-marijuana issue. The pro-Cannabis line-up included Angel Raich, Dr. Donald Abrams, Rob Kampia of the Marijuana Policy Project, and the mother of an emotionally troubled child who had experienced dramatic benefit. The prohibitionists included Dr. Andrea Barthwell, formerly of the Drug Czar's office, and Roger Curtiss, an addiction specialist.

Angel's story came first, accompanied by photos from her scrapbook. As a young mother of two she had been immobilized by a brain tumor, degenerative joint disease, and other maladies. She had been in a wheelchair for four years and couldn't use the right side of her body. "I tried all the drugs, nothing was working. My daughter asked, 'Why can't you do the things other mommies do?'"

In 1997 she had attempted suicide. At that point a nurse asked if she had ever tried medical marijuana. "I was extremely offended," Angel told Montel. "I was very conservative, a mother of two, all I could think of was the cops coming to put me in handcuffs." But out of desperation she tried it, and a year-and-a-half later she was able to stop using a wheelchair. Her inoperable brain tumor stabilized and she became a functioning mom.

Over footage of Angel inhaling mist from a vaporizer, Montel reminded the audience to "Get rid of the image of smoking it. Three days a week I don't smoke it at all, I eat it."

Coming back from a commercial break Montel shook his head in dismay as he noted five million Ritalin prescriptions had been filled last year in the U.S… This was the lead-in to the heart-wrenching story of Debbie Jeffreys, whose son had been put on Ritalin, Adderall, Clonazepam, Clonidine, Depakote, Dexadrine, Imipramine, Mellarel, Neurontin, Risperal, Seroquel, Wellbutrin, Zoloft, and Zyprexa, often with horrendous side-effects. When a California doctor approved marijuana use, the troubled boy's life "changed immediately," according to his mother. "He said, 'Mommy, I feel happy, my head's not noisy.'"

After the next commercial break, the focus was on me. Montel told my story, and I recounted the history of the Federal IND Program. I held my government-issued can of Cannabis, while the camera zoomed in to show the label: "Marijuana Cigarettes... Use twelve per day as directed."

Andrea Barthwell defended the government's approach. She said, "Trying to bring medications to the marketplace through a popular vote is just setting modern medicine back... to when snake oil salesmen handed out medications from the back of stagecoaches."

Montel was on his feet with my can of Cannabis. "We're not handing it out in stagecoaches! The government's sending this out! Your doctors approved the protocol."

"There are some exceptions," Barthwell acknowledged, "and there are other patients that could get it through exceptions." This was not true since the Federal IND Program had been closed since 1992 to any new patients. I was too polite to interrupt. She went on to say, "The research should follow the same scientific principles we follow for all other medications."

That drew me in: "I've been getting this medicine for twenty-two years from the Federal Government, and they don't want to research me. They don't even want to know what's happening with me." I described Ethan Russo's examination of the surviving Federal patients.

Barthwell reiterated: "In looking at the crude botanical, it has not met the test of medicine."

Montel confronted her. "If it hasn't met the test, then you shouldn't be giving it. But since you're shipping it, it must have met some test... You sit here and say we have to still do studies. Well, while you're still doing studies, let the government deliver it to me!" The audience burst into applause.

Montel brandished a bottle of hydrocodone. "I can take one to two tablets every four hours. It takes me twenty of these a day to knock down my pain. I can read in the PDR all the adverse effects of this drug. ...I can barely walk. Why can't the Federal Government expand this program to include people like myself so that I don't have to worry about getting locked up?"

Cut to a commercial showing Peggy Fleming, the champion figure skater, pushing a drug that supposedly gives her "younger bones." During this break and others, I would tell Montel points I thought should be made. Generally, he would start the next segment making the point himself. Montel Williams is a powerful spokesperson for medical Cannabis, and I was glad to be able to join forces and provide him with additional ammunition.

The show ended with Montel calling for moving marijuana from Schedule 1 to Schedule 2. "What is the problem? What is the fear?" he asked.

After the show aired, many people asked what Montel was really like. I would say, "He's just another patient who doesn't want to be called a criminal and chance losing everything because he has an illness that responds best to Cannabis."

Debbie recorded the Montel show on a VHS tape that included an episode of *Penn and Teller's Bullshit,* which I brought to work to show the company attorney. He brought it back, saying "I had no idea... now I understand." From that time on, I've asked and gotten permission to identify myself as a broker with Newbridge Securities when I do interviews.

In October, Jed Riffe released *Waiting to Inhale,* the documentary he had worked on for more than four years. Riffe had filmed many people on both sides of the medical Cannabis issue, including Debbie and myself. His approach was fair and balanced. I thought our message came across well. I encourage everyone to see it.

•

On November 2, 2004, sixty-two percent of Montana voters voted "yes" on a medical marijuana bill. Patients and caregivers were allowed to grow six plants and to possess one ounce of usable marijuana. The program was to be run by the state Department of Public Health & Human Services Bureau of Licensure. That made twelve states! (As a side note, President Bush only received fifty-nine percent of the vote.)

A City for Lincoln

The early part of the year is always nice in South Florida. The cold weather makes me feel bad, so I rarely fly north during the winter months. However this year would be different.

In February 2005, at MPP's request, I traveled to Springfield, Illinois to address a committee of the state legislature that was considering a medical-marijuana bill. The hearing room was packed. The White House sent John Walters, the Drug Czar, to testify, and he was going first.

With tin can in hand, I found a seat at the end of the front row. Standing in front of me was a tall man in a suit with a monitor in his ear. I looked around and realized I was among Walters' entourage.

The Drug Czar started giving his line. When he compared medical marijuana to crack cocaine, heroin, and methamphetamine, it really pissed me off. Why does the other side always compare hard drugs to medical Cannabis? I ostentatiously picked up my plastic bag and took my tin can out and put it in my lap, slowly turning it so the committee and the people around me could see it. This was my way of protesting.

After several minutes the tall man in the suit leaned down to me and quietly said, "I'm a Federal Marshal. What's in the can?" I said quietly, "I'm a Federal patient and I have my Federal Medical Marijuana in the can." He stood back up against the wall and didn't say another word to me.

After Walters spoke, he answered a few questions, and then he and his entourage got up and left. He wouldn't even stay to hear me! How I wish I could have debated him. But government officials don't want to take that chance. Obviously, they're afraid.

Next it was my turn. I said all I could in the allotted eight minutes. (There had been no time limit on Walters' testimony.) I answered questions for about five minutes and then they took the vote, which was seven to four against the bill. Two of the Democratic members who told MPP they were going to vote in favor evidentially bowed to pressure from the White House and voted against it.

•

Some reporters motioned for me to join them outside the hearing room. Before I could start answering their questions, two Capitol Police interrupted and said I needed to go with them. When I asked why, I was told, "It's about what you are carrying in your bag." I said, "I'm carrying my legal medical Cannabis."

With the reporters in tow, (which bolstered my confidence) I accompanied the policemen. My ankle hurt terribly, due to exposure to the cold weather. When we came to a stairwell I told the police because of my bone disorders, I only used stairs in an emergency. They took me to an elevator but would not let the reporters on board.

The elevator descended, and the officers led me down a long corridor. We turned a corner and I could see the reporters and an officer standing by a desk. I was told to turn and walk down another long hallway. I said, "No, I'm in pain and I'm not walking anymore. There is a perfectly good desk and chair where I can sit. I will be glad to assist you, but from that desk."

The police granted my request. They asked for proof my marijuana was legal and I gave them the March 1983 letter from the FDA stating the Federal statute I was under, and the phone number of Tim Estep, the most reasonable DEA agent I had dealt with.

The officers went down the hallway and disappeared. The reporters started asking their questions. I was answering them when two more Capitol Police showed up pushing a wheelchair. They said, "Get in. You said you didn't want to walk anymore, so we got you this wheelchair." I said, "That's okay, I'm going to wait here." They said, "GET IN THE CHAIR NOW." I said, "Am I being detained?" One officer said "yes" so softly the reporters didn't hear him. I loudly repeated my question and the other officer said, "Would you please get in the chair so we can help clear this up."

I got in the chair and they wheeled me down two more hallways with the reporters in tow. We came to a door and I was brought into the Capitol's underground police station. They would not let the reporters in. There were about seven officers in uniform, plus a very tall man in plainclothes who seemed to be in charge. He came over and introduced himself as Captain Somebody. He thanked me for being so helpful with this unusual situation.

I said, "Captain, I just testified before your legislative committee with Federal Marshals, State Troopers, and your own Capitol Police in attendance and they didn't question my Federal exemption. I came to your great state to educate, so that's what I'm doing." He said he had talked to Tim Estep and was awaiting a fax about my case.

He asked several questions about my bone disorders, which I answered. Then the phone rang and I could hear him saying, "Yes, uh-huh, okay, thanks." He then turned and said I was free to go. I asked, "Was there ever a time I was not free to go?" He just smiled.

Back at the hearing room, no one knew what had become of me. Rep. Larry McKeon, D-Chicago, sponsor of the bill was outraged when the reporters told him I had been detained by the Capitol Police. I told him everything was fine, I had just educated ten more officers about medical Cannabis.

We held a press conference and Rep. McKeon blasted the Capitol Police. My detention, he said, was an example of why Illinois needed a medical marijuana law to protect patients.

I said my goodbyes and headed back to Chicago so I could fly home and warm up. On the way we heard a report on the hearing from radio station WLS. It was highly critical of the Capitol Police.

Headlines the next day included "Legal Medical Marijuana Patient Detained After Testifying For Legislation," and "Medical Marijuana Patient Detained After Bill Sinks In State Committee." My situation got more coverage than the Drug Czar, taking away from the real story, being patients in Illinois are suffering and need help. But he, and the powerful forces he represents, kept the bill tied up in committee. To this day the people of Illinois are denied the right to use medical Cannabis.

Censorship in Action

Prohibition could not continue if the American people knew that marijuana was safe and effective medicine. Therefore, the drug companies and others who have a vested interested in keeping it illegal must sometimes resort to outright censorship. The process can be as subtle as involving a threat to withhold advertising revenues.

Los Angeles Times reporter Eric Bailey was assigned by *AARP The Magazine*—a bimonthly with 25 million readers over age 50— to write an article on medical marijuana and the elderly. I did a lengthy phone interview with Bailey in 2003 and expected his piece to have a big educational impact sometime the following year. He interviewed Philip Denney, MD, a Cannabis knowledgeable California doctor, and Republican Congressman Dana Rohrbacher, the co-sponsor of legislation to make the DEA honor state medical-marijuana laws. Bailey also interviewed the Drug Czar John Walters, who said that "feeling better" was not a valid measure of a drug's effectiveness.

Bailey was told the article would run in the fall of 2004, but it got held. In the November-December issue AARP plugged a soon-to-be published article on medical marijuana and published the results of a survey in which seventy-two percent of Americans over forty-five agreed that "adults should be allowed to legally use marijuana for medical purposes if a physician recommends it." Jay Leno based a joke on the AARP survey: "Nearly seventy-five percent of elderly Americans approve of the legalization of medical marijuana. And you thought grandpa used to forget stuff before!" (Again, the fight with stereotyping)

The prospect of an informative article reaching twenty-five million voters moved the Drug Warriors to action, and AARP soon found itself under attack. "From Pot to Porn to AARP: How the Seniors Magazine is Aiding the Dope Lobby" was the headline in the "Accuracy in Media" Newsletter.

AARP Editor Ed Dwyer had worked for *High Times* in the '70s, and this twenty-five-year-old fact supposedly proved that Bailey's piece would be biased! Guilt by past affiliation and by association, are the hallmarks of "McCarthyism."

As a card-carrying member of AARP, I wrote the editors of their magazine: "I cannot think of a good reason for AARP to kill an article about an ancient non-toxic plant that has real and potential therapeutic applications. What's not suitable about this topic for the most mature and experienced American citizens?"

Of course, I never got an answer. Bailey eventually got a release and the *L.A. Times Magazine* published a much shorter version of his article.

Lobbying Day

Tim Estep, the DEA agent who had come to my aid several times, asked me to look him up the next time I was in Washington. The opportunity presented itself May 3, 2005, when I took part in a lobbying effort organized by the Marijuana Policy Project.

Tim invited me to meet at his office in Arlington and visit the new DEA museum. I said, "I feel a little uncomfortable about doing that, I'll be on my way to Congress with my tin can." He proposed a meeting at a nearby Starbuck's. I got there first and sat down at a table. Then he came in and introduced himself—a man in his fifties wearing a coat and tie, I wouldn't have picked him out as a DEA agent. After we'd been there about ten minutes a group of five guys came in and Tim waved them over. "Come over here, I want to introduce you to somebody..." They all had DEA IDs "This is Irvin Rosenfeld, he's one of the patients who gets Federal marijuana."

I had showed Tim my tin can, which he insisted on showing to all of the agents. He pulled the lid off, and said, "Look, this is the marijuana that we send him!" These were high-ranking agents, including some division heads. They had questions, which I was able to answer. It was all very friendly.

No sooner had they left than another five guys came along and Tim waved them over and went through the same routine. He introduced me as a Federal patient, showed them the tin can, and had me answer their questions about the program. I realized he had it all planned.

Then came a third group—three agents this time. While we were talking, Tim noticed another agent and waved for him to come over. "This is Irvin Rosenfeld, he's one of the Federal patients we send medical marijuana to." He opened the tin can and said, "This is the marijuana we send him." It was the same story he gave the other guys, but this time the response was different. The agent glared at Tim and the others, glared at me, and said, "Well, I guess so." Then he did an about face and stormed off.

"What was that all about?" I asked, as they were trying not to laugh.

Tim said snickering, "His one and only job is to oppose medical marijuana." I didn't know what to make of the fact they found this situation funny.

Tim asked if I felt comfortable enough to visit the DEA Museum, which is in a room on the ground floor of their headquarters in Arlington. I said, "Sure."

We went across the street and entered the building. Tim took my canister as I had to go thru a metal detector and then was given a visitors badge with my name on it.

We walked down the hall to the museum. The curator, whose secretary had been on the staff of Francis Young, was planning a section devoted to medical marijuana. I was asked if I would provide four of my tin cans and narrate a video for visitors explaining the Compassionate IND program. I said I would be glad to under one condition: the exhibit also display the opinion of Francis Young on the case of NORML v. DEA.

This turned out to be a deal breaker. The DEA higher-ups want to decide which elements of history should be remembered and which should be erased. That the government provides medical marijuana to (a few) people in need: admirable, that the government refuses to allow medical marijuana use by (many) people in need: mum's the word.

To my regret, I was not allowed to keep my visitor's badge, which was in the shape of an agent's badge. I was very glad, however, to have met Tim Estep, face-to-face. It's good to have a DEA agent on your side and who understands where I'm coming from.

•

I was in Washington to lobby for an amendment to a funding bill that would stop the DEA raids on growers and dispensaries in states that had medical-marijuana laws. First introduced in 2003 by Rep. Maurice Hinchey (D.-NY) and Dana Rohrabacher (R-Cal.) it lost by a 152-273 vote. In 2004 it lost 148-261.

I had a 9:00 am. meeting with Eric Cantor, a Virginia Republican high up in the House leadership. We had some close mutual friends, and I expected he would take me seriously. But I knew as soon as I saw the look on his aide's face I was in for a disappointment. She said the Congressman had been asked by the President to attend an emergency breakfast meeting at the White House. I told her why I had come, and that I looked forward to meeting with Rep. Cantor in the future.

Later that morning I called on a representative of Rep. Bobby Scott, a Virginia Democrat. When I mentioned my meeting with Rep. Cantor had been canceled, he said, "I'll bet they gave you that excuse about an emergency breakfast meeting called by the President."

I asked, "How did you know?"

He laughed. "Because it's true. That's where he was."

As always, the heart of my pitch was my own medical history. With Republicans I often emphasize the rights of the individual, which conservatives uphold in principle. Unfortunately, they vote as if the "War on Drugs" takes precedence over the individual rights of American citizens. Isn't the right to decide what you're going to take into your body the ultimate individual right?

We all did our best by lobbying one on one and doing newspaper and television interviews. It was good seeing a lot of my friends and Montel again.

On May 10, 2005, The *Los Angeles Times Magazine* ran a shortened version of Eric Bailey's article that *AARP The Magazine* had spiked. He described the Federal program as having "seven survivors" and quoted me calling it "the most exclusive club aside from ex-living-presidents." It was even more exclusive than I knew—two of the patients who had maintained their anonymity had died, and our number was down to five.

Bailey noted that pharmaceutical companies are trying to develop cannabinoid-like drugs—which was a good reason to maintain prohibition, according to Drug Czar Walters, but not to the humane Dr. Mechoulam. "During the buildup to prescription forms, the raw plant shouldn't be ignored, said Dr. Raphael Mechoulam, a pioneer in cannabinoid chemistry at Hebrew University of Jerusalem. If it helps the elderly fight pain until prescription drugs are available, he said, 'then why not?'" Again, Dr. Mechoulam had expressed my sentiments exactly.

•

On May 18, 2005, I flew to Providence, Rhode Island to testify on a medical Cannabis bill. I met Rep. Thomas Slater, who introduced the bill, and Rhonda O'Donnell, a Multiple Sclerosis patient and registered nurse, a leading proponent. They were confident the law would get passed, but doubted the governor would sign it. They said they had enough votes to override a veto but it might not be the right thing to do politically. Since I didn't know Rhode Island politics, I didn't question their reasoning.

Members of the Health, Education and Welfare Committee seemed sympathetic as I introduced myself as a Federal patient. I described the IND program and emphasized the Feds had closed it to new patients since 1992. Since no one else who needed Cannabis could become a Federal patient, it was up to the states to provide access.

The bill was passed by the Rhode Island General Assembly, only to be vetoed by Governor Donald Carcieri. The legislators did override the veto, and on Jan. 3, 2006, Rhode Island would become the 12h state to enact a medical-marijuana law.

Doctors could approve patients with cancer, glaucoma, HIV, wasting syndrome, severe pain, nausea, seizures, spasms, Alzheimer's agitation "or any other medical condition or its treatment approved by the state Department of Health." Patients and caregivers could grow up to 12 plants or possess 2.5 ounces of marijuana. The law established a mandatory, confidential state-run registry to issue identification cards. Another victory…I could get used to this!

Gonzalez v. Raich

On June 6, 2005, the U.S. Supreme Court ruled 6-3 against Angel Raich and Diane Monson. The DEA could still arrest anyone in the country who grew or possessed Cannabis, no matter how dire their need, except the five surviving Federal patients.

Angel and Diane were California medical marijuana users who tried to enjoin the DEA from confiscating their marijuana and raiding their suppliers. They argued that the Feds had no jurisdiction to enforce the Federal Controlled Substances Act against them because their activities didn't affect interstate commerce. After failing to get an injunction from a District Judge, they went to the United States Court of Appeals for the Ninth Circuit, which ordered that the injunction be granted. The Bush Administration appealed to the U.S. Supreme Court, which heard arguments in November 2004. The case started out as Raich v. Ashcroft but was decided as Gonzales v. Raich.

Justice John Paul Stevens, who wrote the majority opinion, was joined by Justices Anthony Kennedy, David Souter, Ruth Bader Ginsburg, and Steven Breyer. Regulating the cultivation and use of marijuana in California "is squarely within Congress's commerce power," Stevens wrote. In one of the most remarkable declarations written in a Supreme Court opinion, Justice Stevens and the majority seemed to be encouraging the losing parties, Raich and Monson that they "could seek to have marijuana rescheduled by the DEA" or avail themselves of "the democratic process, in which the voices of voters allied with these respondents may one day be heard in the halls of Congress."

Antonin Scalia wrote a concurring opinion trying to explain why, although he advocated limits on federal power in principle, he did not in this case. (He couldn't come right out and say "the War on Drugs takes precedence over the Constitution.")

Justice Sandra Day O'Connor's dissent repeated Justice Brandeis's famous line "a single courageous State may, if its citizens choose, serve as a laboratory and try novel social and economic experiments without risk to the rest of the country." O'Connor added, "This case exemplifies the role of States as laboratories."

Chief Justice William Rehnquist (Who was author of the Controlled Substance Act) and Justice Clarence Thomas stayed true to their states–rights line by dissenting. Thomas wrote an eloquent separate dissent.

•

Minutes after the verdict was announced I got an interview request from Karen Raffensperger, a producer for CBS Evening News, followed by a request from Aaron Brown of CNN, and many others. With clearance from Newbridge Securities' attorney, I was able to use our conference room for the interviews I gave that afternoon. I did my best to explain the ruling in Gonzales v. Raich did not change any current state laws, nor did it cancel the Federal IND program.

The disappointing ruling in the Raich case was followed in mid-June by a vote in Congress against the Hinchey-Rohrabacher Amendment. This time the vote was 161-264.

Taking On the Sailing Establishment

Victor Brown and I had come in second in our qualifying races at Shake-A-Leg, and planned to compete in the North American Challenge Cup in Chicago in August. We had raced once before in the Challenge Cup, and finished a disappointing twelfth out of fourteen teams. We were hoping to do much better this time.

In July 2005 I got a phone call at work from a woman at U.S. Sailing, the governing body that establishes rules and regulations, organizes races, etc. She said I had not applied for an exemption to use Cannabis during the race in Chicago. I said, "I don't need an exemption. I'm one of the Federal patients." She said, "But, it's a banned substance." I replied, "I know it's a banned substance—except for me and four others." She repeated, "But it's a banned substance." All of a sudden a light bulb went off: "Do you mean like steroids?" "Yes," she said.

She explained the Challenge Cup would be overseen by the United States Anti-Doping Agency (USADA, which drug tests athletes for the Olympics), so I would need an exemption to compete in Chicago. She said, "Just get your doctor to fill out the forms and you should have no problems."

The only problem was time—it might take 30 days to grant the exemption and the races were set for August 4-7. I asked, "Why wasn't I notified about this weeks ago? Why do I need this exemption now when I never needed it before? How come no other competitor had to get an exemption for their banned medicines such as morphine?" All she would say was I had to have an exemption and she would fax me the forms. "You need to get them to the USADA in Colorado Springs as soon as possible," she repeated.

The Challenge Cup is a race for the top disabled sailors in North America, and is quite a media event as well. Thanks to Cannabis, I don't look the part—I'm not in a wheelchair, or visibly crippled. The honchos at U.S.

Sailing and the Challenge Cup must have figured between my normal appearance and my marijuana use, I would not project the proper image. They didn't require people in chairs or missing limbs to get an exemption for their banned substances, but they had manipulated the anti-doping agency to make me jump through this hoop at the 11th hour.

I got the forms and called my doctor in Miami, only to find out he was out of town for ten days. So much for ASAP.

Several days later I got a call from an official in Chicago who revealed U.S. Sailing wanted to revoke my invitation. I warned him I would defend my right to compete in the race. He said, "I will inform Newport (Rhode Island, home of U.S. Sailing)." I thought to myself, "This is not an Olympic class boat. U.S. Sailing has some nerve to try to do this to me!"

I called Harry Horgan at Shake-A-Leg and told him what U.S. Sailing was trying to do. He was as offended as I was. "If you have to sue them," he said, "sue them." I said I didn't want to create problems for SAL. He said, "What they're doing is discrimination against a disabled person. You've stood up for your rights before, and I'm all for you doing it again. What ever you do, call Kerry Gruson right away and let her know."

Let me tell you about Kerry Gruson. She is a writer who in March 1974 was interviewing a Viet Nam vet when he had a flashback and thought she was Viet Cong. He strangled her crushing her larynx and cutting off oxygen to her brain which left her body rigid and confined to a wheelchair. She is brilliant and feisty and one of the top disabled sailors in the United States. She said she would be glad to help rally support, adding, "If they take away your invitation, then we are not going either." I said, "Thanks for your help, but I don't want the rest of you to suffer."

E-mails were sent to all the head honchos from U.S. Sailing around the country spelling out what was happening. Many of these officials were against me, but no one was against Kerry. The next thing you know, I got a letter from U.S. Sailing saying my invitation was not going to be pulled, but if I didn't have an exemption from the USADA, would I please refrain from using Cannabis in Chicago. I read the letter over and laughed. They had some nerve to tell me not to take my medicine, but Victor and I could still go. I would just take my medicine discreetly.

A week before I left for Chicago my doctor returned the forms and I faxed them to the anti-doping agency in Colorado, expecting to get my exemption. I didn't receive an answer before I left.

The races were fun and it was great seeing all my friends. They all supported me against U.S. Sailing and got a laugh out of the fact I was taking my medicine anyway. I'm sorry to report that Victor and I ended up in twelfth place again, as we had in 2003. I guess Cannabis is not a performance-enhancing drug. At least not for me.

I got back home to find a letter from USADA dated August 3, 2005. "Dear Mr. Rosenfeld, The USADA Therapeutic Use Exemption Committee has met concerning your request for a Therapeutic Use Exemption for the use of Marijuana (Cannabis Sativa). Your request has been denied. At this time, you do not have an exemption for the use of the identified substance in competition. If you test positive, you will have committed a doping violation."

I got USADA's top lawyer on the phone—Travis T. Tygart, Esq.—and asked, "Why didn't U.S. Sailing tell you about the banned substances that were used by the other sailors?" He had no answer, of course. His attitude was "Too bad, there is nothing that can be done."

I contacted the newspapers in Newport and Colorado Springs and told them U.S. Sailing had sicced USADA on me. The two reporters verified my account and both their papers ran stories pointing out my rights as a disabled person had been violated. They mentioned my success in obtaining Cannabis from the Federal Government, and the possibility of my suing U.S. Sailing and the USADA to confirm my right to use it.

I soon got a call from Tygart. He asked, "What are you planning to do?"

I said, "USADA now stands to get sued because you were foolish enough to let U.S. Sailing have their way. Here was a sailboat race that had nothing to do with the Olympics, all disabled people, all taking banned substances, and your anti-doping agency had to get involved. I will not rest until I have my exemption."

He quietly said, "If you re-apply and get approved, it would only be for you and not anyone else." I said, "Since I'm the only Federal patient that races sailboats, that would make sense."

I started to re-apply but never finished because on October 24, 2005, Hurricane Wilma devastated South Florida. We were without power for one week at work and at home and the USADA, and their application process, didn't seem important enough to me to waste my time right then. I'll do it later.

Challenging NIDA's Monopoly

A lthough thousands of U.S. citizens were growing medical marijuana for themselves or as legally recognized "caregivers" in twelve states, Mahmoud ElSohly, PhD, of the University of Mississippi, remained the only Federally-licensed grower in America. ElSohly's monopoly, in place for more than three decades, had been challenged in June, 2001, when Lyle Craker, a professor of plant, soil and insect sciences at the University of Massachusetts at Amherst, applied for a DEA license to grow marijuana for use in research by a non-profit research organization based in Cambridge called the Multidisciplinary Association for Psychedelic Research (MAPS). Rick Doblin, the director of MAPS and a friend, had received the FDA approval to study marijuana as a treatment for AIDS wasting syndrome, but the NIDA refused to provide marijuana for the study. (The NIDA previously had refused to provide marijuana to MAPS for an FDA-approved study of vaporization.)

After years of stalling—which is extremely insulting to all of us as citizens and taxpayers—the DEA determined in December 2004 that licensing Professor Craker to grow marijuana would not be in "the public interest." Craker, with backing from MAPS, requested a hearing to challenge the denial of his application. The hearing got underway on August 22, 2005, at the DEA headquarters in Arlington, Virginia. Presiding was Administrative Law Judge Mary Ellen Bittner, successor to the late Francis Young.

Lawyers for the DEA argued, among other things, the marijuana grown for NIDA at Ole Miss met the needs of researchers in terms of quantity and quality.

Craker and MAPS were represented by Julie Carpenter of the Washington, D.C. firm Jenner & Block, with help from Steptoe and Johnson and the ACLU. They argued that "creating an alternative to the current NIDA-controlled monopoly would promote the advancement of science and research by adding competition without increasing the risk of diversion." Also, "the current system does not provide an adequate and uninterrupted supply of marijuana for legitimate purposes."

MAPS presented evidence that the NIDA's marijuana contained sticks and seeds, was harsh to smoke, and less potent than Cannabis available at California dispensaries. Additional hearings were scheduled for December, when El Sohly himself would testify on behalf of the DEA in opposition to Craker's application.

I had a strong personal interest in the case. If the quality of government-issued medicine improved, I could smoke less, and the mild side effects would be even milder. An aspect of medical marijuana use that the Drug Czar and other Prohibitionists won't acknowledge is the higher the concentration of THC and other active ingredients, the smaller the amount required by the patient. If the main adverse effect is damage to lung tissue—as Ethan Russo and other researchers have found—then the less a patient has to smoke, the healthier. Nevertheless, the government regularly issues warnings that "today's pot is much stronger than pot in the 1970s..." as if that made it more dangerous instead of more efficient!

Rick Doblin invited me to testify in support of Craker, but my lawyers at Steptoe and Johnson advised me to decline. The hearing would be wide-ranging, and the government lawyers could ask questions such as "Do you go without marijuana when a shipment is late, or do you find other sources?" Since we had no idea where the questioning might lead, and we all knew the government would love to end the IND program altogether, they felt it was best not to risk it.

My lawyers' fears were borne out when the DEA's attorney tried to get Doblin to name patients involved in the vaporization study MAPS had conducted. Doblin was also grilled about his own marijuana use. Judge Bittner halted the irrelevant line of questioning when Doblin was asked to name the source of his marijuana.

•

In the November 11-17, 2005 edition of the *Jewish News Weekly* of Northern California (formerly the *Jewish Bulletin*) ran a cover story entitled, "Marijuana: Just what the doctor ordered? Jews lead the charge for medical pot." The article started: Irvin Rosenfeld smokes marijuana, a lot of it every day. He also buys and sells stocks, a lot of them every day. And he's up-front about this to all his clients.

He continued to tell my story and the stories of other Jews in the movement. The main point of the article was summed up by sociologist Marsha Rosenbaum: "Jews are more critical and less convinced of official or government rhetoric than the population at large." Attorney Bill Panzer made the same point another way: "Where you find doctors, lawyers and injustice, you find Jews."

•

In late November 2005, I traveled to Madison, Wisconsin to testify before the Assembly Health Committee in support of a medical-marijuana bill. Also testifying was Jacki Rickert, who has Ehlers-Danlos syndrome, a rare genetic disorder in which the body doesn't make enough collagen, the main protein in our connective tissue. Cannabis loosens up her muscles so she can move easier, improves her appetite so she can maintain her dangerously low weight up, and helps with the pain. Jacki was one of the twenty-eight unlucky patients who had been approved by the FDA but had yet to receive marijuana from NIDA when the government closed the IND program in 1992. Her devoted friend, Gary Storck (who has glaucoma), described how Jacki's condition would worsen when her supply of Cannabis ran out, or when they couldn't afford to pay the high prices Prohibition enables dealers to charge. I testified during the same years Jacki was suffering and scuffling for her medicine, I smoked more than 200 pounds of medical Cannabis provided by the Federal Government while she went without.

No vote was taken that day. Gary told me later the bill made it out of committee but didn't pass the Assembly. He and Jacki had long ago formed an organization called IMMLY—"Is My Medicine Legal Yet." Unfortunately, for the people of Wisconsin, the answer is still no.

•

On December 13th. and 14th., 2005, Mahmoud ElSohly testified against the granting of a DEA license to Lyle Craker, his potential competitor. ElSohly claimed the marijuana he grew for NIDA at the University of Mississippi met all the needs of U.S. researchers. It was interesting to learn about the operations of my "caregiver." (Rick Doblin attended the hearing and provided a transcript.)

ElSohly has several contracts with the Federal Government. Much of his time is devoted to testing the potency of thousands of marijuana samples seized by law enforcement throughout the country. He also grows marijuana and extracts THC for pharmaceutical research. He has a contract with Mallinckrodt, a chemical company that hopes to market a generic alternative to Marinol. ElSohly also has patented a THC-extract suppository, which a company called Insys is trying to market.

El Sohly's contract with NIDA runs for five years and was last renewed in 2004. It authorizes him to grow approximately a ton of marijuana. (In the next cycle it would go up to more than four tons, he revealed, much of which would be supplied to Mallinckrodt.) He plants cuttings from various strains in a field on Ole Miss property. After harvest and drying, each strain yields an approximately forty-five-pound "batch" of bud and leaf. "One batch might be two percent (THC)," El Sohly explained to Judge Bittner, "one batch might be four percent, one might be six percent, one might be twelve percent, one might be fourteen..."

His most recent crop was grown in 2002 and averaged about seven percent THC. The dried marijuana is stored in drums lined with plastic in refrigerated vaults until it is requested by NIDA—which could take years. When NIDA specifies the amount and THC content of marijuana going to researchers, ElSohly makes a blend from his various batches and sends it in bulk to the Research Triangle Institute in North Carolina to be rolled into cigarettes.

ElSohly defended the quality of his product and gave several reasons why it was not more potent. He assured Judge Bittner he could grow marijuana higher in THC, but it would gum up the cigarette rolling machines. Moreover, administrators from the University of California's Center for Medicinal Cannabis Research advised him patients in clinical trials could not tolerate marijuana with THC content above 8%. (Hmmm...) Finally, El Sohly assumed all research should be conducted with marijuana similar in potency to the national average: "What makes sense is to look at the national data for potency, for what's out there on the street, and... mimic what's out there and to do research with those kinds of materials."

This was very revealing. The vast majority of research NIDA has sponsored over the years has been aimed at finding the harmful effects of marijuana. For such studies, using marijuana comparable to what most Americans are smoking makes sense. But for research aimed at finding beneficial effects, scientists should be provided with the highest-grade strains available.

ElSohly seemed particularly sensitive to criticism the marijuana he grew for NIDA contained sticks and seeds. He testified he heard Dr. Donald Abrams at a conference "saying it's harsh, it's got seeds, and it's got stuff like that in it." In 2001 ElSohly bought (at NIDA's expense) a de-seeding machine, designed and custom-made in Canada, "specific to the Cannabis plant." Since putting it in operation, ElSohly said, "We're able to provide plant material after going through the de-seeding machine, removing all the seeds, all the stems, all the heavy particles, and have a product that has the right particle size and has no seeds we can ship directly to Research Triangle Institute and they can manufacture the cigarettes without further processing other than blending and humidifying and so on."

Multidisciplinary Association for Psychedelic Studies (MAPS) introduced into evidence the *Journal of Cannabis Therapeutics* article about the Missoula study, which characterized NIDA marijuana as "a crude mixture of leaf with abundant stem and seed components... The resultant smoke is thick, acrid and pervasive." The taste was described as "harsh" and "chemically treated." The article stated clinical research required "a ready and consistent supply of sterilized, potent, organically grown unfertilized female flowering top material, thoroughly cleaned of extraneous inert fiber."

A photograph accompanying the article showed sticks and stems from three cigarettes provided by NIDA to George McMahon. ElSohly questioned the validity of the photo, which had been taken by Ethan Russo. "There is just no way this is material that is actually in the cigarettes," ElSohly testified. "Those things would definitely puncture very thin cigarette paper."

Al Byrne, who had been present when the photo was taken in Missoula, was informed of this statement and promptly provided a sworn affidavit to Judge Bittner: "In my presence a sealed canister belonging to George McMahon was opened... Three of the cigarettes were extracted at random... I observed seeds and stems in that marijuana."

When the judge admitted Byrne's affidavit into evidence, the DEA lawyer asked to cross-examine Al and an additional hearing date was set. I was personally offended. To question Al's honesty was to question my honesty, and George's and Elvy's—not to mention Dr. Russo's. Fortunately, when the DEA realized Al was not afraid to answer questions under oath, they canceled the extra day of testimony.

My Friend Darrell

On March 30, 2006, I headed to St. Paul, Minnesota—another northern state with cold weather—and the next day I spoke at the State House in support of a medical marijuana bill. My friend Darrell Paulson was there.

He is well known around the capitol, having lobbied for years on medical Cannabis and other issues. Darrell has Cerebral Palsy and is confined to an electric wheelchair. Unlike me, Darrell has health problems that are easily visible; and he medicates with Cannabis illegally to treat his muscle spasms, pain, and to increase his appetite.

I talked to Darrell about what I was planning to say and he approved. (I never write a speech in advance. For one thing, I never know what will be said by people who speak before me. Unscripted I have flexibility.)

My turn came and I took my place before the committee with my tin can in hand, behind the microphones and cameras. I looked at each committee member and started speaking, always keeping eye contact. I gave my usual speech explaining who I was and why I took medical Cannabis. People are always amazed to learn the Federal Government actually grows Cannabis and supplies it on a regular basis to a select few.

As I came towards the end of my allotted ten minutes, I held up my canister and said, "As a Federal patient. I can go to any U.S. territory with my medicine and I am not a criminal." Then, pointing to Darrell, I said, "But he IS a criminal." Looking at a State Trooper, I said, "You need to go and arrest him. He's breaking YOUR state law." Then I turned to the woman who was leading the opposition and said, "I don't know about you, but I would sure sleep better at night knowing he's behind bars. Wouldn't you?" Then I looked at my friend who could barely move his body, but his mind and eyes were ready to resist if the State Trooper tried to arrest him, which he did not. Looking back at the committee I said, "That's the problem. Darrell isn't a criminal, but your law makes him one."

Building a Doctor-Patient Alliance

On April 3, 2006, Debbie and I flew to Los Angeles, rented a car and drove to Santa Barbara to attend Patients Out of Time's fourth national conference. The Santa Barbara City College campus overlooks the

Pacific. It was a beautiful setting for our conference. More than sixty health-care providers attended, including thirty doctors and twenty-four nurses. Donald Abrams, MD, was instrumental in arranging Continuing Medical Education credits through UC San Francisco School of Medicine.

Speakers included Robert Melamede, PhD ("Cannabinoids and the Physics of Life"), Mark Wallace, MD ("Efficacy of Smoked Cannabis on Human Experimental Pain"), Natalya Kogan, PhD ("The Current Status of Cannabinboid Research in Israel"), Marta Duran, MD ("The Therapeutic Use of a Cannabis Project in Catalonia, Spain"), Mark Ware, MD ("Canadian Pain and Cannabis"), Marco van de Velde ("Pharmacy Grade Cannabis in the Netherlands"), Donald Abrams, MD ("Cannabis in Pain and Palliative Care"), Melanie Dreher, RN, PhD ("Cannabis Use and Pregnancy"), Steven Hosea, MD ("AIDS and Cannabis"), California MDs Frank Lucido, Arnold Leff, and David Bearman discussing their practices and dealings with the state medical board; and policy analyst Jon Gettman.

I thought Dr. Bearman made an especially important point: "Doctors have at least as much to learn from patients as patients have to learn from doctors." In the typical doctor-patient relationship the doctor is the expert (thanks to a medical-school education) and can advise about dosage, likely effects, etc. But when medical Cannabis users visit a doctor to request approval, the relationship is more equal, since the doctor received no training on the subject, and the patient has personal experience of how the drug affects his or her symptoms.

Daniele Piomelli, professor of pharmacology at UC Irvine, described strategies researchers are pursuing to develop drugs that have Cannabis-like effects minus the psychoactivity. His lab has a compound in clinical trials that prevents the breakdown of one of the body's own cannabinoids.

Debbie's Side of the Story

Not only was I scheduled to speak, but Debbie was going to be on a panel of activists' spouses. It would be a first for her. She was reluctant, but didn't let on. She shared her point of view directly and honestly:

"I'm very fortunate of all the women here, my husband is here to tell you his story himself. [Three other women on the panel were widows.]

"In a lot of ways it's not that different than living with anyone else in any other kind of relationship. As his day goes, so does mine. It's just we live in a cloud of smoke. Living and traveling with Irvin is always an adventure. From a day-to-day standpoint there is always the issue of his needing to take his medicine and me not being able to tolerate the smoke. We have to work out the logistics of which rooms in the house are off limits. (The bedroom is my sanctuary.) How we're going to endure a hotel room, a car ride et cetera, always brings up a big discussion. When we travel together there's always the matter of getting to the airport early. We never know if we'll run into a problem and when he travels by himself, I sit by the phone waiting for his call, waiting to know he got through security and then again he actually made it onto the plane. That wasn't a real concern until Delta denied him access on a flight several years ago. Now I make him call twice.

"There's the constant explaining to our friends and family and new acquaintances about his need to take medicine. Even those who understand and are supportive are not necessarily willing to accommodate. This summer we're supposed to attend a gathering of his family in North Carolina. There's a big discussions already about who we'll stay with—who will be the most lenient about letting him take his medicine. And that's within his family. Some of the friends are not so sure they want to be around medical marijuana. So we're always faced with these dilemmas.

"The children of our friends and Irvin's nieces and nephews are all aware of his medicine. They're fascinated by his story and are big supporters of his.

They're the first to explain to their friends that his is different, it's a medicine, and it's not like people who are using it recreationally.

"Those people who argue what kind of a message we will send to our children if we make marijuana medically available should see these children who have grown up around us. I think we should be more concerned about the message we're sending when we don't give people medicine they need. We keep it illegal because of ignorance and because we're afraid to say we were wrong.

"Irvin and I have been married for thirty-three years. We dated for five years before that. I've seen what marijuana has done to help him, and how it has made our lives more normal and much easier. He used to wake up in the middle of the night screaming in pain, the muscles wrapping round the tumors in his legs. He'd be crawling on the floor just trying to will the muscles to relax. For days after that, he'd have to walk on crutches. It doesn't happen anymore.

"When we moved to Florida and he had to change doctors there was a lapse there. During that time, the screams in the night started again. For those who use Cannabis illegally, there is the constant fear of being caught, taken to jail, losing property and livelihood, and even worse, losing access to that which makes them lead a more normal life. Even someone of Montel's stature has to fear 'What if they come after me?' (Montel had spoken the day before.)

"I've seen Irvin be able to stop using other medications that make him zombie-like and interfere with his ability to work and function as a real partner in our relationship. Irvin—and therefore we—are very fortunate to be one of the few to have legal access to medical Cannabis. We wouldn't be here if not for Alice and Bob. We'll be forever indebted to them for coming public and being willing to educate and help others. It's because of organizations like Patients Out of Time and people like Mary Lynn and Al that this education process has continued. And because of people like Irvin, Elvy and George, who followed in Bob's footsteps and won't be silent. We're all grateful for those of you who have come here and hope you as medical professionals will have the courage to not be silent, too, and to educate those you come in contact with.

"To those of you who are patients, would-be patients, and supporters: speak up, don't be silent, let your voice be heard."

She was walking the walk, as she talked the talk.

Joan Dangerfield

Debbie's panel included Alice O'Leary; Nancy Cavanaugh, widow of Jay Cavanaugh, a Southern California pharmacist who backed Prop 215; and Joan Dangerfield, wife of the late, great comedian who could get no respect. Yes, Rodney Dangerfield qualified as a pro-Cannabis activist. Joan explained why:

"I met Rodney in 1983, and after a ten-year courtship, Rodney and I enjoyed eleven years of marriage. I must admit when I became a part of Rodney's life, I did not approve of his marijuana use. My Mormon background hadn't given me experience with any illegal substances and I was always afraid Rodney would get arrested.

"Rodney was concerned about my feelings and agreed to look for legal alternatives to treat his ailments. Over the years we consulted the best experts we could find in search of legal anti-anxiety and pain medications and even tried Marinol. But nothing "worked" for him the way real marijuana did.

"A couple of years ago Rodney was in the process of writing his autobiography, in which he wanted to be very candid about everything in his life. He even wanted to title the book 'My Lifelong Romance with Marijuana.' I was sure then that Rodney would be arrested. So I looked for, and found, Dr. David Bearman here in Santa Barbara.

"Dr. Bearman examined Rodney and obtained records from Rodney's other doctors for review. In addition to his anxiety and depression, at the time, Rodney's medical conditions included constant pain from the congenital fusion of his spine, an inoperable dislocated shoulder and rotator cuff tear and arthritis. Rodney wasn't able to take traditional pain medications because of their interactions with his blood-thinning medication, Coumadin. It also helped decrease his involuntary ticks, which people thought was part of his shtick.

"We were elated a few days after that initial visit with Dr. Bearman when Rodney's medicinal use was approved. Rodney showed the approval letter to everyone and carried miniature versions in his pockets. Ever the worried wife, I included a copy of the letter in the memory box of his casket in case the Feds were waiting for him at the Pearly Gates...

"After all those years of pot smoking, his memory and his joke writing ability did not suffer and his lungs were okay. He was as sharp as ever. Even moments after brain surgery, Rodney didn't miss a beat. Rodney's doctor came to his bedside after he was taken off the respirator. He said, 'Rodney, are you coughing up much?' And Rodney said, 'Last week, five-hundred for a hooker.'"

It was really a shame he died before he could talk publicly about his use of medical Cannabis.

On a panel devoted to post dramatic stress disorder (PTSD), Al Byrne said the D-word (Disorder) is misleading. "I use Cannabis to cope with post-traumatic stress," he said. "That's what it is—not a disorder but a perfectly logical response to terrifying events." Al experienced unforgettable trauma during combat in Vietnam. Two victims of sexual abuse in childhood, Erin Hildebrandt and Christopher Largen, described their experiences and the relief provided by Cannabis.

•

Al and Mary Lynn had gotten tremendous support from Loren Vazquez, a UC Santa Barbara student who ran the NORML chapter; Joseph White of the SB City College Philosophy Department; and Patrick Fourmy, a local collective Cannabis dispensary founder with a background in journalism who arranged for the conference to be videotaped. (Parts were also filmed by Star Price and Josh Kessler's crew for use in a documentary called "In Pot

We Trust" for Showtime.)

One of the highlights of the conference was a side trip, organized by Patrick, to the immaculate, professionally run Santa Barbara Compassion Center. It was staffed by registered Nurses to help patients choose strains that are best-suited for alleviating their symptoms. It would be appropriate for NIDA to sponsor research along these lines. But if the government won't, the private sector will.

Another highlight was a "photo op" conceived by Al. The purpose was to publicly refute the claim by Mahmoud ElSohly that the Cannabis he grows for NIDA is free of sticks and seeds. George, Elvy and I had all brought unopened cans of government-issued Cannabis to the conference. We were still fuming over ElSohly and the DEA lawyer questioning Al's integrity— and ours, by implication, and Dr. Russo's. As the cameras rolled, we unsealed the cans and shredded some cigarettes to reveal the sticks and seeds. A videotape was sent to Judge Bittner, who had yet to rule on Dr. Craker's application for a DEA license.

•

Not long afterwards, on April 20, 2006, the FDA issued a "statement" to the media, announcing that "no sound scientific studies" supported the medical use of marijuana and it should remain on Schedule 1. Ignored was the fact the FDA never saw fit to study the patients in the Federal IND program in the first place. The FDA said it was issuing the unusual "statement" in response to "inquiries by Congress and the DEA." I wondered why they picked 4/20 as the day to release the statement. Were Drug Warriors in the government trying to needle those of us who want marijuana rescheduled? How unprofessional and juvenile!

The New York Times made the FDA statement a page-one story. Three scientists were quoted disputing the government line. One was Dr. Daniele Piomelli, who said he had "never met a scientist who would say marijuana is either dangerous or useless."

No Withdrawal Syndrome

In late May, I contacted the Bahamian Embassy to find out what I needed to do in order to bring my medicine there. Newbridge Securities was hosting a weekend getaway as a reward for productivity. I earned a spot and was looking forward to being there with the owners and my co-workers.

I was given the phone number of Patricia Rodgers, permanent secretary of the Bahamian Ministry of Foreign Affairs. I called her and explained my situation. She told me to get a letter from my doctor and fax it to her and she would see what she could do.

I did what she asked, but when I called to check on her progress, she would not take my phone call or call me back. So I contacted the *Miami Herald* and the *Sun-Sentinel,* knowing they would call Ms. Rogers.

She then returned my call and said she was still trying, but most likely I would not get permission. I was not happy, nor was I surprised.

The *Miami Herald* ran the story on June 9, the day Debbie and I boarded a boat for Freeport. "No Port For Pot" was the headline. There was a picture of me smoking my medicine in the garage at work and another of my baggie of rolled cigarettes. The caption read: "Irvin Rosenfeld holds a bag containing his prescribed marijuana cigarettes. He smokes ten to twelve joints per day. The Bahamas has refused to let him take the medication with him on a trip to the islands."

Since I wasn't able to take my medicine with me, it was suggested by friends I could buy some when I got there. I said, "No thank you. A lot of people think I'm addicted to Cannabis. This will prove I'm not... Also, I'm not about to break a law in a foreign country."

We enjoyed the trip and appreciated our time with co-workers away from the work environment. I was able to go eighteen hours before I had to start taking muscle-relaxing medications and pain medicine (Flexeril and Percocet). Going without cannabis resulted in no withdrawal symptoms, only muscle tightness and pain. While I didn't crave my medicine, I sure missed it.

It took about four days after I returned to the states for me to feel "normal" again.

Educating Elliott Spitzer

In the summer of 2006, New York Attorney General Elliott Spitzer was running for governor and heavily favored to win. A campaign aide told the media Spitzer was skeptical about the pending medical-marijuana bill—the one I testified for in 2002—because his brother, a neurosurgeon, told him for every illness treatable by marijuana, there was a conventional medicine that worked just as well or better. The pharmaceutical lobbies obviously had done a great job, albeit wrong.

Vince Marrone, a lobbyist employed by DPA (Drug Policy Alliance), was able to arrange a private meeting with the Attorney General. In early August, I got a call from Vince asking if I could fly to New York for the meeting. The other proponent would be UCSF Professor of Medicine Donald Abrams, whose research with medical Cannabis has been well documented. The hope was thru education by Donald a physician, and me, a Federally supplied patient, we could change Spitzer's mind.

On August 14, 2006 Dr. Abrams and I, accompanied by Marrone, met with Spitzer and two of his aides in Manhattan. Spitzer's manner was abrasive. His first comment was "Everyone knows marijuana is not a medicine." (We were facing another uninformed government brainwashed person) I knew I didn't have to respond because Dr. Abrams was there and that question was his lead-in to explain who he was, and what he had done. Abrams talked about his studies and how difficult it had been to get government approval. He talked about his AIDS and cancer patients and said many people are helped by Cannabis who don't respond well to anything else.

At one point Spitzer said, "But it doesn't cure anybody of anything." That was my opening to say, "Well, sir, in reality it has." Then I told him who I was and I explained what I use it for and that nothing else worked and how the tumors I had should be growing but they hadn't for thirty-two years. I showed him my tin can and explained the whole procedure by which the Government supplied me. Since Federal money pays for the program, I thanked him for the share he had contributed as a taxpayer. That got a little smile.

He was shocked. He had no idea that the Federal Government was doing this. I explained how the Federal program had been shut down in 1992 by George Bush senior and no one else had any hope of becoming a Federal patient. I said, "I believe there should be Federal legislation, but until that happens the states are trying to take the crime away from individual citizens by changing state law. And that's why we're here."

He understood, but I had the feeling we still hadn't really gotten through to him so I said, "You know, Mr. Attorney General, New York State doesn't have to pass this law. They really don't need to, because people are doing it anyway. The only advantage of passing this law is now New York State won't have to waste its money prosecuting patients." That seemed to get through to him. He nodded as if to say, "That's right, people are doing it anyway."

When we finished, Spitzer asked Vince Marrone, "What does the bill entail?" Marrone started talking about the bill and I realized how much weaker the sponsors had made it since I testified before the New York State legislature in 2002. I was extremely disappointed.

The meeting lasted forty-five minutes. We would have to wait now to see if our education process was successful. When we walked out I turned to Marrone and said, "Vince, what happened to the bill?" And he said, "Well, this was the best we could do to get something passed."

•

In late November I made my annual cold-weather political pilgrimage, flying to Michigan to testify for a medical marijuana bill. Not much time was left when I finally was called, and I spoke faster than usual. Unbeknownst to me, activist Greg Piasecki taped my testimony and posted it on the internet. If you ever want to hear my story, told fast, it's on **YouTube** and at my website, **potluckrx.com**.

After the hearing, I went to lunch with organizer Tim Beck and about two dozen Michigan activists—a diverse, dedicated group whose work would eventually pay off in November, 2008, when Michigan became the 14th state to pass a medical Cannabis law.

A few months later I made a similar trip to Annapolis, Maryland. Again the hearing at the state house went well... but no vote was taken.

•

Although my emphasis when I give a talk is always on medical use, I often get asked how I feel about "recreational use." Sometimes the question is accusatory, as if talking about medical use is a ploy to advocate "decriminalization" or "legalization" of marijuana. Our opponents are always trying to link the two, but for the patients who are suffering there is only one issue. So my response is: "I really don't have an opinion about the social use of marijuana. As a taxpayer it infuriates me my tax money is going to put non-violent criminals in jail. When a Cannabis user goes to jail, the likelihood is the family goes on welfare—and that costs me money as a taxpayer. There is also the exorbitant cost of incarceration. In Florida, and probably in your state, too, the jails are overcrowded. If we weren't jailing people for Cannabis offenses, we'd have room for all the violent criminals... But I really don't have an opinion about social use."

•

According to the FBI Uniform Crime Report the number of Americans arrested for violating marijuana laws in 2006 was 829,627. Most of these arrests—738,916—were for possession. These arrest statistics have risen steadily through the years. The "War on Drugs" is the main reason the U.S., with four percent of the world's population, has twenty-five percent of the world's prisoners. There have been twenty million marijuana arrests in America since 1965.

It always amazes me when I hear how long the sentences are that are handed out for "Cannabis crimes" compared to violent crimes. You can assault someone and not go to jail, but don't you dare provide a sick person with Cannabis...

An example of this unfairness is a little known penalty facing college students who apply for, or who are receiving financial aid, and are convicted of a drug offense. Titled the "Aid Elimination Penalty," and added to The Higher Education Act in 1998, this penalty denies loans, grants, and work-study options to college students who have been convicted of drug offenses (even if the offense occurred back in high school). Some 200,000 students have been made ineligible for financial aid thanks to this penalty. These students already have been punished through the criminal justice system. Will forcing them to drop out of college make them more likely to develop into productive citizens? What was Congress thinking? Students today already face great difficulties. They incur levels of debt that limit their options in life and create inescapable anxiety just when they should be confidently embarking on careers, planning to start families, etc.

The "Aid Elimination Penalty" does not apply to crimes due to alcohol, or murderers, rapists, or thieves, only to drug offenders—the vast majority of whom were arrested for marijuana possession. "The War on Drugs" is mainly a war on marijuana users; look at the statistics.

An organization called Students for a Sensible Drug Policy, headquartered in Washington, D.C., made the elimination of the Aid Elimination Penalty its key goal. Their hopes were raised when Democrats won control of Congress in the 2006 elections, but they would not achieve success in the upcoming session.

"The Public Interest"

On Feb.12, 2007, five-and-a-half years after the case was filed, DEA's Administrative Law Judge Mary Ellen Bittner issued her "Opinion and recommended ruling, findings of fact, conclusions of law, and decision in the matter of Lyle E. Craker, PhD" Just as DEA's Chief Administrative Law Judge Francis Young had done almost twenty years earlier, an arbiter appointed by the DEA, wound up telling the DEA to stop obstructing research. Bittner concluded that the NIDA's refusal to provide marijuana to some qualified researchers proved the existing supply system was not adequate.

Competition among producers would be in the public interest, Bittner wrote. The DEA argued the existing system involved competition because Craker (and others) could submit a bid against ElSohly every five years when the NIDA contract came up for renewal. Bittner observed, "The NIDA contract requires the contractor to analyze samples of marijuana supplied by law enforcement agencies, a separate activity from cultivating marijuana for research purposes, and a requirement a qualified cultivator may not be able to fulfill."

It was gratifying a judge recognized and called attention to the conflicts of interest inherent in Mahmoud ElSohly's operation at the University of Mississippi. But I reminded Rick Doblin not to get his hopes up the DEA would heed the Judge's recommendation. As this book goes to press, a new administration is promising meaningful change. Allowing Professor Craker to grow Cannabis for research purposes would be just that.

Another meaningful change would be removing Cannabis from Schedule 1. The scientific literature now contains hundreds of articles showing Cannabis is safe and effective medicine. A study led by

Donald Abrams, MD, proving Cannabis relieves pain, was published in the February 13, 2007, issue of *Neurology,* a prestigious peer-reviewed journal. HIV patients smoking Cannabis experienced a thirty-four percent reduction in intense foot pain—twice the reduction reported by patients who smoked placebo. That study, by itself, is sufficient to invalidate placement of Cannabis in Schedule 1 of the Controlled Substance Act because it disproves the third factor, that there is a "lack of accepted safety for use of the drug…under medical supervision."

A feature story by Stephanie Armour in *USA Today* dated April 17, 2007, dealt with the very important but under-publicized issue of medical Cannabis use and employment. It ran on the front page of the "Money" section under a headline that read, "Employers grapple with medical marijuana use—Ethical, liability issues rise as more states make it legal." New Mexico had just become the twelfth state to do so.

I was Exhibit A, a person who could smoke more than a half-dozen joints during the workday and still function without loss of efficiency. There were photos of me taking my medicine in my car (parked), and at my desk. "All my clients know I use it," I was quoted. "Without it, I wouldn't be able to work."

My employers were not afraid to stand up for me. "Newbridge Securities is resolute in its support of his on-the-job use of medical marijuana," Armour wrote. "Company officials say they aren't concerned about legal liability issues because they say Rosenfeld's use of the drug doesn't have an impact on his ability to work. He also discloses to every client that he uses the drug.

"'He's a quality stockbroker, and he does a great job,' said Phillip Semenick, executive vice president and branch manager."

Thanks, Phil. (Phil left the firm in February 2009.)

Exhibit B was Joseph Kintzel, 41, of Golden, Colo., a respiratory therapist who ran his own business but occasionally worked for companies that knew he used medical marijuana. Kintzel had endured "four back surgeries for ten herniated discs… and has thirty-two pieces of titanium holding his spine together." He had used morphine, Percocet and Vicodin but was unable to work for several years, until he tried marijuana.

As in my case, heavy, regular use eliminated the emotional high. "After getting a doctor's authorization, Kinzel began using marijuana regularly," Armour reported. "Within six weeks he was off the narcotics and began riding a bike. A few months later he was back at work. He says he gets no euphoric effect from marijuana." Kintzel told USA Today he was working sixty to sixty-five hours a week and had had "one sick day in the last four years."

One advantage I had as a Federal patient was economic. Kintzel, who got marijuana from a card-holding caregiver, consumed an ounce every ten days, at a cost of $200-250 an ounce.

Companies with federal contracts are much less tolerant, Armour reported. She cited the firing of Robert Washburn, a lumber-mill worker who had a doctor's approval and a card from the Oregon Medical Marijuana Program. Washburn did not medicate while on the job. He smoked before bedtime, to relieve pain and be able to sleep. "He was never impaired at work," his lawyer stated. Washburn sued for reinstatement and back pay. The case went to the state supreme court, which ruled for the mill owners.

Armour's article was reprinted in a Japanese newspaper, which she sent me as a souvenir. I thought she did an excellent job of showing how far our medical Cannabis use had come in terms of acceptance in the business world. "Even in New York and other states that do not allow medical marijuana, companies are beginning to debate the issue," Armour noted.

I hope that debate is guided by common sense, not prejudice. Researchers have found the effects of smoked marijuana peak in about 15 minutes and wear off entirely after three-four hours. No medical user should be fired just because the metabolites of THC are in his or her system. The real issue is whether or not the person is impaired. A patient almost always knows what he or she can do on the medicine and adjusts accordingly—just as people learn to do with other prescribed medicines.

One thing employers may learn to their surprise is, for certain people in certain jobs, marijuana is a performance enhancer. (but not in sailboat racing!)

New York State of Mind

In New York, the Democratic-led Assembly passed a bill that would let doctor-certified patients cultivate, possess and use marijuana. A New York Times story dated June 14, 2007—"Legislators Grapple Over How To Legalize Medical Marijuana Use"—noted Governor Spitzer, the former Attorney General, had changed his position and was now in favor of the bill. "On many issues, hopefully, you learn, you study, and you evolve," Spitzer was quoted in the *Times*.

According to Vince Marrone, Spitzer was telling people he had been educated by "two of the experts in the country" on medical Cannabis. Knowing Donald Abrams and I had made a real difference made me dance for joy. "I hope he remembers when he runs for President," I told Vince.

Now, how the mighty are fallen. Elliot Spitzer had to resign after his hiring of a prostitute came to the attention of law enforcement.

•

The possibility of New York enacting a medical marijuana law was the theme of Fox TV's "Morning Show with Mike and Juliet" on June 20th. I had spent the night at a midtown Manhattan hotel and was at the studio well before air time (9:00 am). The featured guest, Montel Williams, had not yet arrived.

The producers engaged me in a brief discussion of the subject. They explained Mike and Juliet would be on the stage with Montel and a spokesperson for the Partnership for a Drug-Free America. I would be sitting in the front row of the audience, miked, along with an AIDS patient and a New York doctor (who was also a patient). I said "Fine," was taken to makeup, and then sat in the hall waiting.

About 8:45 am. Montel showed up. We said our hellos and I gave him a gift—two of my empty Cannabis tins to auction off for his Multiple Sclerosis Foundation. He gave them to his bodyguard, who said he would guard them with his life. "Fortunately," I reassured him, "I can re-place them."

When Montel emerged from make-up the producers told him the plan for the show. Evidently it was different than the plan he had agreed to the day before in discussions with the main producer (who on this morning was attending her son's fifth-grade gradua-tion). I could hear Montel saying he wasn't going to do the show. I looked at my cell phone and saw that it was 8:58 a.m.

It was past 8:59 am., when one of the producers grabbed me and started running down a long hallway. "There's been a change," she said. "You're going to be on stage." We rushed onto the set and she pointed me to a stool. Mike and Juliet showed their surprise, as did the other guest. They'd been expecting Montel.

I was taking my seat as the director said, "Three, two, one, we're live." Mike and Juliet looked at the Teleprompters and starting read-ing: "Welcome Irvin Rosenfeld..." When they identified me as a Federal patient, the Prohibitionist spokesperson seemed very un-easy.

As we debated over the next twelve minutes, I felt I had two tre-mendous advantages over him: first-hand knowledge of the subject (a lifetime dealing with a serious illness) and visible proof that even the Federal Government recognized the medical potential of mari-juana (my gleaming tin canister).

Leading into a commercial, Juliet said, "When we return, Montel Williams will be joining us." I got up to join the audience, but the director said, "No, you stay up there; that's what Montel wants." He turned to my adversary and said, "You need to go join the audi-ence." He was not happy about his dismissal.

Montel came onto the set, all smiles. We shook hands and then it hit me: he must have set this whole thing up! He had pulled that prima-dona act to give me the opportunity to go one-on-one with the authority from The Partnership for a Drug-Free America! I looked at Montel and laughed. We sat down and the last segment started. Montel took up where I left off in demolishing the arguments that uphold the Federal marijuana prohibition. I set him up with a few lines and greatly enjoyed playing sidekick to such an articulate, forceful star.

After the show the Partnership spokesman yelled at the two producers about the fact he never agreed to debate a Federal patient. They came over to me and said, "I guess everyone is mad at us except you." I said, "I thought the show went rather well."

Before I flew home I went to the Carnegie Deli and got a huge, hot corn beef sandwich for the flight. I finally had a nice trip speaking in a warm climate!

History Lessons

On July 9, 2007, "In Pot We Trust," a 90-minute documentary produced by Wolper Productions, debuted on Showtime. Filmmakers Star Price and Josh Kessler originally planned to make a documentary about the surviving Federal patients, but the more they learned about the scope and significance of the medical marijuana movement, the more they expanded their focus. The final version was an excellent overview of the movement. I expect the DVD, with additional footage, to be even better if and when it comes out.

•

On August 1, 2007, I told my story on a 24-minute news special, "Seniors and Medical Marijuana," on Retirement Living TV. Also interviewed was Deputy Drug Czar Bertha Madras, who said she "didn't care how many anecdotal testimonies" confirmed Cannabis was effective medicine, because "that's not how we in the United States decide if a substance is medically beneficial."

If it had been a give-and-take format, I would have challenged Dr. Madras's dismissal of "anecdotal testimonies." It is extremely disrespectful of the government to imply that millions of American citizens are liars. When anecdotal evidence is coming from so many people, and their reports are so consistent, the government, through its scientific agencies, should evaluate our claims with rigorous studies instead of dismissing them contemptuously. As Dr. Lester Grinspoon said, "What did we do to decide what was a medicine before we had double-blind studies"?

The show ended on a shot of me sailing with Shake-A-Leg and saying, "Medical marijuana has been a lifesaver to me. They can't arrest everybody. And people are going to use it. The more we educate people about the benefits of it, the more they're going to try it. When you're in pain, you get to a point where you say 'well, heck, I'll try it.' And once they try it and they find out it works, then you're going to have more voices saying, 'Why is there hysteria about this? This isn't bad. This is helping me, not harming me.'"

•

My 25th anniversary in the IND Program,—November 20, 2007—was getting near. I contacted Al Byrne and we put together a release announcing a press conference to commemorate the occasion. We sent it to media outlets far and wide.

On the historic morning I woke up in sunny Fort Lauderdale and thanked God for my health. I drove to work early so I could get my orders in line and free up an hour to hold my press conference. Somewhat to my surprise, I hadn't heard back from any reporters or assignment editors.

At 9:30 am. I made the short drive to the Westin hotel, the site of the press conference. The 10:00 am. starting time arrived and the room was still empty. Just me and my stack of press releases, an urn of coffee and some pastries the hotel provided. I waited half an hour but no latecomers showed up. Had the media decided my story was no longer newsworthy? Were they losing interest in the medical Cannabis issue? Or had the movement become so big the Federal IND program no longer seemed significant?

Only my hometown newspaper, the *Virginian-Pilot,* took note of my 25 years as a Federal patient, and they did it with a "Whatever happened to?..." article about that once well-known "medical pot recipient from Portsmouth." The piece was written by an old ally, Tony Germanotta, who reported I no longer ran the bases in softball, but I could still hit, and with the help of pinch runners, I was still playing.

The thought of my old friends and acquaintances reading this article was consolation for the fact history was obviously moving on. Without the support of my hometown, Portsmouth Virginia, my story would have ended many years ago.

It Takes a Movement

On December 5, 2007, I flew to New Orleans to attend the Drug Policy Alliance conference, which drew almost 1,000 activists. Funded primarily by financier George Soros, DPA's premise is "the war on drugs is doing more harm than good." Unlike NORML, Patients Out of Time, the Marijuana Policy Project, and Americans for Safe Access, which are all about changing the marijuana laws, DPA takes on the whole "War on Drugs" issue.

At the conference there were talks and sessions on sentencing reform, drug treatment, drug testing, race, needle exchange, the political situation in other countries, and many other aspects of the Drug War, including, of course, marijuana prohibition and how to end it.

This was my first trip to New Orleans since Hurricane Katrina, and it was a tragic sight. I had seen the destruction that Hurricane Andrew brought to parts of South Florida. But the total devastation in New Orleans was on a much larger scale because of the flooding. If only the state of Louisiana and the Federal Government had devoted their resources to maintaining the infrastructure of the waterways instead of imprisoning citizens for non-violent drug offenses, perhaps the levees would have held.

It was good to see old allies from across the country, and encouraging seeing hundreds of new faces. DPA has a scholarship program that enables students and others who could not afford the fare to attend. DPA recruits and supports activists from the African American community, and the conference was noticeably better integrated than some I had attended. (Everybody who protests the "War on Drugs" risks their respectability, but African American activists are in a double bind because by going public, they seemingly confirm the racist charge that African American people are "into" drugs. African American people are no more into drugs than Caucasian people, but they are imprisoned at quadruple the rate.)

A quarter century of political activism had convinced me there are limits to what a soloist can achieve. Changes on the scale of ending marijuana prohibition are achieved by groups of people working towards a common goal. We may treasure our individuality, but we need allies and co-workers to change society.

As you may recall, changing society was the furthest thing from my mind when I first tried to obtain a legal supply of (confiscated) marijuana from Chief Boone back in Portsmouth. My goal was strictly personal: survival. When Bob Randall helped me achieve it, he gave me a new one: to help other seriously ill people get legal access to Cannabis. This goal was political, but it still seemed finite and readily achievable. The government convinced me otherwise by closing the IND Program to new patients in 1992.

•

On December 13, 2007, we lost Corinne Millet. I would talk to her about once a month. She was always so excited to hear news of the movement—I should have called her more often.

Corinne had remained in Nebraska with her children and grandchildren rather than travel about carrying the message as Elvy, George, and I had done over the years. "It's very frustrating for me to know," Corinne once told Mary Lynn Mathre, "that there are all these people out there that have no idea what they should do. They're going blind, they're losing their sight—they know they are. They don't know what to do. They don't know who to write to. They don't know who to call. They don't know what they have to have. This is very upsetting to me, because these people are desperate as I was desperate. I don't want to be blind. I don't want to be any more handicapped than I already am. And I don't feel that this is justifiably honest for this country to deny these people this information. And who is doing it? Who? Why? I don't know."

Who is upholding the marijuana prohibition when seventy-five to eighty percent of the American people want medical use to be legal? Who stands to lose if prohibition ended? The drug companies, the liquor industry, the prison-industrial complex, and other powerful forces. It's going to take powerful forces to overcome them. It's going to take a movement.

The Future

Writing this book has been a labor of love. I hope it will open people's eyes and hearts to the needless suffering that marijuana prohibition has brought on our country. We are kinder to our pets than we are to each other.

The job of the FDA is to protect the American people from harm—not to protect the pharmaceutical companies from competition. The fact that marijuana is an herb and contains hundreds of different compounds should not prevent the government from recognizing its medical usefulness. If marijuana doesn't fit their criteria for approval, they should change their criteria.

It angers me when the FDA says, "We don't decide what is a medicine from anecdotal statements." Hundreds of thousands of Americans are using marijuana for medical purposes, safely and effectively. Doctors in California and the other states where it is legal have documented their patients' experiences. Why won't the Federal Government respect the evidence? There have been no deaths, no pattern of dangerous reactions. The single biggest

side effect of widespread marijuana use is one I experienced personally: reduced consumption of opioids and other pharmaceutical drugs.

This, obviously, is what frightens the drug companies and their allies: you
can't patent a plant.

As for harmful side effects, every medicine the FDA approves has many
side effects which are stated on every commercial and every pamphlet required by law to be given with each prescription. The FDA could allow
medical Cannabis to be promoted in the same way—with realistic warnings.
I had to sign a release before my protocol started saying if I got lung cancer
from the Cannabis, I couldn't sue the government. My response was, "With
all the tumors already in my body that could kill me, I should live so long
as to die of lung cancer."

All those years ago, my decision to use Cannabis to treat my bone disorder was my own, based on input from my doctors. That's how it should be
for everyone. Patients and doctors should have the right to make their own
treatment decisions, and the options should include Cannabis.

•

How can we achieve that goal? Our new President has pledged to bring
about "change." Could there be a more dramatic change than ending medical Cannabis Prohibition?

I would like to see Congress pass a law allowing physicians the right to
recommend a medical herb called Cannabis. Patients would have the right
to procure it any way they see fit. They could grow their own, have someone
grow it for them, or buy it from a dispensary. Producers and vendors should
be allowed to compete in a free market. Even State Governments and the
Federal Government could grow and sell Cannabis. After all, competition is
what our economy is based on. Government at the local, state, and federal
levels could generate billions of dollars of revenue by taxing medical marijuana sales.

If I were running the movement, I would ask competent lawyers to draft
the appropriate legislation and call it the "Robert Randall Medical Cannabis

Act." Instead of hiring Washington, D.C. lobbyists, I would ask Al Byrne and Mary Lynn Mathre to organize truth squads made up of experts—doctors, scientists, nurses, and patients—to present a condensed Patients Out of Time conference in the office of every single member of Congress. The truth squads would also give public forums and conduct seminars and teach-ins on college campuses. It's not enough to educate the politicians. They need to know their constituents are educated, too, and mobilized around the medical-marijuana issue.

They also need to know they can't stay in office if they go against the will of the people. After the House and Senate vote on our medical-marijuana law, members who uphold medical Cannabis Prohibition should be challenged in their districts by pro-medical Cannabis candidates. This is a huge undertaking, and will require funding and organization; but it is achievable.

I know from personal experience, and you know from reading my story: goals that seem almost impossible can be reached. Against great odds, I have lived a long, full life and made a dent in the wall of Prohibition. Now it's time to bring down the wall.

You may reach me at **potluckrx.com** and to order more copies of the book, visit **mymedicinethebook.com**.

Cannabis works as a medicine. I'm living proof.

ACKNOWLEDGEMENTS

For years, people had been telling me that I needed to write a book about my experiences with having a severe bone disorder and how Cannabis came to play such an important part in my life.

People said that a book could speak for me and reach millions more then I had already educated. I knew they were right. And since I wasn't getting any younger, I started.

I can now say, "I know what 'a labor of love' means. While I put a lot of time into writing and researching, it was well worth it. I came away with a greater appreciation of how many people had helped me get to where I am today.

There are many people I want to thank and I apologize in advance for the ones I forgot.

I want to start with my parents, Robert and Thelma (deceased) Rosenfeld. They were always there for me and were my biggest supporters. It was their love and understanding that helped make me who I am. It wasn't easy for my parents to watch one of their children suffer physically, however they helped me mentally to deal with my condition. It was easier for me as a child to have dealt with my condition then it was for my parents. Kids can deal with sickness easier because they don't know any better. So to all parents with a child who has a physical problem, be there for them, involve them in their treatment, but know that it's harder on you.

To the rest of my family, thanks for being there and understanding. From my sister's Gayle and Susan and their families, to all my nieces and nephews, who turned out fine even though they were exposed to Cannabis since their birth.

To Debbie, my wife of 36 years. You knew me since I was 15-years-old and you were 14, which was years before I discovered Medical Cannabis. You knew how bad I was physically before Cannabis and how much better I was with it. You've stuck by me when others might have 'cut bait' and run.

I don't know what my life would have been like without you and I'm glad I don't. We have been a team that's had its ups and downs, however as a team, we have prevailed. Thank you, my love.

To Debbie's parents (both deceased), Michael and Beatrice Glick, thanks for your understanding. Debbie's mother was a second mother to me and someone I greatly respected. To sisters Carolyn and Janet and their families; we go back a long way and I have appreciated all of your support. To Carolyn's son, my nephew, Raymond Schwarzkopf, who has done a bang-up job on my personal website, **potluckrx.com,** thanks.

To my Great-Uncle, Dr. Shipley Glick (deceased) and my Uncle, Dr. Sigmond Stein (Siggy) (deceased); thank you for getting me to Boston Children's Hospital, and for helping me learn about the history of Cannabis in our country. Also, for helping me deal with all the physical problems and understanding how difficult it was going to be dealing with such a devastating disorder. They along with my other doctors made it much easier for me by being completely honest about my condition. Remember, kids can adjust easier then parents.

To Dr. William Green and Dr. Henry Waive, both deceased; Dr. Green taught me what I needed to learn and do to survive. He also taught Dr. Waive to become a brilliant and caring physician. Without them, I wouldn't be alive today. How I wish Henry was still alive. He would have been so proud of me.

To Dr. Charles Goldman; you believed in me and helped me get to where I am today. I don't know to this day if you realized how important what you did for me was, nor how important for a nationwide movement. You made the quality and quantity of my life better. What more could a doctor ask for?

To Dr. Sanchez-Ramos; you came along and took over my protocol and made a real study out of it. It was nice finally meeting a physician that wanted to help me and had a great knowledge on how and why Cannabis worked.

To Dr. Ethan Russo; thanks for doing our study in Montana and proving how right we were in knowing how well Cannabis worked with no negative side effects. Also thanks for being there when I need a medical question answered.

To my present physician; I understand why you have never gone public. I just hope you know how important you have been to me and all the good you have done. You have saved my life. What more can a doctor do?

I think that takes care of my physicians.

Now to the other people that have helped make me who I am today.

From my Little League baseball coach, Roger Howington, (deceased) to Paul Butler, who was my main teacher during the five years that I was home-bound, to all my friends in AZA and BBG, to Paul Herrera, (missing) my best friend in college, to Bill C, (deceased) the person who helped me get Cannabis before I was legal, to Marc Silverberg, a life long friend, to Karen Mitchell, Kerry Gruson, Harry Horgan, and all my friends at Shake-A-Leg, to my firm, Newbridge Securities where I mostly wrote this book and for all the paper I went through, to Dara Jennings, my sales assistant, for help with the spelling, to my fellow co-worker, Mike Grande and his dictionary, to my Sunday softball guys, to ProCon.org, who helped with some history, to John Schwerin, my neighbor who's is like a brother to me, and his daughter Stacy, to Jeff Jones, Richard Lee, Angel Raich, May Nutt (deceased, and all my other friends in "The Movement," I say thanks for helping and putting up with me.

A special thanks to the Founders of "Patients Out of Time," Al Byrne and Mary Lynn Mathre. Keep up the good work!

To Patrick Fourmy, my friend, agent, and the person who helped produce this book, "well done." Thanks, George Delmerico, for the wonderful designs.

To Serafin Gonzalez, my pharmacist and his staff, including Steven Murphy, thanks for being the conduit between my physician and the Government, and Steven for the great pictures.

Now my attorneys: Richard Bonnie, from UVA, who was a big help in bringing the government to hold hearings for me, to Christopher Sharp and Georgetown Law School who helped me sue Delta Airlines, and to Andy Hefty, Mark Black, and everyone at Steptoe and Johnson, who has represented me in the past and hopefully will be their for me in the future, and to Ralph Smith, our attorney with Patients Out of Time, thanks to all for doing a great job.

To all the media people through the years, I want to thank you for helping to tell my story and helping educate people on Medical Cannabis.

To my fellow Federal patients; Barbara and Kenny Jenks, (both deceased) Corrine Millet, (deceased) Barbara Douglas, George McMahon, and Elvy Mussika, we have a special bond which only we know. Thanks to all of you.

And to Fred Gardner, my co-writer who did a great job helping me with the first draft. Fred is a wonderful writer and was easy to work with. Thanks, again!

There are two people which I purposely left out until now. They are Robert Randall (deceased) and Alice O'Leary. I owe a lot of people for what they have done for me in my life, however this book would never had been possible without Bob and Alice. I don't think I would have ever become a Federal patient without them blazing the trail and helping me navigate the maize.

For that reason, I am dedicating my book to them. Some of my information came from books that Bob and Alice wrote so I highly recommend that you read their books. They made "one hell-of-a-team."

The last thank you is to God. Many times he has been there for me. He put me in this position and showed me how to best deal with it for myself and others.

I've written this book to the best of my memory along with all my articles that I quoted. I talked with a lot of the people that I talk about in my book and got mostly the same answer, "I don't remember."

I wanted this book to tell my story and to tell the history of the Medical Cannabis movement in this country as seen through my eyes. I hope you enjoy *My Medicine*..

More Praise for *My Medicine*

Irv Rosenfeld has a rare disease and a rare gift—eloquent, dignified integrity amidst great pain. Diagnosed at the age of 10 with Multiple Congenital Cartilaginous Exostosis, a potentially lethal disease causing 200 tumors all over his long bones, he was told he'd have to battle this disease for the rest of his life. He did not know, then, that the battle would have to be fought against vast government bureaucracies, police, airlines, and many others. He did not know that medical cannabis would save his life. *My Medicine* is his story, beautifully told, plainspoken truth, no bull. Parts of it made me cry. Parts of it made me shout for joy!

His memory unimpaired, his intelligence manifest in every line, Irv is "living proof" that medical cannabis works very well, that the government gives medical marijuana to patients while denying that it has any medical value whatsoever, and that the government doesn't want to know how well it works, or want us to know. He is the longest-surviving legal Federal cannabis patient, now reduced to 4 people of the original 13, and last year Patients Out of Time—the national advocacy organization for medical cannabis patients—named him the "World Record Joint Smoker," having consumed more than 115,000 cannabis cigarettes in the past 27 years, all of it supplied by the National Institute on Drug Abuse from the Federal cannabis farm at the University of Mississippi.

What's surprising is that the schwag supplied by the government—grown intentionally badly (low potency), frozen for as long as 13 years, packed loosely into cigarettes and given to him in a metal canister—actually did work. This explains the large amount he must smoke to survive, 10 to 12 joints every day.

NIDA had the perfect opportunity to do full scale double blind clinical trials of the medicinal value of marijuana on the Federal patients, and refused, hoping to sweep it under the rug rather than risking "living proof" that the government flat-out lies about marijuana. It was left to Ethan Russo, MD, editor of the now-defunct Journal of Cannabis Therapeutics, to study the small group of patients who fought their own battles to force the government to recognize their plight and grant them the only medicine that worked. Russo found no significant adverse effects from daily cannabis use among any of the Federal patients. Strikingly, Irv's lung capacity was rated at 108% after smoking cannabis for 39 years. He's one of the best spokespeople the reform movement has ever had.

My Medicine is one man's story that changed America for the better. It's a page-turner that cannot be ignored, a sail unfurled in the winds of change, and a great read!

—*Michael R. Aldrich, Ph.D.*